P9-CFU-349

PETER SHAFFER   THEATRE AND DR
AMA

MACMURRAUGH-KAVANAGH, M. K. M
ADELEINE K.   1965-

PR6037.H23Z76 1998

SE

PETER SHAFFER: THEATRE AND DRAMA

Peter Shaffer
Theatre and Drama

M. K. MacMurraugh-Kavanagh

First published in Great Britain 1998 by
MACMILLAN PRESS LTD
Houndmills, Basingstoke, Hampshire RG21 6XS and London
Companies and representatives throughout the world

A catalogue record for this book is available from the British Library.

ISBN 0–333–68168–1

First published in the United States of America 1998 by
ST. MARTIN'S PRESS, INC.,
Scholarly and Reference Division,
175 Fifth Avenue, New York, N.Y. 10010

ISBN 0–312–21183–X

Library of Congress Cataloging-in-Publication Data
MacMurraugh-Kavanagh, M. K. (Madeleine K.), 1965–
Peter Shaffer : theatre and drama / M.K. MacMurraugh-Kavanagh.
p.   cm.
Includes bibliographical references and index.
ISBN 0–312–21183–X
1. Shaffer, Peter, 1926– —Criticism and interpretation.
I. Title.
PR6037.H23Z76 1997
822'.914—dc21   97–38024
                                                                        CIP

© Madeleine MacMurraugh-Kavanagh 1998

All rights reserved. No reproduction, copy or transmission of this publication may be made without written permission.

No paragraph of this publication may be reproduced, copied or transmitted save with written permission or in accordance with the provisions of the Copyright, Designs and Patents Act 1988, or under the terms of any licence permitting limited copying issued by the Copyright Licensing Agency, 90 Tottenham Court Road, London W1P 9HE.

Any person who does any unauthorised act in relation to this publication may be liable to criminal prosecution and civil claims for damages.

The author has asserted her right to be identified as the author of this work in accordance with the Copyright, Designs and Patents Act 1988.

This book is printed on paper suitable for recycling and made from fully managed and sustained forest sources.

10   9   8   7   6   5   4   3   2   1
07 06 05 04 03 02 01 00 99 98

Printed in Great Britain by
The Ipswich Book Company Ltd
Ipswich, Suffolk

For my Mother

Contents

List of Plays and Play Premieres

The Salt Land (television drama), 8 November 1955 (ITV).

The Prodigal Father (radio drama), 14 September 1957 (BBC Radio).

Balance of Terror (television drama), 21 November 1957 (BBC); 27 January 1958 (CBS).

Five Finger Exercise, 16 July 1958, Comedy Theatre, London. 2 December 1959, Music Box Theater, New York.

The Private Ear (with *The Public Eye*), 10 May 1962, Globe Theatre, London. 9 October 1963, Morosco Theater, NY.

The Public Eye (with *The Private Ear*), 10 May 1962, Globe Theatre, London. 9 October 1963, Morosco Theater, NY.

The Merry Rooster's Panto, 17 December 1963, Wyndham's Theatre, London.

The Royal Hunt of the Sun, 7 July 1964, National Theatre at Chichester. 26 October 1965, ANTA Theater, NY.

Black Comedy , 27 July 1965, National Theatre at Chichester. 12 February 1967, Ethel Barrymore Theater, NY (with *White Lies*).

White Lies (with *Black Comedy*), 12 February 1967, Ethel Barrymore Theater, NY. 21 February 1968, Lyric Theatre, London (*White Lies* revised as *White Liars*).

The Battle of Shrivings (revised as *Shrivings*, 1974), 5 February 1970, Lyric Theatre, London.

Equus, 26 July 1973, National Theatre, at the Old Vic Theatre, London. 24 October 1974, Plymouth Theater, NY.

Amadeus, 2 November 1979, National Theatre, London. 17 December 1980, Broadhurst Theater, NY.

Yonadab, 4 December 1985, National Theatre, London

Lettice and Lovage, 27 October 1987, Globe Theatre, London. 25 March 1990, Ethel Barrymore Theater, NY (revised as *Lettice & Lovage*).

Whom Do I Have the Honour of Addressing? (radio drama), May 1989 (BBC). 19 November 1996, Chichester.

The Gift of the Gorgon, 5 December 1992, The Pit Theatre, Barbican Centre, London.

Preface

I was first introduced to the plays of Peter Shaffer by a truly inspired teacher when I was in my mid-teens; I have never forgotten the impact these dramas had on me and the areas of thought and feeling they opened. With the necessary exams passed and with further studies embarked upon, I continued to return over and over again to the texts, each time finding some new reverberation or meaning in the words. It is the intention of this book to communicate some idea of the sheer pleasure to be gained from a reading of these plays, and to suggest ways in which this pleasure can be deepened by placing them in the contexts of academic debate and of the theatrical imagination.

The reader's knowledge of these plays at the level of plot (gleaned from a reading of the work or from seeing performances of it) has been assumed in this book. Given the tight word-limit in operation here, it makes little sense to provide outlines of stories when words can be spent on more valuable analysis. To understand the ideas presented here, then, readers should read or view the plays first. Viewing the film adaptations of them will be of little help as the film scripts often bear scant resemblance to the stage versions of these plays.

This book is divided into nine chapters, each taking a specific theme in Shaffer's work, discussing its relevance, and applying the ideas outlined in the preliminary section to two or three plays from his canon. The plays are not discussed in chronological order but are introduced into chapters when their impulses or themes have a direct relevance to the analysis. Dealing with the plays chronologically would hamper discussion of the major themes at stake and would preclude the drawing of interesting parallels between two plays (as in Chapter 4) simply because they happened not to follow one from the other in date order. The book is therefore organized around broad areas of debate rather than around a sequential analysis of individual plays.

Beginning with general topics of interest, the book first discusses Shaffer's life and writing career and places him in the context of post-1945 British theatre. Critical assessments of him are also summarized in this introductory chapter. Chapter 2 continues with the general and investigates Shaffer's use of the theatrical environment; this section incorporates some basic and necessary discussion of Shaffer's apparent debt to two of the most significant theatrical theorists and practitioners of the twentieth century – Antonin Artaud and Bertolt Brecht.

The book then moves towards more specific themes and topics in Shaffer's drama beginning with the much discussed theatrical preoccupation, communication. Here, discussion of Shaffer's earlier plays (*Five Finger Exercise, The Private Ear, The Public Eye* and *Black Comedy*) is applied to the ideas raised. Chapter 4 then looks at the related emphases on dysfunction, identity and alienation in these plays, drawing a comparison between two of Shaffer's protagonists, Mark Askelon of *Shrivings* and the eponymous Yonadab.

Chapters 5 and 6 (the centre of the book) both deal with *The Royal Hunt of the Sun, Equus* and *Amadeus*. These are, of course, Shaffer's most famous plays and are the most frequently performed and studied – one good reason for devoting two chapters to the analysis of them. In the first, Shaffer's use of religion and myth and the idea of 'worship' are themes that predominate; in Chapter 6, these themes are again featured in a discussion which views the plays as clear demonstrations of Shaffer's theatre of conflict and disjunction. The crucial debates centring on the Apollonian-Dionysian impulses in Shaffer's drama are addressed here.

Chapter 7 introduces a theme that has not been sufficiently explored in criticism of Shaffer's plays: that is, the role of the female protagonist in his drama. Here, discussion begins with a brief consideration of this playwright's female protagonists through the years, and then focuses on two plays in which female presence is at last fully registered and realized: *Lettice and Lovage* and *Whom Do I Have the Honour of Addressing?*

In Chapter 8, Shaffer's connection between myth and morality is explored in an extended analysis of Shaffer's most recent full-length play, *The Gift of the Gorgon*. An entire chapter has been devoted to this drama because there is, at present, little published discussion of it for students or playgoers to refer to. Finally, the conclusion presents a brief discussion of the cinematic adaptation of Shaffer's plays and offers a framework in which Peter Shaffer's work for the theatre can be understood and, above all, enjoyed.

Readers will, it is hoped, emerge from this book with a clear understanding of the way in which Shaffer's theatre 'works' both theatrically and dramatically. It is also hoped that students and playgoers alike will respond to an insight that stands central to Shaffer's work; that is that 'meaning' is not purely intellectual, but resides, above all, in emotional and psychological territories of experience.

I would like, finally, to express my warm thanks to Peter Shaffer for co-operating with such generosity in the writing of this book. During a particularly hectic period of his life, his courtesy never flagged as, even in a less busy man, it surely had a right to do. Both he and his plays have made the writing of this book an enlightening and extremely pleasurable experience.

MADELEINE MACMURRAUGH-KAVANAGH

Acknowledgements

My thanks must first of all go to Peter Shaffer whose help and encouragement in the writing of this book has been invaluable. I am extremely grateful to him for agreeing to meet me and to spare the time for a series of entertaining and illuminating interviews held in London and Chichester in the autumn of 1996. Discussing his work with him has been a joy.

My thanks, in addition, to Charmian Hearne at Macmillan who has been so supportive of me as a writer and whose professional eye has steered me calmly through the publishing process.

In addition, I would like to thank Ron Knowles at Reading University for encouraging me to write this book and for his assistance in making the initial approach to Macmillan. His advice and help has been much appreciated over the years that I have known him. I would also like to thank Brian Edgar, an extraordinary and gifted teacher, who first introduced me to these plays and who taught me to think in mature terms about literature and history.

Finally, my heartfelt thanks to my family and friends. To my mother in particular, my special thanks for her generosity, love and support over the years: she is a remarkable woman without whom I would have achieved nothing. And to Mark, of course, for his kindness and patience.

1
Introduction

A member of an elite group of dramatists including Harold Pinter, Alan Ayckbourn, and Tom Stoppard, Peter Shaffer is an internationally recognized and highly acclaimed writer who occupies a privileged position in contemporary British theatre. His work has been consistently performed for over 30 years in subsidized and commercial, metropolitan and provincial, professional and amateur arenas; his plays have scooped the top theatrical and film awards and the world's finest actors scramble for roles in his dramas which are guaranteed to play to packed houses wherever they are performed. The extraordinary popularity of Peter Shaffer's work in front of worldwide audiences is, in short, nothing less than a cultural phenomenon.

Since his emergence as a dramatic writer of formidable theatrical intelligence in 1958, certain characteristics of his writing, which alert us to the reasons for this popularity, have sharpened and developed. With his first 'serious' full-length stage play, *Five Finger Exercise*, he demonstrated a control over dramatic dialogue and a verbal dexterity that has remained a constant feature of his style; linked to this is his comedic flair (evident in the 'darker' plays as well as in his 'lighter' work) which incorporates Machiavellian irony, Wildean wit and Ortonesque farce as well as word-play and one-liners. In an era where articulacy is drifting into extinction, Shaffer's drama satisfies a hunger for crafted dialogue that leaves his audience craving for more.

His plays are 'crafted' pieces in more senses than this alone. Noting that Shaffer expresses a predilection for the term *'Playwright'* (with its connotations of artistry and workmanship), Simon Trussler suggests that it is as a *'maker'* rather than merely as a 'writer' of plays that Shaffer 'has made a distinctive contribution to contemporary theatre'.[1] This contribution lies in the insistence we find in these dramas on the principles of the 'well made play' where structure and development are central to the writer's concerns. In Shaffer's case, this becomes integrated with a musical

1

sensibility, as is clearly revealed in the playwright's statement: 'I like plays to be like fugues – all the themes should come together in the end'.[2] In the very construction of his plays, then, Shaffer consistently demonstrates a control over character and situation which suggests an earlier, more literate drama from which contemporary theatre has perhaps strayed too far.

Connected with this skilful dramatic technique is another audience-pleasing accomplishment: the ability to weave a compelling story. Shaffer is an undisputed master of 'telling tales', forcing the audience into involvement with his dramas through detective-story suspense, human identification, and the presentation of complex conflicts. The playwright is fully aware that story-telling is central to the dramatist's art, stating 'It is my object to tell tales; to conjure up the spectres of horror and happiness [...] to perturb and make gasp: to please and make laugh: to surprise'.[3] This, he understands, is the role of the dramatist in whatever medium he/she is working, but in the theatre, where all drama relies on human interest, it assumes a position of priority. An audience gripped by a story, played out live before them, never forgets the experience: it is little wonder that Shaffer's audiences return for more and more.

This playwright's dramatic skills do not end here: we should also consider his unusual generic dexterity where farce or satire appear as natural forms for him to write in as do tragedy or Epic. Further, his writing moves easily between the stage, the page, the television screen and the cinema as if the techniques required for each were equally automatic to him. Nor does he refuse a dramatic risk, frequently rejecting the comfortable or easy expectation audiences may have of his work and presenting them with something entirely different. He confounds their preconceptions, challenges their 'facts' and their attitudes, and startles with unexpected dramatic moments and potentially unfamiliar themes. Such a high-risk dramatic strategy leads Walter Kerr to label Shaffer a 'gambling man', a writer who seems not to care about 'what kind of chances he takes': these 'chances' usually pay off in spectacular fashion.[4]

So far, discussion of the popularity of Shaffer's plays in front of audiences has focused on his dramatic 'craft'. Equally central to his appeal, however, is his theatrical intuition. Above all else, and despite his work in other media, Shaffer is a writer for the theatre whose dramas find their ultimate meaning in this environment alone; returning to the 'craftsman' metaphor, Shaffer himself alludes to this when he states his desire to 'make theatre, to make something that could only happen on stage'.[5] With the ability to utilize every resource available to him in this arena (lighting, music, choreography, communal atmosphere, and so on), Shaffer involves his audience *imaginatively* in his drama where metaphor, allusion and illusion prevail. For this playwright, it is not enough that the audience should respond purely intellectually to his work; it is his desire that they should be caught up in, and surrender to, the magic and the mystery that differentiates live theatre from any other dramatic experience. The emotional and the psychological realms are therefore of paramount importance to his theatre where the unconscious must be triggered for its significance to be fully registered. Every staging device has, over the years, been wielded by Shaffer to these ends, while his recurrent dramatic themes of the search for worship and the conflict between reason and instinct pitch the intellect at a level where more primitive and more elemental territories of imagination and experience can be accessed. It is for this reason that John Russell Taylor describes Shaffer as a 'theatrical thinker', a dramatist who is able to create plays into which the communal imagination of the audience flows.[6]

All of which helps us to understand Shaffer's popularity with international audiences over a 30-year period. Simultaneously, and perhaps paradoxically, it also provides clues as to why he has consistently met with critical hostility, particularly from English academics and commentators. For these critics, Shaffer's very popularity seems suspicious since it hints at an accessibility that apparently implies intellectual hollowness and a tendency to pander to the audience. As a result, a constant refrain in critical reactions to Shaffer over the years has been the charge of superficiality and the complaint of 'popularism' which, of course, carries darker connotations than the still dubious label 'popular'. His success has, moreover, been attributed to his directors (notably John Dexter), with the implication that the weaknesses in Shaffer's dramas are consistently concealed by theatrical masters.[7] Further, critics have complained of a certain pretentiousness in Shaffer's style, arguing that his rhetoric blinds audiences to insuffiencies in terms of ideas in his plays: meanwhile, the charge that he abuses historical 'fact' has been a long-standing criticism of his work, though critics have frequently had to backtrack hastily on this charge when Shaffer's material has been validated by concrete evidence.[8]

The result of this critical antipathy to Peter Shaffer's work is that a curious split has opened up between audiences who flock enthusiastically to his plays and critics who habitually denigrate them.[9] A situation has evolved in which it is not somehow 'correct' to 'admit' an admiration for this playwright, as though, when we do so, we are revealing that we are members of some misguided mass who have been duped by rhetoric and stage effects. However, when we examine this issue more thoroughly, it appears that critical hostility to Shaffer's plays seems to be based on little more than cultural snobbery; since his dramas appear not to be 'political' in the manner, for example, of David Hare or Howard Brenton, critics feel that their approbation must be withheld as if this is the standard by which all else is measured. In addition, if audiences respond in droves to the work, if it is not 'difficult' to respond to, the critical establishment seems to feel that there must automatically be something 'wrong' with it. This is, of course, a wholly illogical situation which is based on a mistrust of commercial triumph above all else (Shaffer comments that the British Press 'can't stop talking about money').[10] One reason why Shaffer's plays may have received a far less antipathetic critical reaction in the United States is surely that America is not known for its suspicious attitude towards success. In the States, popularity is an indication that the playwright has done his work well: in England, 'popularity' is still taken as an indication that the playwright has, literally, 'sold out'. For Shaffer himself, however, popular success simply means that 'the problems one has tried to solve have in some ways been solved', and 'validation' has resulted.[11]

None of this is to argue that Shaffer's plays are without problematic elements and the playwright is himself aware that certain weaknesses dog his writing. Following the failure of *The Battle of Shrivings* (his first commercial flop), he was alerted to the 'danger in my work of theme dictating event', while 'a strong impulse to compose rhetorical dialogue was beginning to freeze my characters into theoretical attitudes'.[12] He therefore admitted the 'justness' of the critical verdict, though he detected 'none at all in the palpable pleasure with which it had been delivered'.[13] So while flaws do mark this drama (and it would be futile to argue otherwise), it is nevertheless true that the critical evaluation of it is often far from balanced and is frequently delivered with an ill-disguised relish. Shaffer has, however, had over 30 years to become used to this reaction and to understand that, with drama, it is what happens in front of audiences, rather than what happens in newspapers and journals, that finally matters to the playwright: after all, as Shaffer emphasizes, his drama is written '*for* the public', and is realized '*with* the public'.[14]

A brief biographical survey of the playwright's life and career may be useful at this point. Peter Shaffer was born, together with his twin brother Anthony, in 1926 in Liverpool. His family was middle class and the sons were educated in Liverpool and later in London where the family moved when Peter Shaffer was ten years old. Following school years at St Paul's, Shaffer was conscripted as a Bevin Boy in 1944 and spent three years working at a coal mine; as he told Brian Connell in 1980, this experience gave him 'an enormous sympathy and feeling of outrage in contemplating how a lot of people had to spend their lives'.[15] Between 1947 and 1950, Shaffer studied History at Trinity College, Cambridge, spending much time co-editing the student magazine *Granta* with his brother. Simultaneously, the brothers were embarking on their fledgling career as writers of detective stories, the first of the three novels they produced, *The Woman in the Wardrobe*, being published in 1951 under the pseudonym 'Peter Anthony'. Asked in later years why he was reluctant to publish under his own name, Shaffer responded: 'I had a sense that I wasn't going to continue as a detective writer [...] I just felt that I would rather reserve whatever writing I did of a more serious nature for my own name'.[16]

The second of the detective novels, *How Doth my Little Crocodile?*, was published in 1952 by which time Peter Shaffer had left England to live and work in New York for three years between 1951 and 1954. Taking a variety of jobs including a bookseller in Doubleday's, a salesman in a department store and a librarian in the New York Public Library Acquisitions Department, Shaffer appears to have drifted from job to job, feeling slightly on the edge of life, and trying to gather the courage to commit himself to a career as a full-time writer. One problem that Shaffer had to overcome in deciding on a life as a dramatist was the idea he had absorbed from his father that 'work' involved a serious profession while 'writing' constituted something of a hobby. In one interview, he notes that 'my father regarded writing as a leisure activity, not central to life and not a profession':[17] as a result, as he told Brian Connell, 'I denied myself the pleasure of writing plays for a very long time'.[18] Though nowhere in any interview does Shaffer express resentment about his father's attitude, the regular appearance in his plays of domineering fathers who attempt to impose their own visions on sensitive, easily-bullied sons (in characters including Stanley Harrington, Frank Strang and Leopold Mozart) perhaps has its genesis here.

Returning to London in 1954, Shaffer began work at the music publishers, Boosey and Hawkes. By now, however, he had realized that if he failed to commit himself immediately to a writing career, he would never do so; he resigned his job and decided to 'live now on my literary wits'.[19] Existing on a small allowance from his father, and earning extra money by working as a literary critic for a weekly review, *Truth*, he began writing in earnest and was rewarded for his efforts in 1955 by the sale of a television play *The Salt Land* to ITV. In the same year, his final detective novel, *Withered Murder*, was also published. Two years later, Shaffer sold *Balance of Terror* to BBC Television and another play, *The Prodigal Father*, to BBC Radio. Peter Shaffer's writing career was, a little belatedly, well and truly underway.

Of these early pieces, little is worth discussing here in any great detail. The novels were light-hearted romps involving one of two detective characters (Mr Verity and Mr Fathom) and, as is always the case in this genre, the interest was less focused on 'whodunnit' than on *why* 'it' was done. This preoccupation, of course, later emerges as central to dramas such as *Equus* and *Amadeus*. The early plays, meanwhile, were well-written exercises in social realism though, in *Balance of Terror*, a tale of cold war espionage, Shaffer also demonstrated an early ability to weave a gripping yarn. *The Salt Land* is also interesting for its attempt to construct a Classical tragedy from events taking place in modern Israel.

What is really important about this work, however, is that Shaffer had placed himself in a position where he could launch himself into the theatrical arena which he always regarded as his true home. Martin Esslin explains that the media boom of the late 1950s not only encouraged an expansion in dramatic writing, but also provided a training ground where young writers could 'first acquire professional experience in radio, and advance from there to television', finally using these platforms as 'a spring-board to theatre and cinema'.[20] Esslin here describes exactly the path that Peter Shaffer's writing career was to take.

His first major theatrical success came in 1958 when *Five Finger Exercise* was staged at the Comedy in the West End; the play ran for 610 performances which, as Oleg Kerensky notes, constitutes an extremely long run for a 'serious drama'.[21] A 'semi-autobiographical play', in Shaffer's words, *Five Finger Exercise* seemed to militate against the dramatic trend which had been set by John Osborne's *Look Back in Anger* two years earlier (whether the two plays are, in fact, as dissimilar as they seem is a question addressed in Chapter 3).[22] Shaffer's focus was on a bourgeois country house where a battle raged between middle-class members of a privileged family; it was 'well-made' in terms of structure and dialogue, naturalistic in form, and apparently traditional in all its aspects. The critics warmly approved but at the same time labelled Shaffer a 'Tory Playwright, an Establishment Dramatist, a Normal Worker': these were labels that Shaffer objected to and has since found difficult to shake off.[23] *Five Finger Exercise*, however, established Shaffer's name in the commercial sector and simultaneously established him as a writer of well-structured, crafted dramas.

Between 1961 and 1962, Shaffer indulged his second passion, music, becoming music critic for *Time and Tide*.[24] At the same time, he was writing the first of his double-bills, *The Private Ear* and *The Public Eye*, which appeared on stage in 1962. The first of these dramas was hardly alien to what audiences may have expected from the author of *Five Finger Exercise*, but the second of the plays risked disorientating the public with a part-farce, part-whimsy, part-realist, part-existential drama. The reaction to the play was, as a result, uncertain. However, Maggie Smith and Kenneth Williams triumphed in the leading roles and audiences seem to have approved of the dramas more warmly than did the critical establishment.

In the following year, Shaffer co-wrote the film script of *The Lord of the Flies* with Peter Brook, and contributed two sketches to BBC's satirical show, *That Was The Week That Was*: 'But My Dear' and 'The President of France' revealed the playwright's ability to write in the form of satirical farce, an early demonstration of his generic flexibility. That his dazzling epic, *The Royal Hunt of the Sun*, should be the next work to appear in 1964 demonstrated his range even more spectacularly. No audience member who had witnessed any of Shaffer's earlier dramatic offerings could have been expecting this 'intellectual spectacular' which, in Alan Brien's words, could be described as 'a de Mille epic for educated audiences, an eye-dazzling, ear-buzzing, button-holing blend of *Ben Hur*, *The King and I*, and *The Devils*'.[25] Rejecting traditional naturalism, Shaffer had embraced the theories of Bertolt Brecht and Antonin Artaud (see Chapter 2) to produce what one critic decided was the 'great[est] play [...] written and produced in our language in my lifetime'.[26] *The Royal*

Hunt of the Sun was subsequently adapted as an opera and produced at the Coliseum, London, in 1977.

But as if to refuse categorization yet again, Shaffer in his next play produced the totally unexpected: *Black Comedy* (1965), written to accompany Strindberg's *Miss Julie* at the Chichester Festival Theatre, was a light farce, ingenious, physical, and almost determinedly frivolous. The play was a huge success and was later presented in another double-bill with *White Lies* (later, *White Liars*, and later still, *The White Liars*); this play, however, was by far the weaker of the two pieces and, despite constant revisions, has never found unanimous approval among audiences and critics. Even so, the play was not a commercial failure, a fate Shaffer had not yet suffered. In 1970, however, it was pay-back time and *The Battle of Shrivings* proved to be Shaffer's biggest and most damaging dramatic failure. Like *White Lies*, the play was revised extensively and the rewritten version is now published as *Shrivings*; but so deeply does the entire experience of the original play's failure seem to have wounded Shaffer that this play has never been performed subsequently and remains comparatively unknown.

By 1973, though, Shaffer had sufficiently recovered from a 'huge writer's block' that followed the failure of *The Battle of Shrivings* to produce one of the most commercially successful and influential plays of contemporary theatre: the mighty *Equus*.[27] Christopher Ford dubbed the drama 'the most quickly successful serious British play ever' and noted that, by 1976, it had been staged in half the countries of the developed world.[28] Collecting practically every theatrical award available (winning all the New York awards in the same year, the first play ever to do so), this drama involving a psychiatrist's relationship with a young boy who has blinded six horses remains a haunting classic of British theatre. Shaffer had truly arrived on the international arena and his position as one of the foremost writers of modern times was enforced by the equally influential *Amadeus* in 1979. Again suspected by the critical establishment, attacked for its refusal of the Mozart myth, and scorned for its massive worldwide popularity, *Amadeus* has nevertheless joined *Equus* in the ranks of contemporary classics.

In the years that followed, Shaffer more than ever divided his time between the subsidized and commercial sectors. Though *Yonadab* in 1985 received a critical battering, the biblical epic ran successfully for several months at the National Theatre where it was first staged. A triumph equal to his earlier hits was then again scored with the joyful comedy, *Lettice and Lovage*, which was premiered in the commercial theatre in 1987 and ran for nearly three years at the Globe in the West End (the title of the play became *Lettice & Lovage* upon its New York debut as a result of a revised ending).[29] Again turning in the opposite direction to that taken in his previous play, Shaffer returned to muted realism in this warming tale which wittily and humanely investigates the relationship between past and present, and between instinct and reason. Its female focus was continued into a 1989 radio drama, *Whom Do I Have the Honour of Addressing?*, which was developed as a stage play in 1996 at Chichester Festival Theatre. Finally, from the contemporary and the 'everyday', Shaffer turned towards a grand fusion between Classical theatre, realism and epic in his huge drama, *The Gift of the Gorgon* (1992): a controversial play incorporating staging effects derived from cinematic technique, this drama divided the critics more than ever before. As in all his earlier dramas, there are no easy answers offered or arrived at in this complex moral investigation. But despite the critical storm that greeted the play upon its debut (see Chapter 8), *The Gift of the Gorgon* is scheduled for production in several capital cities worldwide and completes Shaffer's canon to date.[30]

Most of the plays described here have transferred from London to New York where Shaffer has scored further triumphs on Broadway.[31] Most have also been adapted into cinematic films though, it must be added, with mixed results. But the visibility that Shaffer has enjoyed as a result of this international audience has confirmed his position as among the foremost playwrights of his generation; and unlike many of the writers with whom he shares this honour, he has in addition demonstrated that he is unwilling to stick to safe formulae in an effort to safeguard his position. Quite the opposite: Shaffer has in fact risked everything time and time again in his eagerness to experiment with new techniques, esoteric ideas, and different genres. In addition, he has refused to follow the trends of literary fashion preferring instead to listen to a mainstream audience and to satisfy, anticipate, and even create its needs.

The difference between 'literary fashion' and mainstream demand can easily be assessed by placing Shaffer's dramas in the context of the years in which they were first performed and relating the patterns inherent in them to the prevailing attitudes of the time. As we saw with *Five Finger Exercise*, Shaffer's first major stage success did not accord with the contemporary fashion for social realism of the 'Angry Young Man' school. However, much as this drama was beloved by critics and élite audiences, mainstream audiences never warmed to its aggression and to its refusal of the 'entertainment' ethic. The demand was still for literate, bourgeois drama which investigated less the class system and social issues than the individual within that most intimate grouping, the family. This is not to suggest that contemporary attitudes went unreflected in the mainstream drama of the time, but simply to note that mainstream taste preferred matters such as youth's revolt against the outmoded principles of their elders delivered in a more subtle form than Osborne *et al.* believed to be necessary. Nowhere was this taste more evident than in the West End commercial sector and Shaffer's drama, which dealt with such issues in a digestible, crafted form, accorded perfectly with the mainstream mood of the time.

In doing so, of course, it removed him forever from what John Russell Taylor refers to as 'the new drama' as defined by writers such as Ann Jellicoe, John Arden and Harold Pinter.[32] Such writers produced drama that was either directly 'political' and/or revolutionary in terms of form and content. Shaffer's drama was neither 'political' nor 'revolutionary' and though debate raged at the time about to what extent this mattered, by the 1970s, Taylor could admit that such debate, though 'serious', was 'rather pointless'.[33] Categorization by the means that he had attempted in 1962 was, he seems to have realized, essentially reductive and was based on stereotyped assumption; in addition, since Shaffer himself appeared to care little about 'the new drama' and his place within it, debate on his exact position was always futile.

Never interested in dramatic fashion, then, Shaffer from the beginning of his career concentrated on responding to the needs of the mainstream audience (in whatever sector) and rejected the precepts of literary opinion. That following literary fashion is, besides any other consideration, a hopeless task is a point demonstrated by *Equus*, a play whose critical reception demonstrates the fickle nature of critical appraisal. In this drama, Shaffer had responded to the prevailing *zeitgeist* of the early 1970s, a period when, following the confused excesses of the 1960s, society seemed to turn inwards on itself and embrace psychological exploration of the human condition. Further, as C.J. Gianakaris points out, 'Shaffer's concern for metaphysical absolutes', as demonstrated in *Equus*, 'was in tune with the mainstream existentialism then dominating intellectual thought'.[34] All of which suggests reasons for the huge popularity of the play in front of worldwide audiences. However, ten years later, one critic can suggest that 'recent opinion' has 'lowered' the play's 'estimation', not because of any structural objection, but because of the 'suspicion that it is an élitist throw-back to the days of "non-committed" theatre'.[35] To satisfy 'fashion' in one era, then, is not necessarily to guarantee fashionable opinion in another. Shaffer is surely correct to avoid this minefield altogether and respond solely to his audience's needs as well as to his own theatrical intuition.

The success of this strategy is clearly demonstrated by *Amadeus*. Fully in line with the 1980s predilection for spectacle, this play packed audiences into the National Theatre creating, in Peter Hall's phrase, 'an atmosphere like a football match' at each performance.[36] Further, the play appears to have satisfied an almost tangible need in its audiences since, as Simon Callow (recalling his experience playing Mozart) notes, 'a hunger' seemed to emanate from the auditoria to which he played, this communicating to the actor 'a feeling that [audiences] were getting something they'd done without for too long'.[37] In an era where directly 'political drama' stalked the subsidized sector, and where mindless musicals as produced by Andrew Lloyd Webber dominated the commercial arena, *Amadeus* forged a path between the two presenting a drama which asked searching questions and which 'entertained' as it did so. Sensing his audience's needs, Shaffer had produced a play which entirely expressed the spirit and demands of the age.

Shaffer, then, has never strayed from his self-made path of rejecting literary fashion in favour of mainstream taste. This has, as we have seen, handed ammunition to his critics who detect in this a tendency to pander to his audiences whilst maintaining a solidly right-wing position. In fact, it is far from easy to pigeon-hole Shaffer politically since 'politics' as such never intrude onto his stage. His concerns transcend this area focusing instead on metaphysical issues such as the relationship between man and God, man and himself, man and eternity. Despite this, many critics have succumbed to the urge to classify him in party political terms, using his position within commercial and subsidized theatre to argue that here is a man who is firmly on the Establishment side or who is, at the very least, suspiciously apolitical – a position of which no self-respecting critic can allow himself to approve.

However, a brief inspection of the plays suggests that, if we really feel it necessary to align Shaffer with a political camp, we must place him to the left, rather than to the right, of centre. *The*

Royal Hunt of the Sun clearly reveals an anti-Imperialist position and, while neither Capitalism nor Communism emerge as admirable philosophies in this play, the former undoubtedly fares worse at Shaffer's hands. His attitude towards homosexuality is unambiguously liberal in plays such as *Black Comedy* and *White Lies*, while *Amadeus*, despite being labelled a 'sincere radical right-wing play' by Peter Hall, reclaims the Mozart myth from bourgeois ideology.[38] This whole exercise is, however, essentially redundant since labels such as 'right-wing' and 'left-wing' simply provide a codified route to preconditioned response; in addition, they have nothing at all to do with Shaffer's dramatic impulses and should never intrude into our assessment of the plays themselves. The desire to classify writers in political terms is a post-1956 phenomenon and should be resisted in relation to Peter Shaffer and his work or reductive analysis, as manifested so consistently in journalistic criticism, will inevitably result.

As far as academic criticism of Shaffer's theatre is concerned, the writers cited in this book fall into clearly identifiable camps. Gene A. Plunka concentrates almost exclusively on his thesis that these plays demonstrate the playwright's concern for role-playing; he argues that they are based on a clash between a protagonist who bows to convention to his cost and a protagonist who rejects convention in favour of independence and autonomy also, ultimately, to his cost. Dennis A. Klein, following an alternative route, examines instances of game-playing in Shaffer's plays, emphasizing the playwright's love of tricks and stratagems which are reminiscent of his early detective novels. Critics such as Jules Glenn and Sanford Gifford, meanwhile, focus on the notion of 'twinship' in relation to the drama, an approach which is adopted with far more dramatic intelligence, and thus success, by Michael Hinden. C.J. Gianakaris provides thoroughly interesting analyses of the plays, usually paying close attention to the text and to impulses such as the Apollonian-Dionysian dialectic; he also writes extensively on the adaptation of this drama to the cinema and on the question of Shaffer's historical accuracy. Barbara Lounsberry and James Stacey, on the other hand, concentrate closely on the metaphysical nature of these plays, producing fascinating and incisive essays on the philosophical and mythlogical bases of Shaffer's drama. Rodney Simard analyses Shaffer in terms of postmodernist aesthetics, while John Russell Taylor is more concerned with Shaffer's work as it relates to the dramatic trends of post-1956 British theatre. These and several other critics too numerous to detail here have much to contribute to the analysis of Shaffer's work and are referred to regularly in the discussion that follows.

This book incorporates areas of the debates outlined above in the interests of introducing readers to the meaning and significance of Shaffer's drama. In addition, it presents ideas which have previously been neglected in critical discourse such as the problematic nature of communication in these plays, unexplored connections between certain dramas, and the role of the female protagonist on Shaffer's stage. However, the concern here is also to draw attention to levels of meaning that relate as much to the *experience* of Shaffer's drama as to its intellectual patterns: the ability to create a theatre that moves audiences onto an altered imaginative plane is, after all, what differentiates Shaffer's work from that of his contemporaries in absolute terms.

Readers are asked to put aside 'fashionable' opinion as they approach the plays of Peter Shaffer and respond to them honestly and instinctively. After all, as the playwright himself reminds us in *The Public Eye*, 'There is no sin more unpardonable then denying you were pleased when pleasure touched you. You can die for that'.[39]

2

'Of the Theatre Theatrical'

Speaking in 1958, in the wake of his first stage success with *Five Finger Exercise*, Peter Shaffer described his theatrical project: 'I want to revive the magic and the rhetoric, all the things that make the audience go "Ooh!"'.[1] For audiences who had seen Shaffer's breakthrough play, this may have seemed a curious statement given the determined and even old-fashioned naturalism of this drawing-room drama; six years later, for those who had experienced *The Royal Hunt of the Sun*, it would seem more curious still that a playwright who had created this 'total' theatrical experience could ever have written in the naturalistic format in the first place.

Such startling dramatic versatility is a hallmark of Shaffer's work, as also is his maximization of a range of theatrical devices. From the apparently conventional naturalism of the early plays, the work then journeys through the territories of symbolist, 'total', 'epic' and Classical theatre using a variety of staging strategies including the splitting of time and space, 'doubling' of characters, mimes, masks and rituals. Regardless of the genre within which he is writing, Shaffer's consistent desire in his work for the theatre is to create an experience that is *entirely and only theatrical*.[2] That he has largely succeeded in this agenda is indicated by John Russell Taylor who describes Shaffer's most celebrated plays as works that are 'of the theatre theatrical', adding that they could belong to no other medium.[3] This crucial remark invites speculation as to what exactly is meant by the term 'theatrical' and, in defining this, we simultaneously have to address its relationship with the term 'dramatic'. This in turn yields clues which explain the popular success of Shaffer's work and which help to account for the peculiar power of its means of communication.

The starting point to this examination is to decide why the labels 'theatrical' and 'dramatic' can rarely be regarded as synonymous. 'Dramatic' elements in plays are usually taken to include aspects such as structure, characterization, plot development and exposition, all of which can be recorded in a text and subsequently

14

analysed. This is the sense in which the words 'drama' and 'dramatic' will be used in this book. The difference between the terms 'drama' and 'theatre', however, is that where 'drama' can be written down, 'theatre' cannot because the word connotes a range of experiences that cannot be expressed in terms of stage directions or descriptions of sets. So 'theatre' refers to the total emotional, psychological and intellectual experience of a production, its atmosphere, the effects of communal spectatorship, the fact of live performance, and the direct channel of communication between stage and auditorium. This is the range of elements that the word will be taken to connote in this discussion. 'Theatre', then, is more than either the text or the staging alone, and yet it is created by both: put another way, 'theatre' is an entire experience and one that finally evades concrete definition.

What is unique about Shaffer is that his theatrical intelligence resides on both 'dramatic' and 'theatrical' levels, his plays skilfully tuned to systematically build tension and release their shocks at key points dramatically, the stage functioning as an arena where lighting, movement and sound coalesce to intensify and express this drama, and where a combination of representational devices conspire to create a communal experience that is unique to 'theatre'. In Shaffer's work, the dividing line between 'theatre' and 'drama' becomes indistinct since each conditions, and motivates, the other. The variety of ways in which this is effected is the subject of this chapter. Details of staging strategies will not be discussed here since such comment appears regularly in a number of volumes on Shaffer's work; instead, the aim in this section is to examine Shaffer's concept of what theatre 'is' and of what it can potentially 'do', to describe and explore a total context wherein this 'drama' merges with 'theatre', and to outline a framework in which Shaffer's work can be read, interpreted and understood.

The perception that Shaffer is a playwright who successfully combines 'theatre' with 'drama' is not necessarily shared by the critical establishment who cannot accept that a mutually expressive relationship between 'theatre' and 'drama' is possible. Frequent charges against the playwright, delivered with unimaginative regularity, include the complaint that though the plays may be fine pieces of 'theatre', they are shallow dramatically, the former being a mask to the latter. Jack Kroll, for example, in a particularly glib assessment, defines the 'typical' Shaffer play as 'a large-scale, large-voiced treatment of large themes, whose essential superficiality is masked by a skilful theatricality reinforced by the extraordinary acting, designing and directing resources of Britain's National Theatre'.[4] Other critics similarly emphasize the playwright's theatrical skill whilst dismissing his dramatic achievement by complaining that the dramas fail to live up to the standard of their productions; for these commentators, 'drama' connotes normative intellectualism of a purely mainstream nature while 'theatre' connotes staging detail they wrongly interpret as extraneous to it. Their attitude is parodied by the dramatist in his play *The Gift of the Gorgon* where Jarvis' preconditioned response to Edward's play directly recalls the consistently narrow assessment of Shaffer's work: 'Clever pictorialism is no substitute for serious insight'.[5]

In fact, Shaffer's achievement has been to redefine 'drama' in terms of 'theatre'. In these plays, we find that the drama of a situation is simultaneously expressed in terms of what is often called 'stagecraft', the drama conditioning the effect and the effect contributing to the meaning of the drama. For example, Alan Strang's tortured psyche is dramatically explored through key episodes of increasing tension in *Equus*, and while the audience becomes progressively gripped by the mysteries that the drama explores, its absorption in and understanding of the drama is intensified by the penetration of Alan's mind through amplified noises and changes of lighting that condition representation and clarify meaning. 'Drama' and 'theatre' here conjoin to create an experience that is produced symbiotically, and neither could find full meaning without the other. Numerous similar examples are scattered throughout Shaffer's plays, all suggesting that, for this playwright, 'theatre' and 'drama' are interchangeable, mutually-involved terms.

However, this point has escaped most critics who persist in their charge that Shaffer's work prioritizes the 'theatrical' over the 'dramatic'; 'theatricality' thus becomes a pejorative label, an inherently illogical situation as Shaffer indicates here:

> People who quite like one's work but want to put it down a bit say 'well, it's very theatrical, of course'. I always find that very odd. It's almost as if you are making a pejorative remark about a painter by saying of course it's very painterly. My quarrel with a lot of London is that it's not theatrical enough. I am tired of seeing a one-set play with two people whining at each other all night or delivering a sequence of lectures to the audience. It doesn't seem to me to be what theatre is for.[6]

What theatre 'is for', in Shaffer's terms, is a complex matter but certain 'functions' become clear through an examination of his work and comments. In the first place, he believes that theatre should startle and absorb an audience, involving it directly in the drama and in the theatrical experience of its expression; in 1973 he commented: 'I passionately believe that people come to the theatre to be surprised, moved and illuminated. They're not interested in simply what they're *hearing*. They're receiving what you say viscerally'.[7] In other words, for Shaffer, theatre should not necessarily involve itself with the territories of experience concerned with logic or rationality, but should satisfy audience needs associated with instinct and intuition. The theatre thus becomes a site of mystery where levels of experience denied access in daily life attain expression. Here, metamorphosis is a fact of production, time does not hold its conventional ground, and 'reality' is an ever-shifting category of perception. For Shaffer, then, theatre should lend the audience 'a sense of wonderment, and while entertaining reveal a vision of life'[8]; or, to quote from *Black Comedy*, theatre should resemble a 'magic dark room' where tricks are not only played but where they are also eagerly believed.[9]

If the theatre becomes a realm of mystery for Shaffer, then it also becomes a place of worship, an arena in which communal needs are channelled into a space where rite and ritual dominate. In the modern context in which 'God is Dead' and where a vacuum exists in worship's place, Shaffer seeks to express the spiritual in the one area where the irrational cannot be displaced – the theatre. As he notes in *The Gift of the Gorgon*, theatre is 'the only religion that can never die', adding that for centuries, 'the theatre gave us faith and true astonishment – as religion is supposed to do'.[10] In the theatre, the audience willingly believes the unbelievable and suspends rational response in a surrender to a form of 'faith' embedded in the communal psyche. In these terms, even a form of transubstantiation becomes possible, as Shaffer notes in relation to the funeral masks used in *The Royal Hunt of the Sun* which, despite being of fixed expression, apparently mutated in the course of the production, seeming to 'reflect joy, hope, gloom' according to the reactions of the spectators.[11]

Related to the idea that theatre fulfils functions closely akin to rituals and experiences associated with acts of worship, is Shaffer's belief that theatre also releases in the spectator a type of primeval memory buried deep in the communal unconscious. A long-term admirer of the work of Carl Jung (as *Equus* reveals), Shaffer's interest in the notion of archetypes contributes to his perception of what theatre is 'for' and also of what it can *do*. In his words, 'theatre is more than words or dialogue, it is a place for cathartic release of archetypal drives', an arena wherein an audience can connect with its 'memory' and purge itself of the drives associated with it.[12] Further, the theatre is by its nature archetypal in that actors exorcize through performance latent demons imbued in the unconscious, much in the manner of priests performing a religious ritual.[13] As we will see later, such ideas have a great deal in common with those found in the theoretical writings of Antonin Artaud and suggest a significant debt to him.

For Shaffer, then, theatre is 'for' expressing and experiencing territories of being alien to modern existence and is at its most eloquent when its imaginative resources are pitched at this level. Hence the full exploitation of theatrical devices such as music, mime, and movement: all contribute to the creation of a 'magic' the audience would respond to in no other realm. But the use of such devices would fail to achieve emotional and psychological impact if they were not expressed in a form accurately attuned to them: if experience did not match expression. A point that the critics cited above have failed to note is that they would be blind to the 'theatricality' of Shaffer's plays if inherent dramatic qualities were absent from them: in praising the effect, they are inadvertently responding to the means of achieving it dramatically. Would the rising of the huge sun at the end of *The Royal Hunt of the Sun*, for example, achieve any kind of theatrical effect if it did not express the death of hope in Pizarro? If the audience did not receive this meaning dramatically, and if it cared little about this 'death' because the drama had been flawed, the theatrical image would leave it cold. The fact that the rising sun, glaring out into the auditorium, proves a profoundly moving image demonstrates the extent to which drama and theatre are, in this play, symbiotic.

Shaffer is fully aware that 'theatricality' must be conjoined with certain structural rules if the potential of the environment is to be exploited. 'Effect' would not alone be enough. As a result, from his earliest plays, Shaffer has exhibited a tight control of structure and expression whilst simultaneously exploring the possibilities of experimental currents in terms of representation. Stating that the 'quality of *shape* is very important to me', Shaffer consistently demonstrates a control over the form of his work by constructing plays which are notable for their symmetry and rhythmic pattern-ing.[14] Frequently planning the structure of his work while seated at a piano keyboard, a musical quality pervades many of his dramas either overtly (as in *Five Finger Exercise* and *Amadeus*), or less obvi-ously in plays such as *Black Comedy* and *Equus*. Certainly, Shaffer's musical training and knowledgeability leads naturally to this sense of shape, just as it also suggests an innate awareness of rhythm and tempo, so clearly demonstrated in a play such as *The Royal Hunt of the Sun*. Whether in the early naturalism or in the developed 'epic' mode, or in any of the forms we could isolate during or since, the sense of musical accuracy, operatic structure, and symphonic pace is always evident in Shaffer's work and invariably exerts an iron control over the shape and internal movement of the 'total' play.

A further musical influence may also be detected in Shaffer's in-sistence on collaboration during the production of his plays where the director, designer, writer and actors conjoin to carve out a play in the medium where it is to find meaning. Testing what works and what does not work in the theatre, Shaffer rewrites his material throughout the rehearsal period, tuning the play by conducting the actors in the stage space. Here, form is the priority, a point noted by Simon Callow who observed the playwright in action throughout the preparations for the London production of *Amadeus*:

> ...the play changed so much by the first readthrough that it was scarcely the same play. It was to change again almost completely by the time we opened. It is still changing. Peter is the opposite of a lapidiary writer. The form of his work is open to constant im-provement. Its theatrical essence remains unaltered.[15]

The tight construction this gives rise to simultaneously serves another purpose; in moulding the material into a flawless 'musical' shape, Shaffer is also ensuring that this shape is *entirely and only theatrical* since it is dictated by environment. Composed external to the site of ritual, the play is essentially alien to its systems of com-munication, but transferred into that medium, form as well as content become moulded to its precepts. Here we see that in the act of composition, 'drama' again becomes 'theatre', and 'theatre' becomes 'drama' in Shaffer's work since both are inextricably con-nected at the point of writing which is also the point of realization.

The allegiance to form is perhaps more clear in the plays which suggest the traditions of naturalistic theatre, though it should be

understood that form becomes an intensified, though less conspicu-
ous, preoccupation of the later plays. Naturalism is, of course, a
mode that offers structure as a prerequisite of meaning; insisting
on an adherence to the precepts of the 'well-made' play, its characters behave credibly within a recognizable socio-cultural situation
(which is evoked with scientific accuracy), and a clear progression
from beginning, through middle, and towards end is evident. The
norm of mainstream, mainstage theatre since Ibsen and Shaw, the
naturalistic mode was still dominant in 1950s theatre, so dominant,
in fact, that even a 'revolutionary' play such as John Osborne's *Look
Back in Anger* (1956) failed to shake off its representational idiom.

With naturalism reigning supreme on the West End stage (the
'temple' of commercial success), it is hardly suprising that Shaffer
felt compelled to write within its conventions, even though his
preference for alternative forms of representation was already fer-
menting by the mid-1950s. But still a relatively inexperienced
dramatist, the playwright could hardly risk attempting to stage a
play such as *The Royal Hunt of the Sun* (in composition prior to *Five
Finger Exercise*) when his theatrical experience was so limited and
when he enjoyed only minimal recognition in the wake of his radio
and television plays. As a result, Shaffer's earliest stage successes
remained within the naturalistic tradition; *Five Finger Exercise*, for
example, centred on a typically bourgeois, middle-class family
waging a bloody war of attrition in their country retreat. The naturalistic emphases on heredity and environment are central to the
drama while the Ibsenian technique of journeying from past to
present in the course of the play gradually explains the situation
we stumbled upon as the curtain rose. The play moves carefully
towards crisis point through the skilful placing of key moments,
usually at the end of an Act, these moments increasing in intensity
as the play moves clearly (even predictably) forwards to the point
of closure.

However, while it remains true that *Five Finger Exercise* belongs
within the naturalistic tradition in many respects, it is equally true
that it has been too easily accepted that this play is little more than
the work of a mainstream playwright learning his craft and producing work that is 'traditional' in all its major components. Upon
closer examination, it becomes clear that Shaffer's breakthrough
stage success is not as conventional as it seems. To begin with, as
John Russell Taylor points out, the play is organized less through
dialogue than through a system of monologues or 'self-revealing

tirades', these being antithetical to the 'well-made' pattern of evenly distributed exchange; such monologues draw attention to the 'theatricality' of the play, removing it from the naturalistic emphasis on a mimetic representation of 'reality'.[16] Secondly, *Five Finger Exercise* exhibits distinct signs of symbolist activity where words or objects assume significance external to their apparent function: the emphasis on Walter's hair, caressed by both Mrs Harrington and Clive alternately, might be considered as an example of this, as might also Walter himself. A network of symbolist signs weaves through this play and alerts us to the fact that what we have too easily accepted as 'normal' is strange indeed.

Thirdly, the intensity of psychological penetration evident throughout this play again suggests that Shaffer is attempting to do something more with his drama than its form immediately implies. The use of monologue is involved again here, but more important still is the fact that the psychological activity that these monologues reveal is presented in terms that involve stripping each character bare (with the exception of the solidly uninteresting Pamela), much in the way that Clive dreams he is stripped physically bare by his father who removes blankets from him one by one. As this process of psychological stripping develops, it becomes clear that what we are witnessing on stage is not a middle-class family indulging in trench warfare but a group of bloodthirsty cannibals bent on destroying any intruder. Psychological exploration is by no means inimical to the traditionally oriented stage drama prevalent at this time (it is even central to it), but the manner of charting this exploration in *Five Finger Exercise* surprises us in its primitive savagery.

So the apparently conventional West End drama which achieved solid commercial success becomes a rather more complex piece of theatre than it at first seems. The play in effect fools us into believing that what we see here is familiar territory with its drawing-room stage interior and its family of 'types'; it fools us again into thinking that we have seen all this before on countless mainstream stages. But in fact this play succeeds in undermining our theatrical assumptions because where its structure suggests conventional dramatic substance, its content suggests impulses running counter to it. Here we see the first tentative flowering of dramatic experimentation which was to achieve full expression in the later work: *Five Finger Exercise* is an appetizer.

Shaffer's interest in exploring new representational techniques was revealed a little more confidently in each new play that followed. Gradually, his reputation as a dramatist was increasing and this allowed him greater freedom not only to experiment, but also to ensure that his experiments would be staged in the mainstream, commercial theatre, an environment that had traditionally proved hostile to innovation. In his double-bill of one-act plays, *The Private Ear* and *The Public Eye* (premiered in May 1962 at the Globe Theatre), Shaffer's theatre expanded in new directions whilst still apparently remaining within familiar dramatic territory in its examination of close-knit social groups. In the first play, an extended mime elevated the apparently conventional examination of alienation into a new region of theatrical experience; Michael Wall was one of several critics who indicated that the resulting emotional release proved powerful:

> ...at the end of *The Private Ear*, as Terry Scully and Maggie Smith, in beautifully timed and acutely observed performances, falter their way to making love while the Love Duet from Madame Butterfly fills the squalid attic room, one could have stood and cheered – if it had not been so intensely moving.[17]

Wall is here responding to a combination of visual and aural triggers, the preceding drama having created the conditions in which 'effect' can create maximum theatrical impact. The mime is a moment of catharsis commenting on the trap of idealism in which Bob is caught where reality is squalid but possible and where dream is perfect but impossible. The mimed seduction shatters Bob because he is forced to confront this irresolvable disjunction, but his tragedy is not expressed verbally because words have always proved insufficient to him: instead, the amalgam of music and movement communicates the hopeless farce of his situation and the profound despair that accompanies it in a manner more direct and expressive than a section of dialogue, no matter how eloquent, could ever achieve. This is an early example of 'drama' conditioning 'theatre', and of 'theatre' expressing 'drama'.

The musicality of *The Private Ear* is manifested on a number of levels in ways that will become familiar in Shaffer's later plays. Here, music is used as a means of communication, as a way of 'speaking' emotion and experience and as a way of extending that intuitive discourse into the auditorium. It is also used thematically with Bob's inability to exist within drab reality and his subsequent alienation being expressed in his retreat into a musical world where language and interaction are redundant. Finally, music grounds the play in a structural logic since, as Walter Kerr notes, three identifiable movements (which he labels, 'the skirmish, the scramble, the scratch') are involved here: he adds, 'if the little play is, in any plausible sense, a sequence of three emotional non sequiturs, it works as a piece of clever music might, in movements that assert themselves as contrast'.[18] Music, in other words, organizes the play thematically, emotionally and structurally just as it will later do in *Amadeus*.

The Private Ear in addition displays a range of devices which will again be developed in the later dramas, the 'freezing' of characters, disrupting the internal logic of time and space, being one of them. In a related strategy, the speeded up chatter of the dinner party echoing round the theatre on tape allows the audience to penetrate Bob's subjective perception since he receives the conversation only as meaningless babble while time moves at an irrational pace in imitation of the noise. Bob can make sense of neither and the audience hears what Bob perceives. In each example, it becomes clear that Shaffer is in this play attempting to fuse 'drama' with 'theatre' since none of the effects discussed here are isolated from the context of plot direction or psychological development. In short, *The Private Ear* constitutes a significant step in the playwright's search for representational modes capable of uniting theatrical 'effect' with dramatic 'effectiveness'.

But while such theatrical experimentation met with approval from many critics, the response to *The Public Eye* suggests that there was a limit to how far Shaffer could go within the confines of traditional representation. Again focusing on a dysfunctional relationship catalysed by an external force, this Ortonesque 'farce' sought to entertain whilst simultaneously posing fundamental questions related to communication and identity. Onto a familiar stage interior waltzes Julian Christoforou, a sugar-crazed elf-cum-redeemer who proceeds to reveal Charles to himself and to reunite him with his wife by insisting that he speechlessly observe her over a number of weeks to discover who she really is. The play works at a number of levels, tight verbal play producing pace and recondite enquiry producing depth, but what puzzled critics was that what the play *seemed* to be appeared to be in conflict with what it actually *was*. John Simon is typical in his assessment of the play, mistakenly attempting to resolve the conflict in terms of genre: 'It cannot quite decide whether it wants to be Peter Sellers's type of farcical comedy verging on dropping pants, or something more Metaphysical and "absurd" in the manner of Ionesco, which leads to contradiction and eventual wobbliness'.[19]

A certain 'wobbliness' is certainly evident in this play though the problem is less to do with genre as Simon decides than to do with an uncomfortable collision between form and content. It was time for Shaffer to make his theatrical intentions clear in a drama that risked stepping out of the familiar world of contemporary interiors and into a theatrical context where form could be united with content and where 'theatre' could be fully fused with 'drama': the result was *The Royal Hunt of the Sun*.

First produced by the National Theatre at Chichester in 1964, this play was to have an enormous impact not only on those who saw the production, but also on Shaffer's subsequent career; in addition, it forced the mainstream stage into new perceptions about what it could present and suggested a recalculation in relation to its audiences' 'needs'. Critical evaluations of Shaffer's work would be conditioned by the play from this point on, a fact that has not always worked to his advantage as we have already seen. In *The Royal Hunt of the Sun*, Shaffer's ideas about what theatre could do finally became concrete while his dramatic obsessions were placed centre stage; the search for meaningful worship, the desire for immortality coupled with the devastating effects of time, questions of identity, and notions of experience and existence, all of which were impulses present in the earlier plays but buried by limitations imposed by form, achieve bold statement in this spectacular assault on the senses and the emotions.

Incorporating a wide range of theatrical effects including mime, chant, dance and bird-cries coupled with stagecraft involving lighting, costume and choreography, *The Royal Hunt of the Sun* has largely been analysed critically in terms of its apparent debt to the dramatic theories of Antonin Artaud and Bertolt Brecht. Before assessing the usefulness of this overworked approach, it is necessary firstly to outline the theories of the two playwrights who so many believe to have had such a direct influence on Shaffer, particularly in this play and in *Equus*.

In his manifesto, *The Theatre and Its Double* (*Le Théâtre et son Double*, 1938), French director, author, poet, actor and theorist Antonin Artaud outlined the concepts which defined his programme for a new drama named 'Theatre of Cruelty'. Artaud's vision of theatre was located in metaphysical regions and aimed to create a mystical experience where an audience's primal energies could be communally purged through a stage event based on an alternative 'language' which forsook the merely verbal. The intention was to create a theatre that impels self-scrutiny through witnessing stage action that forces 'us to see ourselves as we are, making the masks fall and divulging our world's lies, aimlessness, meanness, and even two-facedness'.[20] This was to be effected through a 'language' composed of 'everything filling the stage, everything that can be shown and materially expressed on stage, intended first of all to appeal to the senses, instead of being addressed primarily to the mind, like spoken language'.[21] Based on the precepts of Eastern theatre (specifically, Balinese), Artaud's theory of theatrical event therefore centralized gesture, sound, music and movement, all coordinated with 'the solemnity of a holy ritual', and designed as an 'exorcism to make our devils FLOW'.[22]

At this point, Shaffer's debt to Artaud's theories seems significant: in *Equus*, sound corresponds with gesture in the acoustic and stylized representation of the horses, while in *The Royal Hunt of the Sun*, we find an insistent 'appeal to the senses'.[23] The concepts of exorcism and of 'holy ritual', outlined above, are also echoes of Artaud. Further, a concept central to 'Theatre of Cruelty' is the idea that the stage action should take place *around* the audience, involving each directly with the other: again, this is echoed in *Equus* where, with the audience placed both in the auditorium and in on-stage tiers, the drama actually takes place *between* the spectators rather than in front of them with all the emotional and psychological consequences that this positioning implies. Artaud's insistence on 'continual amplification' of sounds and noises, and his demand that lighting should be used to influence and suggest, are also strategies employed in Shaffer's three best-known works: *The Royal Hunt of the Sun*, *Equus* and *Amadeus*.[24]

'Theatre of Cruelty', Artaud was keen to stress, did not necessarily involve violence as its title suggested, but was intended instead to refer to a 'sense of drastic strictness' effected through an 'extreme concentration of stage elements'.[25] The aim was to release the audience from unthinking adherence to the laws of social life, to connect it with unconscious energies associated with dream and imagination, and to purge it of violent destructive tendencies which lead to riot and murder. The first project he devised for his new theatre was to be titled 'The Conquest of Mexico', a historical play pitching Christianity against Paganism and contrasting 'the tyrannical anarchy of the colonisers with the deep intellectual concord of those about to be colonised'. Artaud continues: 'From a social point of view, it demonstrates the peacefulness of a society which knew how to feed all its members and where the Revolution had taken place at its inception'.[26] Little wonder then, that several critics have found in Shaffer's *The Royal Hunt of the Sun* an apparent homage to the theories of Artaud since not only does its theme seem to tally with this planned production, but its means of theatrical communication seem to be predicated upon the principles of 'Theatre of Cruelty' which 'The Conquest of Mexico' was intended to demonstrate.

The connection between the two has, however, been over-emphasized, as has also the extent to which Shaffer has been influenced by Artaud's theatrical theories. To begin with, Shaffer is as much indebted to William Prescott's book, *The Conquest of Peru*, as he is to Artaud's planned 'The Conquest of Mexico', Shaffer having stated that the effect that Prescott's work had on him was enormous. In addition, Artaud had insisted that 'The Conquest of Mexico' should 'stage events rather than men', since men should be regarded only in the light of the parts they played in the scheme of wider social and historical events.[27] Even a cursory examination of Shaffer's play shows that *The Royal Hunt of the Sun* does precisely the opposite, the drama focusing on the relationship between Atahuallpa and Pizarro and on the linked ideas of divinity, worship and immortality that this relationship comes to represent. The greed of Spain and its eventual downfall, 'gorged with gold', together with the contrasted socio-economic systems of Communism and Capitalism, are certainly emphases, but they are not ultimately central to the thesis of the play.[28]

Further, the relationship between the two men is expressed through a blend of dialogue and gesture, the verbal being particularly central to the expression of Pizarro's despair. Here we find Shaffer's most significant departure from Artaud since where Artaud insisted that psychological theatre is dead and that words are essentially external to theatrical experience, Shaffer insists that psychology is a seam of dramatic enquiry that has hardly been mined and that words are the basis (though not the whole) of theatrical communication.[29] In his introduction to *Equus*, Shaffer makes it clear that 'words' conjoin with a range of elements to produce a 'total' theatrical 'experience': 'That experience is composed, of course, not merely of the words [the audience] heard, but the gestures they saw, and the lighting, and the look of the thing'.[30] In short, for Artaud, stage 'language' prioritizes 'theatre', but for

Shaffer, stage 'language' unifies 'drama' *with* 'theatre' since neither is complete without the other.

That Shaffer has absorbed several of Artaud's theories is not in question, but the idea that he is in some sense a 'disciple' of Artaud, following his precepts unthinkingly, is erroneous.[31] In the case of *The Royal Hunt of the Sun*, it can even be argued that the Artaudian disciple is less Shaffer than his director, John Dexter, whose notions of performative athleticism and adherence to the precepts of 'total theatre' are clearly derived from Artaud.[32] 'Theatre of Cruelty' is certainly a context that should be considered in relation not only to the Inca play, but also to later work such as *Equus* and *The Gift of the Gorgon*, but it should never be taken to be the whole story. Apart from any other consideration, there is another theatrical influence to be considered – the work and theories of Bertolt Brecht.

As in the case of Artaud, several critics have pointed to aspects of Shaffer's plays which suggest Brechtian influences, but again, this apparent debt has been over-emphasized. Brecht's concept of 'Epic Theatre', which derived from his allegiance to Marxist ideology, attempted to stage a socio-political reality which forced the audience to think actively and self-consciously about what it was witnessing. Rejecting naturalism on the grounds of its inherently bourgeois focus which automatically expressed the establishment view of reality, Brecht formulated a theatre of alienation (*verfremdungseffekt*) where the audience was discouraged from identification with character and was therefore persuaded to respond to events intellectually rather than emotionally. This involved a continual smashing of the fictional frame to remind the audience that the performance was a performance *only*, and that the issues raised in the course of the play remained in need of urgent and direct action. As such, alienation techniques include the use of a narrator (an inherently non-naturalistic device), recourse to placards announcing 'scenes', and the incorporation of songs, tableaux and movement which express or announce issues of particular significance. Brecht's theatre was thus pointedly didactic, manipulating the audience through a range of devices towards a specific point of view, refusing ambiguity in an insistence on intellectual accord, and forsaking closure to emphasize the need for socio-political action external to the theatrical environment.

In 'Epic Theatre', then, the audience become critics who are asked to observe and analyse rather than lose themselves in emotional and psychological reaction. Brecht here differs radically from

Artaud who had wanted the spectator to become absorbed in the performance to the extent that he/she was elevated to a psychic level of experience. Despite this difference, however, there is an overlap between the two theories of theatre in that both writers rejected orthodox naturalism in their attempts to address a failed socio-political context, both felt words to be insufficient to the expression of their agendas, both attempted to conjoin 'drama' with 'theatre' realizing that neither is complete without the other, and both understood that the 'meaning' of theatre is largely contained in, and created by, its communality.[33]

Brecht's concept of 'Epic Theatre' apparently infiltrates several of Shaffer's plays, *The Royal Hunt of the Sun* and *Equus* most obviously. In both, we find the use of a controlling narrator, the use of song, mime and dance in the earlier work, and the positioning of the audience as observers and even inquisitors in the later work where spectators behave as witnesses in a trial or as observers at a clinical lecture. Both plays also develop episodically, this being reminiscent of Brecht's concept of *gestus* where each 'scene' is designed as a separate piece of a wider 'story', and *Equus* in particular demands a concomitant level of intellectual awareness if the episodes are to be pieced together and interpreted with any degree of analytical sophistication.

However, labelling either play 'Brechtian' (in their apparent resemblance to 'Epic Theatre') is as misleading as labelling them 'Artaudian' since while certain elements may suggest Epic influence, more elements suggest significant departures. Shaffer is not, for a start, emerging from a specifically ideological position in his drama and, as a result, didacticism in socio-political terms is neither the intention nor the effect of his plays.[34] Nor does didacticism condition his means of expression in the way that it does Brecht, so that while Shaffer may insist on analytical absorption in *Equus*, this is not the 'total' effect he aims for. Instead, he intends (and achieves) a balance between mental attentiveness and emotional engagement, this giving rise to a dramatic and theatrical experience which is wider than either Artaud or Brecht envisaged. And while performative elements may seem to insist on a consistent awareness of the fictional frame, it remains true that most audiences quickly acclimatize to the 'theatricality' of Shaffer's staging and, by the end of the play, fully accept the alternative mode of reality that has been created throughout the performance. Finally, Shaffer's narrators are more than simply guiding or explanatory devices as they are in Brecht's theatre; Old Martin, Dysart, Salieri and Yonadab not only unify and comment on each episode, they also condition our intuitive responses *to* them through their participation *in* them. Emotional and psychological identification, so despised by Brecht on ideological grounds, naturally arises as a result leading us to respond more to character than to context or situation: as before, it is Pizarro's despair that the audience remembers more than Spain's Imperialist terrorism, just as it is Dysart's existential disintegration that penetrates our consciousness more than the implications of a socially-imposed (and thus arbitrary) definition of psychosis.

The problem is that though the labels 'Brechtian' and 'Artaudian' take us some way towards an understanding of Shaffer's theatre in theoretical terms, they can never proceed beyond a certain point because, not only does 'theory' in principle have little to do with 'theatre' in practice, but also the labels become inappropriate when dominant elements in the plays fail to fit the theories. It seems that Shaffer has selected certain ideas from both dramatists and adapted them to create a version of theatrical drama (or dramatic theatre) that is unique to him so that any attempt to categorize his means and methods always flounders. An additional problem is that Shaffer's influences are wide-ranging and eclectic so that the techniques of Chinese opera are relevant to *Black Comedy*, the Shakespearean chronicle play relevant to *The Royal Hunt of the Sun*, Classical theatre relevant to *Equus* and *The Gift of the Gorgon*, satyr or 'revel' drama to *Lettice and Lovage*, opera to *Amadeus*, and so on. Finally, classification by theory or 'school' becomes a self-defeating exercise since it inhibits analysis and thus leads to reductiveness. This is a trap that Gene A. Plunka falls into when he decides that '*Equus* works well on stage because it is effective Theatre of Cruelty as Artaud suggested it should be performed';[35] Plunka misses the point that no piece of theatre can be fully effective solely as a theoretical demonstration and that a range of dramatic and theatrical elements are more fundamentally involved in causing the play to 'work well on stage' than theory can ever account for.

Shaffer is himself aware of the dangers of 'labels' in their application to theatre and drama, a position he made clear as early as 1960 when he stated:

I do not want to classify, or be classified by others, especially since the classifications are not only irrelevant but often quite perverse [...] As a playwright, I'm scared of the too well-defined identity – of being either publicly or (even worse) privately its prisoner [...] if I knew how to formulate it, I would like to propound an Artistic Theory of Indeterminacy [...] I am beginning to be uneasy about a climate of belief that makes me feel a slight guilt because I want to do many different kinds of things in the theatre.[36]

For Shaffer, then, labels not only lead to preconditioned and stock response in relation to drama, they also inhibit the writer who feels defined and thus trapped by them. Examining Shaffer's theatre by way of theory (whether naturalism, 'Theatre of Cruelty' or 'Epic') will take us to a certain point, but will always lead to an eventual dead end. Instead, we need to approach the matter of 'theatricality' from another angle and, of the alternatives available, Shaffer's use of dramatic language is potentially the most illuminating.

As discussed above, Shaffer views language as central to the theatrical experience, words triggering audience responses which a range of staging effects enforce and intensify. Often accused of over-writing and of a tendency towards rhetoric, Shaffer in fact demonstrates impressive dexterity in juggling a range of communicative devices including monologue, stichomythia (dialogue in alternate lines), song and dialectic. As always, the form that the dialogue takes depends on the emotional and psychological effect he aims to produce and is always conditioned totally by the dramatic and theatrical situation.

Shaffer's control over a range of communicative strategies is perhaps best demonstrated in *Equus*. This play proceeds through question-and-answer examination (though who is being examined is permanently open to question) and, to express this structure dramatically, Shaffer incorporates regular stretches of stichomythic exchange into the dialogue. Forming an inherently non-naturalistic rhythm, these exchanges serve multiple purposes, increasing the pace of the 'investigation', dramatizing the duel between hunter and hunted (and rendering the question of who occupies these roles ambiguous), and encouraging a sense of tension and danger that comes to fill the theatre. The following extract provides an example of these effects in action:

DYSART: Was she friendly?
ALAN: Yes.

DYSART: Or stand-offish?

ALAN: Yes.

DYSART: Well which?

ALAN: What?

DYSART: Which was she?

[ALAN *brushes harder.*]

Did you take her out? Come on now: tell me. Did you have a date with her?

ALAN: What?

DYSART [*sitting*]: Tell me if you did.

[*The boy suddenly explodes in one of his rages.*]

ALAN [*yelling*]: TELL ME!

[*All the masks toss at the noise.*] [37]

The audience here is effectively identifying with Dysart since it is equally eager to discover the explanation for Alan's crime: we too analyse the boy's responses, and react to the increasing pace of this exchange by demanding yet more pace as the tension mounts towards an inevitable explosion of some kind. At the same time, we feel for the hunted boy who is desperately trying to conceal and keep private that which can no longer be hidden. The tossing of the masks simultaneously reminds us of this private worship and marks an explosion of violence that will later be directed in terrifying terms at the masks (or horses) themselves.

This stichomythic pattern characterizes key sections of *Equus* in an imitation of the 'detective' format where the desire to reveal is pitched against the desire to conceal.[38] Meanwhile, the haunting stage images contrast clinical efficiency (the set resembling a dissecting theatre circled by analytical observers) with passionate experience (the boy abreacting in a mimed field of mist): again we find that the drama and its theatrical expression are mutually dependent since the disjunction that this representation denotes is at the heart of Dysart's existential dilemma.

The stichomythic patterns in this play are placed in counterpoint to their rhetorical opposite: sections of monologue addressed by Dysart to the audience who now become the analysts of the analyst. It is perhaps Shaffer's use of monologue that moves the audience onto an altered emotional plane; again suggesting the antithesis of naturalism, these passages often contain sections of remarkable poetry that prove moving on grounds that are largely indefinable. In *The Royal Hunt of the Sun, Equus, Amadeus, Shrivings* and *Yonadab,* these monologues appear at structurally significant points, comment on events, and express moments of deepest emotion, elation and despair.

In *Equus*, for example, Dysart's lengthy addresses to the audience begin both acts and open with the same sentence: 'With one particular horse, called Nugget, he embraces' (p.209, p.267). The words are visually enacted by the accompanying image of Alan engaged in acts of worship with the horse; neither the words nor the image make much sense in the opening moments of Act 1, but both are beginning to do so by the start of Act 2. After a few lines in each monologue, Alan leads the horse from the stage and Dysart is left alone to continue his speculations and to explore his reactions. What proves so powerful in these moments is a combination of elements that deserve analysis since they extend our understanding of how Shaffer's mode of communication works on both theatrical and dramatic levels.

The first element to note is the structure of the key sentence; use of punctuation paces the line, causing a pause at its centre (the choice of the name 'Nugget', as in 'core', also locates this clause as crucial). The words are simple and the line is short, but the word 'particular' alerts us to the strangeness of what we are witnessing while its pedantic specificity contrasts sharply with the 'extremity' of the visual image. Secondly, the image we see on stage completes the audience's psychological and emotional response to the sentence, the stark drama implied by it (and by its utterance in monologue form) finding corresponding visual expression. The words would make no sense without the image and would achieve less impact, and vice versa. 'Drama' is again fused with 'theatre', and 'theatre' with 'drama'.

Finally, the repetition of the line at the beginning of both acts unifies the drama and provides a verbal and visual demonstration of the extent to which the image of the boy and the horse haunts Dysart's psyche since he cannot purge it from his mind. The combined effect haunts the audience in the same way. Dysart is then left alone on stage to express, in increasingly urgent terms, the devastation he feels as a result of his encounter with this 'case', expressing his terrors in sentences of complex rhythms and ideas alternated with lines of stark simplicity: key-words such as 'extremity' recur, sentence structures repeat, the whole building to a final desperate bid to rationalize that which can never be converted into logical response.

Here, heightened expression produces an emotionally charged atmosphere which characterizes Shaffer's concept of 'theatrical drama'. The monologues which litter this text are simultaneously elements of the play's 'drama' (since the isolation of their delivery proclaims alienation) and elements of the play's 'theatre' (since the response they trigger is located in the communal imagination). Similarly, the stichomythic exchanges express dramatic impulses (the detective format and the relationship between hunter and hunted) and rely for their impact on the effect of their rhythms in the theatrical arena where rite and ritual dominate. Language in this play, specifically in the interplay between stichomythic exchange and monologic delivery, therefore becomes the link between the two communicative levels and attests to the extent of their mutuality.

In this example, which reveals a pattern that is replicated in so many of Shaffer's plays, the attempt to create an alternative form of imaginative reality is clear. What we find here is a version of 'poetic drama' that is unique to Shaffer since it relies for its effect on a network of triggers located in the pattern of words, the form in which they are delivered, on the communal nature of their reception, and on the visual images or aural sounds which accompany and complete them. In effect, we have here a demonstration of an aesthetic process described in *Amadeus* where Salieri asks: 'Could one catch a realer moment? And how except in a net of pure artifice?'.[39] Shaffer's theatrical drama resembles such a 'net' in its intricate fusion of words, music and stagecraft, all of which conspires to express the 'realer moment'. It is this 'net' which finally brings the audience 'right to the edge of experience'.[40]

That this combination of elements is unique to theatre is proved by the fact that the adaptation of Shaffer's plays to the cinema has led to unsatisfactory results, the one successful film (in commercial and critical terms), *Amadeus*, having been rewritten and reformulated in transition to the screen. To remove Shaffer's drama from the theatre is to destroy it because, as throughout, the symbiotic relationship between the two means that it can achieve complete expression in no other arena. As we have seen, this 'expression' is based neither on the verbal level nor on the performative level in isolation, but is predicated on a powerful interrelationship between the two. The 'failure' of the adaptations alone attests to this defining co-dependence in Shaffer's work.

The immense range of theatrical strategies in these plays is too vast a subject to consider in detail here; the operatic structure of

Amadeus complete with stichomythic patterning, the consistent technique of 'freezing' characters to allow space for comment, monologue and analysis, the use of music to condition reaction and interpretation, the manipulation of stage space to represent dual scenes (in a theatrical equivalent of the cinematic split screen), and so on, are all strategies that should be considered when analysing and understanding Shaffer's work.[41] The concern in this chapter has been to place these strategies within a wider context to explain how and why this body of plays triggers such intense response in the spectator; it has suggested that the answer lies in the unique fusion between 'theatre' and 'drama' as is made clear through a consideration of Shaffer's use of language.[42] Finally, though, any attempt to rationalize theatrical response will always have to concede that there is a certain point at which logic must be abandoned. Nowhere is this more clear than in Shaffer's theatre where a form of 'heightened waking' characterizes audience experience.[43]

As these plays so eloquently suggest, neither words nor logic can explain every level of response, and the attempt to make them do so limits rather than expands understanding. It is to the issue of words and their limits that the next chapter turns.

3

Words and their Limits

The previous chapter discussed the relationship between Peter Shaffer's use of language and his concept of theatrical communication and argued that 'meaning' did not arise from verbal discourse alone. Here, the matter of communication is examined from another point of view in an analysis of the way in which it operates as a theme in several of these plays. The idea that words alone may not be enough to effect true communication, expressed theatrically in this body of work, is continued into the action of the plays themselves where words are consistently seen as a block to understanding, meaning and truth. This chapter traces the many ways in which this modernist concept is illustrated concentrating largely on Shaffer's earlier plays where the theme is foregrounded, but incorporating some discussion of the later work where the theme also infiltrates stage action.

Central to a complete interpretation of plays such as *Five Finger Exercise* and *The Public Eye* is the idea that words are not only insufficient when it comes to the expression of emotion, but that they are also an impediment to true knowledge and understanding either of a situation or of a person. Words contained in speech are excellent weapons when they are used to divide and destroy, and they are useful for lies and evasions, but Shaffer shows in his plays that they are more suited to concealment than they are to revelation. As a result, consistent emphases in his early plays include the extent to which silence may 'speak' louder than words and music may 'speak' louder than both since both silence and speech are constantly misinterpreted according to the prejudices or needs of the listener.

The plays examined in this chapter first appeared on stage between 1958 and 1965 and should be placed within the dramatic context of these years. The issue of the instability of language, of its dubious relation to meaning and truth, was widely explored in the drama of this time, a move potentially initiated by John Osborne's *Look Back in Anger* in 1956. In this deeply influential play, husband

and wife battle within a domestic interior using words as their weapons: Jimmy speaks obsessively in an effort to make himself heard while Alison retreats into a silence she knows will hurt him more than speech could ever do. A massive communication failure results though both, in effect, 'speak' incessantly. Harold Pinter was also achieving widespread recognition with plays such as *The Birthday Party* (1958) and *The Caretaker* (1960), both of which focused on the relationship between language and power as well as on the gap between what people say and what they really mean. Here, language becomes a tactic, a means of avoidance, and only in silence does true communication occur. These dramatic emphases are clearly detectable in Shaffer's earlier work and place the plays within an identifiable cultural moment, but this playwright's concern with the vagaries of language arguably extends further than either Osborne's or Pinter's work implies. In Shaffer's plays, words and their limits become an obsession as the need for communication, and the impossibility of it in verbal terms, is placed centre stage.

It is with the dramatic and thematic nature of this obsession that this chapter is concerned. Before looking at the communication issue in relation to the early plays, it is worth mentioning a few of the ways in which it recurs throughout the entire work. For a start, communication is implied in Shaffer's characteristic interest in word-games and puns (see, for example, the titles of *The Private Ear* and *The Public Eye*). The playwright is aware that word-games expose language as a fraud since they reveal the fact that 'meaning' is not fixed; such verbal play interrogates the very notion of 'language' since it illustrates its essential instability and converts it into a kind of joke where meaning cannot be guaranteed.[1] It therefore draws attention to the reasons why any form of communication that relies purely on words is sure to fail, and the inclusion of word-games and puns in a play such as *Five Finger Exercise* carries this perception to the heart of the text.[2]

A second emphasis related to this issue characterizes Shaffer's work, and that is the recurrent use of the question-and-answer format which survives from the early detective novels and which pitches the desire to reveal against the desire to conceal. Interrogations and interviews scatter the plays whether conspicuously as in *Equus* or less obviously as in *The Public Eye* and *The Gift of the Gorgon*. Usually, the interrogator is attempting to interpret the past and rationalize the present through the answers that he or she seeks, though the questioner often turns into a self-questioner in the process, in the manner of Dysart. The respondent, meanwhile, often answers in the spirit of confession and purgation, releasing torments that have been repressed too long as a result of various communication failures. Lies, which in Shaffer's plays signal the most fundamental abuse of meaning, are often implicated in these failures, hence the consistent emphasis on forms of dishonesty and deception here. Words are the means by which these frauds are perpetrated, as is made clear in *Yonadab* in particular.

Also related to communication failure in these plays is the frequent incorporation of an obsessive communicator, one who is driven to speak and to make himself known: Pizarro, Dysart, Mark Askelon, Salieri and Yonadab all fall into this category. These characters feel compelled to speak, to reach out for understanding, absolution or contact, but they often find that words actually aggravate their existential distress rather than alleviate it. For example, Mark Askelon has used words as a substitute for experience and when he comes to realize this, words lose all meaning for him. Similarly, Dysart is so 'reined up in old language and old assumptions' that he is unable to experience passion, this placing him in direct contrast to Alan who has passion but no 'language' with which to express it.[3] Salieri, meanwhile, is painfully aware of the limits of spoken language since not only does his sardonic wit attempt to conceal the 'truth' (and is thus an evasion), but his anguish derives from the fact that he has only ever heard God 'speak' in Mozart's music. In each case, communication is attempted compulsively but since these protagonists have come to understand that 'meaning' has little to do with 'words', the attempt itself becomes problematic.

This is perhaps indicated most clearly in *Amadeus* where a number of issues revolving around 'words' and their limits are raised. To begin with, Salieri's role as narrator, interpreter and mediator (between past and present, stage action and audience response) places the matter of interpretive meaning at the heart of the text.[4] Do we believe Salieri's version of events as he asks us to, or do we interpret the subjective account of the interpreter to arrive at an alternative, objective conclusion? In addition, the play is constructed in the detective genre, as indicated by Salieri's chosen title for his final work: 'The Death of Mozart' or 'Did I Do It?', so that the theme of the play again insists on interpretation.[5] Further, rumour, as personified in the Venticelli, is thematically central to the play and suggests a wild exaggeration of fact which spreads like wildfire; each example provides an extension of the difficult relationship between words, communication and truth.

But this ambiguous relationship is most clearly expressed in *Amadeus* through the use of music, and here we find the repeat of an emphasis that had existed in Shaffer's work as early as *The Private Ear*. Where words block and distort meaning in both plays, music focuses and distils it. In *Amadeus*, Mozart's music transports Salieri because it reaches beyond the limits of the verbal (and the emotions that can be expressed this way) and stretches towards territories of experience which escape words. As a result, Mozart's scatological nonsense-language is actually a direct echo of his music which also renders language nonsense because it is able to articulate profound meaning in a way that words cannot. Also, one of the reasons why Mozart fails to penetrate Salieri's web of deceit is that he can make 'no sense' of the 'nonsense' verbal world of dishonesty, only truly understanding the language of music which, by definition, cannot lie: as Salieri tells us, 'A note of music is either right or wrong – *absolutely*!'.[6]

Words, however, can be both 'right' and 'wrong' simultaneously, as Clive discovers in *Five Finger Exercise* (the musical implications of the title are not accidental), a play concerned almost exclusively with the painful gap between words, communication and meaning. Here we find that the impulses outlined above achieve their earliest dramatic expression in Shaffer's stage work. Described by Peter Roberts as 'a devastatingly true picture of the way human beings suffer and yet remain isolated and totally unable to understand each other', *Five Finger Exercise* centres on the range of ways in which communication within a family group becomes a painful impossibility, and numerous levels of dishonesty are incorporated into its stage action in the interests of illustrating its motivating idea.[7] Meanwhile, the perception that, as Peter Griffith notes, 'language in use demonstrates a struggle for power' (an emphasis we would usually associate more with Pinter than with Shaffer) here becomes prominent.[8]

The theme of communication gaps and blocks is announced immediately in this play; reading the text, we find that we are introduced to Stanley Harrington in terms that draw our attention to his inability to connect with others and which indicate that his manner conceals his true nature and fears: '*there is something deeply insecure about his assertiveness*'.[9] Similarly, Walter is initially described as '*secret, diffident*' (p.19). In both cases, we detect a gap between what these characters seem to be and what they actually are; neither will dare to reveal themselves through speech but will use words instead as an evasive device designed to keep either themselves or their deepest fears hidden.

The first skirmish of the play, which occurs only minutes into the action, emphasizes the extent to which words are wielded by these characters as defensive or offensive weapons. Stanley and Louise are engaged in a form of guerrilla warfare where each attempts to gain an advantage in a struggle they can barely define. While they bicker and snipe, they do not actually express the cause of their dissatisfaction, as Pamela astutely recognizes when she struggles to explain their situation to Walter in Act 2: 'With Mother and Daddy the row is never really *about* – well, what they're quarrelling about' (p.57). In this undefined battle, Clive is a prisoner-of-war sought by both parties who try to capture ground by manoeuvring him into a position where he must declare allegiance to a 'side'. This is, of course, attempted via words and one of the earliest encounters of the play suggests the extent of the communicative difficulties that arise as a result. Louise tells Stanley to 'keep your ideas to yourself' on the grounds that 'we don't want to hear them', but Stanley responds to the attempt to silence him by introducing an obviously familiar weapon:

STANLEY: We? Clive agrees with me.
LOUISE: Do you, Clive?
CLIVE: Well, yes, I mean, well, no. Isn't it a bit early for this kind of conversation?
STANLEY: You said last night you thought a tutor was ridiculous.
CLIVE [*unhappily*]: Well, not really ridiculous ...
LOUISE: Just get on with your breakfast, darling.

(p.15)

Taking pity on him (and feeling that Clive is being of little help to either side), Louise silences her son just as she had tried to silence her husband. Here, Clive is caught in a situation where every word seems to condemn him in the eyes of one of his parents. He lapses into confused, nervous explanation using the phrase 'I mean' which recurs throughout the play, always at a point where a character is experiencing difficulty in converting thoughts, ideas or emotions into the clumsy mode of speech. 'You know what I mean', 'Do you understand?', 'I didn't mean it', are connected phrases which litter this text, and they each express the inability to articulate clearly and unambiguously through the medium of speech.

As the stage action shifts from our defining encounter with the elder Harringtons, we are introduced to Walter and Pamela through the tutor's doomed efforts to persuade his student to conjugate the French verb *parler* – to talk. The irony of this choice of verb cannot be over-emphasized given the scene we have just witnessed where 'to talk' was a bloody and painful business. The emphasis on foreign languages in this play again links with the communication issue in a number of ways. Hearing a language you are unable to understand should prove the profoundest block to communication, but in this play it is suggested that the link between 'language' and 'meaning' is not as simple as this. In Act 1, scene 2, Louise asks Walter to recite some poetry in German and when Clive points out that, since she does not speak the language, this may be a little futile, Louise responds:

> It's not the meaning, it's the sound that counts [...] when you speak it I'm sure I'll feel exactly what the poet wanted to say [...] even more than if I actually knew the language and had to cope with all those miller's daughters and woodcutters and little people. It's difficult to explain – but you know what I mean.
>
> (p.39)

Louise again takes refuge in that phrase of frustrated communication as she insists that 'meaning' may have little to do with verbal understanding. The same concept is expressed in the idea that while 'meaning' may arise from an unfamiliar language, 'nonsense' may arise from words spoken in a language which the listener ostensibly 'understands'.[10] Clive speaks English and so do his family, but it is only when he reaches Cambridge that he finds people communicating in an intellectual and emotional 'dialect' that he understands. As he explains to Walter: 'I suppose one of the thrills of travel is hearing people speak a foreign language. But the marvellous thing about this is hearing them speak my own for the first time' (p.38). Clive is here making a similar point to Louise since, like her, he is pointing out that words, communication and meaning have no innate connection.

'Foreign' language also becomes a thematic emphasis in Walter's refusal to teach German even though this is obviously the subject at which he is most expert. In Act 1, this becomes interesting from more than one point of view since the communication issue is implied at every level of his refusal. Pamela introduces the subject into the conversation, and thus to the audience, by asking Walter why he does not teach his own language: 'Walter, I never asked before – but why not? I mean you'd make more money doing that than anything else'. The following stage direction then informs us that Walter *'shakes his head slowly "No"'* (p.22). Walter's trauma about his Nazi background, we later learn, accounts for his refusal to teach his native language: he cannot bear to be reminded of his childhood and of the guilt he feels about being in some way implicated in the atrocities he connects with his country's genocide and with his father's brutal participation in it. That he marks this trauma through a retreat from his language is deeply significant, as also is his silence in response to Pamela's question. For Walter, the German language 'means' guilt and shame but he cannot communicate this chain of association to another person so deeply is he scarred by its connotations; instead he seeks refuge in non-communication and silence.

Clive's perception that only upon entering Cambridge did he hear a 'language' that he 'understood' is validated through what we see and hear of his relationship with his father. Pamela states that Clive has spent his whole life 'not being listened to' (p.57) and his encounters with Stanley in particular certainly suggest that father and son are speaking 'languages' that the other cannot (or will not) 'understand'. Shaffer's point that words may have little to do with communication is made explicit in these frustrating exchanges as Clive attempts to make his father understand his vision of life and as Stanley refuses to receive his 'meaning'.[11] A particularly interesting example of this breach occurs in Act 1, scene 2 when Clive tries to explain why an Indian friend at Cambridge 'matters' to him so much:

CLIVE: That's why he matters – because he loves living so much. Because he understands birds and makes shadow puppets out of cardboard, and loves Ella Fitzgerald and Vivaldi, and Lewis Carroll; and because he plays chess like a devil and makes the best prawn curry in the world. And this is him.
STANLEY: Do you want to be a cook?
CLIVE: No, I don't want to be a cook.

STANLEY [*bewildered and impatient*]: Well, Clive, I'm glad to know
you've got some nice friends.

(p.51)

Stanley clearly does not understand a word of what his son is
saying and he desperately grasps at the last idea that Clive introduces in an effort to concretize values that he cannot understand:
hence the comic question about cookery. Clive has tried to express
the essence of a person's 'being', but his father can only understand
this in terms of career aspirations which to *him* define a person's
'being'. When this interpretation is closed down, he withdraws into
impatience and patronage. The communication gap between them
seems hopeless since, as Clive points out, Stanley is somehow
proud of not understanding his son 'almost as if it defined' him
(p.52);[12] further, Clive notes that the failure is reciprocated: 'Has it
ever occurred to you that *I* don't understand *you*?' (p.52).

By the end of the play, though, it appears that Stanley and Clive
understand each other perfectly on a level that has nothing to do with
words and the tensions and failures of meaning they cause. It transpires that though Stanley has used Clive's lie concerning his
mother's infidelity with Walter to dismiss the intruder, he has not believed a word of it. Perhaps, like Clive, he has realized that just as the
'truth' may be used for dishonest purposes, 'lies' may be more 'true'
than they seem. In a play that is littered with falsehoods and evasions,
Clive's lie concerning the intimacy he says he has witnessed between
Louise and Walter is potentially the most damaging and appears to
have no rational explanation. Several critics have explained Clive's
motivation here as being grounded in Oedipal and/or homosexual
territory, but Clive's explanation of the lie (which may not be true, of
course) is equally illuminating.[13] To his mother, Clive defends his
actions by stating: 'I told a lie, yes. But what I felt under that lie, about
you and Walter – was that so untrue?' (p.91). Clive's ability to 'see
what's true and just what isn't' (p.48), which he had earlier told
Walter was his 'one real talent' (pp.47–8), is demonstrated here. As
we have seen, Clive is correct; Louise had been attracted to Walter
and, as such, Clive has simply converted his 'feeling' which was 'true'
into words which were 'false'. Again, the ambiguous relationship
between language and truth, together with the gap between 'feeling'
and language, becomes foregrounded.

Where words are used in this play to block meaning, construct
deceits (even if they are fundamentally truthful), evade and

destroy, silence also proves to be an unreliable form of communication. Silences are often interpreted here in accordance with what a character either wants or needs to believe, and they are therefore as prone to blocking 'meaning' as are words. A dominant example of this occurs in Act 2 where Louise suggests to Clive that he is jealous of Walter and that he is worried that the personable tutor with the hair of a poet will displace him in her affections; this interpretation relieves her of the necessity of having to explore more painful reasons for Clive's strange behaviour so she imposes her analysis on Clive and takes his subsequent silence for agreement. When she leaves, we are told that Clive experiences *'bitter disgust'* with himself, not merely because he loathes the idea of being an object of sympathy, but also because he has used silence as an evasion just as he has previously used words. Walter's earlier silence about his childhood and refusal to teach German finds a parallel here since both he and Clive 'speak volumes' in their *refusal* to 'speak', but at the same time reject the option of direct communication. Another parallel is also forged between Clive and his father when Stanley silently withdraws from the room when Clive asks him why he has acted upon a lie he had not believed; here again, Stanley's silence implies a refusal to bridge the communication gap and is eloquent in its evasion.

When direct, unambiguous communication is approached in this play, its consequences are perceived to be terrible. By the end of Act 2, in the wake of Louise's discovery of Clive's lie, a violent verbal exchange occurs between mother and son in which 'truths' too disturbing to speak are finally converted into words. Louise turns on Clive, asking him a chain of questions in a threatening manifestation of the interrogation format; she asks him why he lied and why he is so disturbed by Walter's dismissal when this is surely what he had wanted. Finally, the furious Louise approaches the issue of incestuous desire causing Clive to beg her to stop because her words are 'killing' him (p.93). In the silence that ensues, he is 'saved' from hearing the articulation of painful truth by the sound of Walter's record that has stuck and not been moved on, this alerting them both to the fact that something is badly wrong. Silence allows for evasion once again, an evasion that is more desperately needed than ever since, this time, words have refused to lie.

Lies appropriately end the play as 'truth' is retreated from at breakneck speed: when Pamela asks what the problem is with

Walter, Clive uses language in the way he know best and tells her
that he has simply fallen and hurt himself. We assume that the
family will regroup and assimilate their crisis through continued
evasion, again using language as a smokescreen to feeling. The
communication gap between Clive and his parents (or between his
parents and Clive, given that this is a two-way breach) can never be
healed while understanding is mediated through words that lie and
conceal. While Clive and Stanley potentially 'receive' each other's
'meaning' on an intuitive level, they will never be able to do so in
spoken dialogue with each other. The theme of words and their
limits therefore both begins and ends the play.

Despite the extensive range of ideas and impulses related to this
issue in *Five Finger Exercise*, Shaffer's creative interest in the relationship between words, communication and meaning had not
been exhausted by 1962 when he came to write his double-bill of
one-act plays, *The Private Ear* and *The Public Eye*. On the contrary,
his interest in this question had been extended into new territories.
In the first play, the perception so dominant in *Five Finger Exercise*
that words evade both truth and meaning is converted into a
metaphor where music potentially becomes the only form of direct
communication possible; in the second play, the breakdown of
communication within marriage (in a further echo of the
Harringtons) leads to a solution where words are finally made redundant. In both, the connected ideas of language, speech, knowledge and self-knowledge are developed into a dramatic impulse
that first achieved expression in *Five Finger Exercise*.

In *The Private Ear*, the communication issue is largely expressed
through a contrast between the fluidity and expressive potential of
music, and the awkwardness and artifice of verbal dialogue; the
gap between the two modes of communication is only narrowed
when Bob talks *about* music and finds that his usual conversational
unease disappears. At all other times, Shaffer uses the alienated,
isolated Bob to demonstrate that dialogue is a tricky business, and
one that is fundamentally ill-equipped to express emotion and instinct; by cramming his play with numerous examples of communication gaps and failures, Shaffer enforces this underlying idea. This
emphasis extends from the opening minutes of the play where we
notice Ted's easy domination of the introductory dialogue, Bob's
glibly confident companion finding conversation unproblematic
because he is blithely unaware of its limits. When naive Doreen
later compliments him on his 'gift for words', Ted immodestly

comments that he has always been skilled with words and 'languages' (p.37); though this is largely intended ironically, he is not essentially incorrect since communication for him is not hampered by the knowledge of the contingent relationship between 'words' and 'meaning'.[14]

Bob, on the other hand, is fully aware of the pitfalls of verbal communication and has retreated into a realm where words are secondary to music, music offering the purest distillation of expression and 'meaning'. But this has simultaneously aggravated his sense of estrangement and thus, necessarily, his difficulty with spoken language so that in the opening moments of the play he can offer only single-line responses to Ted's patronizing comments which are delivered from the position of a 'man of the world'.[15] Further, when he had taken Doreen to a coffee bar following the concert, he had found that he had nothing to say to her and, anticipating a similar difficulty over dinner, has asked Ted to stay and 'help out with the talk' (p.17). Only once in these early moments are Bob's short responses developed into extended and fully expressive communication, but his articulacy (which is of a type that Ted can neither understand nor reciprocate) meets with a similar response as had greeted Clive's description of a person's 'essence' in *Five Finger Exercise*: here, Bob tries to explain the meaning of the word 'carriage' which, he suggests, cannot be learned because to have it someone must 'love the world. Then it comes out'. Barely listening and hardly interested, Ted replies: 'I see. Have you got any redcurrant jelly?' (p.19). For Bob, as for Clive, verbal communication invariably fails at the point of its clearest expression, but for both, the failure is not necessarily of their own making.[16]

The play evolves from this early positioning into a sequence of set pieces which all extend the examination of communication failures within language. Both Bob and Doreen exhibit signs of ventriloquism, Bob attempting to offer Ted's words and thoughts as his own (realizing that they are more suited to 'conversation' than anything he can produce), and Doreen quoting her father's clichés at any given opportunity (since she has developed few original thoughts of her own). The phrase 'do you see what I mean?' also recurs frequently here, just as it had done in *Five Finger Exercise* where it was used in a comparable way to indicate the difficulty of attempting to express complex emotions or thoughts in words. For example, when Bob tries to explain to Doreen why he loves Bach he concludes with this phrase, and the fact that Doreen patently does *not* see what he 'means' is indicated by the fact that *'she gives him a quick, tight smile, but says nothing'*, retreating to the non-committal and confused safety of silence (p.28). Bob's attempts to communicate with Doreen inevitably dwindle into similar silences, as in the following painful exchange:

> BOB: I don't think imagination's a thing you can cultivate, though, do you? I mean, you're either born with it or you're not.
> DOREEN: Oh yes, you're born with it.
> BOB: Or you're not.
> DOREEN: Yes.
>
> (p.22)

Again, Doreen can merely echo Bob's words as the lines become progressively shorter in a skilful expression of conversational crisis. Bob is speaking to her in the manner in which he wants her to respond, but even when he realizes that she is not the person he thought she was, he refuses to loosen his grip on the ideal image of her that he has constructed. He persists in his attempts to connect with her at a level at which she does not function, and both conversation and communication flounder as a result.

Shaffer's stock of devices through which to explore the gap between words, meaning and communication is still not exhausted. In the wake of Ted's departure, Bob and Doreen speak in stichomythic rhythms of question, answer and statement as Bob attempts to gain control over his emotions and as Doreen tries to analyse the implications of Ted's departure. Here, neither is saying what they want to say and their mutual disappointment is expressed in choppy tones of nervous aggression. Later still, following Bob's longest and clearest verbal articulation in the entire play where he explains his vision of life and tries to communicate the emotions that music 'frees' in him, he is again met with a wall of non-response as a stunned Doreen can offer only a finalizing, uncomprehending 'Well' in response (p.44). Separated now by an unbridgeable gap, they embark on an exchange wherein neither listens to the other because both are pursuing their own lines of thought; Doreen insists that she must leave as her father will be worried about her:

> BOB: Does he worry that much about you?
> DOREEN: Yes, he's a natural worrier.

BOB [*urgently*]: Well, how about one more record before you go?
DOREEN: Worries about everything.
BOB: One for the road.
DOREEN: Old people always do, don't they?
BOB: Something more tuneful and luscious?[17]

(p.45)

The separate conversations occur on alternate lines; Bob's question is initially answered, his second question is ignored, and Doreen's rhetorical question is finally met by another question that is totally unrelated to her own. Here, the gap between words and communication is at its widest point.

Little wonder, then, that words are subsequently abandoned altogether in the speechless mime that immediately follows this exchange. Here, '*silence hangs between them*' (p.47) as Bob attempts to seduce Doreen using the only language he truly understands – music. When this also fails, Bob's immediate instinct is to lie, again appropriating Ted's words in the assertion that he has a fiancée called Lavinia who enjoys the quality of 'carriage': here, in the dying moments of the play, communication finally becomes possible between Bob and Doreen, though this is of a form that neither had desired: the word 'carriage' alerts Doreen to the fact that Bob is lying since Ted had used it in relation to her earlier in the evening. She realizes that 'Lavinia' is another example of Bob's tendency to quote his friend, his echo of Ted's comment about the depressive effects of alcohol having been noted by her earlier. Similarly, Bob has correctly interpreted Doreen's interest in his workplace as the desire to know where she can contact Ted. Though both are inept with words in their own different ways, both have nevertheless penetrated each other's verbal strategies to arrive at an accurate understanding of their respective unspoken 'meanings'.

But where Doreen allows Bob the comfort of delusion and pretends that her belief in 'Lavinia' is total, Bob draws attention to Doreen's deceit in the last words that he says to her. For one who is so uncomfortable within verbal language, Bob has throughout the play been remarkably unafraid of the painful consequences of articulation, this in contrast to Ted who we may have assumed to be more courageous in this respect than Bob. But though Ted is fearless within language, he retreats in panic from communication, and that Bob occupies the opposite position is made clear in the hostile confrontations between them. In the first encounter, Ted is struck dumb with surprise by Bob's statement that he is 'dead ignorant', this being delivered in a tone of *'calm contempt'* (p.30). In the second confrontation, Bob (loosened by alcohol) tells Ted that his glib phrases are empty before dismissing him from his life: the stage directions tell us that Ted *'tries to say something – to patch it up – make a joke – anything – but nothing comes'* (p.41). Words finally fail Ted as their limits become apparent.

For Bob, communication with both Doreen and Ted has further aggravated his sense of profound and irretrievable alienation. Like his hero, Peter Grimes, Bob has 'visions about what life should be' and has longed to find someone with whom he can 'share his life' (p.29); but when his attempt to express his vision fails, and when communication with the person he believes to be his soulmate is blocked, he rejects not only words, but also connection through music. His vicious vandalism of his record destroys the operatic melody of *Madam Butterfly* as it echoes around the auditorium just as Bob's vision has itself been destroyed. At the final curtain, then, all routes to communication have been seen either to connote deepest pain and disillusion, or to fail in absolute terms.

Where *Five Finger Exercise* had dramatized the unstable relationship between words, communication and meaning, *The Private Ear* takes the idea one stage further by suggesting the final impossibility of each in isolation. In the first play words blocked meaning and in the second music finally suggested disconnection. In *The Public Eye*, Shaffer explores a concept closely related to the impulses of both plays and asks whether the clearest communication resides neither in verbal nor aural territory, but at the level of intuition.

Intuition is, of course, a form of knowledge that relies less on words than on 'vibrations, psychic vibes, unverbalized and indeed unheard of messages'.[18] In the second of these one-act comedies, Shaffer stresses the fact that there has been an intuitive communication between Julian Christoforou and Belinda from the moment that the 'public eye' first saw her. Remembering that she was standing alone, shrouded in the mists of Hyde Park, he states: 'There was something about your loneliness that filled my eyes with tears! I tasted at a distance the salt of your solitude!'.[19] Their relationship develops on the same intuitive level with Julian and Belinda taking it in turns to follow each other over a period of three weeks, finding out about each other by wordlessly showing the other person the things they most love. A profound intimacy arises between the two since they are connecting at a level that cannot be accessed through words. As Belinda states, 'because there aren't any words, every-thing's easy and possible' (p.82).

Hostility and resentment, however, intrude into this relationship as soon as Julian breaks the silence and makes verbal contact with Belinda. Recriminations naturally follow Julian's exposure as a de-tective hired to spy on her and Belinda's feelings of betrayal are ex-pressed in their new communicative currency of words. When Belinda angrily demands that Julian stop using 'magaziny lan-guage', the detective again draws attention to the intuition that had existed between them when they had known each other through silence stating, 'I should never have talked. When I was dumb we understood each other' (p.89). This is, of course, the logic behind his solution to the communication gap in Charles and Belinda's marriage since he realizes that meaningful connection can only be made between them when they stop hiding behind the misleading smokescreen of words and 'understand' or 'know' each other at a level that words habitually block.

Julian is, despite his instinctive alienation, a born communicator whether at the level of intuition or at the level of words. His witty, energetic and idiosyncratic speech-patterns suggest an obsessive desire to communicate which locates him as a benign precursor of characters such as Salieri and Yonadab. Giving far more informa-tion about himself than he needs, indulging in endless speculations and non sequiturs, he is placed in obvious counterpoint to Charles, a man who has been introduced to us in terms that are reminiscent of Stanley Harrington:[20] Charles is, we are told, *'exact and almost finicky in his speech, with a fairly steady line in pompous sarcasm'* (p.55), this again suggesting the extent to which he, like Stanley, uses words as a self-defence mechanism and as a barrier against others. But Charles's frosty interiority is quickly broken down by Julian's communicative skills, and he soon finds himself unwillingly gripped by Julian's 'chase' story, subsequently revealing to the de-tective the whole history of his marriage to Belinda.

Charles is convinced that Belinda has taken a lover because a massive communication gap has opened between them. He de-scribes how 'whole meals go by in silence, and when she talks, she appears not to be listening to what she herself is saying' (p.69). However, when Belinda finally enters, we realize that the commu-nication gap between them has obviously been present even from their earliest meeting; on one of their first dates, Belinda remem-bers, Charles 'had already explained to me the Theory of Natural

Selection, the meaning of Id, Ego and Super-Ego' and was 'halfway through the structure of Bach's Fugue in C Sharp Minor, Book One, *Well-Tempered Clavier'* (p.77). At the time, she had been thrilled with his knowledge because she felt herself released from 'that hot, black burrow of feeling' through facts, ideas and reasons, but in retrospect, it has become clear that the transmission of knowledge is purely one way and that facts, ideas and reasons have eliminated spontaneity and instinct in Charles (p.77). The range of communicative problems that we now see between them all emanate from these two basic issues.

For example, Charles's use of 'morning-suit language', delivered in his 'iceberg voice' (p.75), is an attempt to ward off experience with words: in effect, he converts both into formulae so that, for him, the word 'wife' 'means' a category of behaviour and a predetermined emotional attitude, neither of which take account of individualism or spontaneous response. As a result, Belinda is continually being asked to tailor her words and actions to comply with the criteria of an inhuman definition, and since she cannot possibly hope to fulfil all of its precepts, she constantly feels guilty in Charles's presence, telling him, 'I feel I have to defend myself in front of you' (p.78) (an echo of Clive's feelings towards his father in *Five Finger Exercise*). Finally, she realizes that silence and withdrawal offer the best chances of avoiding judgement and she stops even trying to communicate with her husband. Admitting that her visit to him was not a whim that seized her as she happened to pass his office, she states: 'I wanted to talk to you. No, not talk. I knew that wouldn't be any good. I wanted to – I don't know – give you something. These flowers' (p.82). Words, she now knows, are 'no good' when it comes to communication, so she attempts connection another way, through a gift.

Julian sums up the difference between Charles and Belinda as the split between 'spirit' and 'letter': 'You've got passion where all he's got is pronouncement' (p.91). To unite the two, he insists on the course of action that has led to his own redemption since, when following Belinda, he had suddenly begun to 'feel' his feelings, the silence between them allowing his own emotions to grow. Understanding that the breach between husband and wife has been both caused by, and expressed in, words, he realizes that it can never be healed while words literally come between them. Hence his final demand, 'End of words. Start of action' (p.94); like

Eurydice and Orpheus, Belinda and Charles will find their way back from Hell, and will know each other and connect at the level of intuition alone. Where *The Private Ear* had suggested that words, communication and meaning were a final impossibility, *The Public Eye* suggests that once the barrier of words is dispensed with, communication and meaning automatically arise.

Shaffer's next double-bill of one-act plays extends his meditation on words and their limits into new and darker territory – physically and metaphorically. *White Liars* and *Black Comedy* are dramas that centre exclusively on lies; here, characters deceive either others or themselves (and often both) through a network of complicated untruths which the audience must unravel and interpret as the action develops.[21] One lie leads to another as characters conceal motives and identities; as soon as one lie is uncovered, another is offered in its place. Finally, the truth is revealed to the audience who by this time can barely distinguish honesty from dishonesty; it has learned that it can hardly believe a word that has been said and it has simultaneously realized that the most direct communication has taken place in the space *between* words, in what has been left *unsaid*.

Since *White Liars* is a 'darker' play than *Black Comedy* (where darkness is converted into a physical motivator of farce action), the connotations of communicative failure through lies and evasions are far more sinister here. At first, lying is presented as a fairly harmless and comic activity in Sophie's slogan 'Lemberg Never Lies', this being an unlikely claim given her status as a fortune-teller and thus as a professional charlatan. The dubious grounds of her claim are immediately revealed in her call of 'true' when Frank presents her with a coin he has spun which he asserts has landed on 'heads' giving him the right to consult with Sophie before Tom – the coin had, in fact, landed on 'tails'.

From this point on, lies build upon lies as Sophie listens to Frank's story (which is a fabulous falsehood), interspersing his tale with dishonest accounts of her own background and identity. When the trick they play on Tom fails, we realize that it was itself based on another trick, Tom's silent corroboration of Frank's romanticized idea of his past. Tom explains to Sophie how his true identity had become buried by illusion, revealing his accent and manner to be fake working-class in response to what Frank and Sue had required of him; Sophie is appalled by his confession that he lives life as 'one enormous great *lie* from morning to night', a situation which she finds '*Unimaginable!*' (p.123). The obvious irony here, of course, is that Sophie is the last person who should find this beyond imagination since her own life is also a fraud based on deception and self-deception.

But here, Shaffer creates a strange situation which extends the difficult relationship between words and truth even further; the lie that Sophie and Frank have devised fails because it was itself based on a lie. Further, Tom's lie was not simply verbal but was also contained within silence; he tells Sophie that he had often allowed a shrug to 'articulate' a falsehood so that when Frank himself answered his own questions about Tom's childhood, Tom's silent shrugs implied tacit confirmation of a range of deprivations and miseries. Even so, the real damage was inflicted verbally, Tom noting that 'Once I'd spoken – actually spoken a lie out loud – I was theirs' (p.130): the untrue words he offers Frank amount to a surrender of his entire identity.

Sophie cannot bear to hear this saga of deception and fraud because it reveals to her the extent of her own dishonesty. Finally she can take no more and silences Tom with her agonized cry, 'Words on words on words on words' (p.131), this placing the relationship between words, communication and meaning centre stage once again. Her sentence actually converts the idea of 'words' into a nonsense (any word that is repeated often enough loses its sense) and the relationship between words and 'meaning' simultaneously becomes contingent. Her cry also suggests that 'words on words' have concealed truth and have finally rendered it an impossibility. She is forced then to examine the nature of her own 'words', and can ultimately desert the fiction of her identity by revealing the truth of who and what she is. But now, when words are finally wielded to reveal rather than conceal, communication breaks down since Tom has left the room and Sophie's truth is therefore delivered into a void. At least 'meaning' results since Sophie's new motto, '*Plotkin Never Lies!*' (p.136) suggests that now she has acknowledged her true identity, she will forge a new connection between words, communication and truth.

Sophie had been misled not only by Frank's words (he is, as Tom notes, a 'mad talker', p.127), but also by his appearance; she has mistakenly concluded that he is a 'giver' where Tom is a 'taker' (p.126), having confused what *seems* with what *is*. This is another reason why Sophie feels her moral universe collapse when

Frank finally reveals the great truth behind his great lie and, *'in agony'* admits that he had handed Sophie his pack of lies not to keep Tom away from his girlfriend, but to keep Tom in his own bed (p.133). Sophie is forced to examine her entire scale of judgement in the light of this 'confession' and her final commitment to communication through truth suggests that, for her, re-evaluation is possible.

In *Black Comedy*, however, no character makes such a commitment. The second half of this double-bill continues the interrelated themes of deceptive appearances, lies, tricks and communication failures. In Brindsley's 'magic dark room' (p.196), Shaffer presents a farce world where the 'light of truth' dawns only in darkness through a series of exchanges which fully illustrate the gap between words, communication and truth or meaning. The situation we find at the start of the play is a fraud-in-progress; in full light (stage darkness) Brindsley and his appalling fiancée move easily within their artificial world of strategic affection which is in the process of being made more artificial still with the addition of furniture 'borrowed' from their neighbour. Brindsley and Carol are constructing a 'set' in which her father will be fooled into believing that Brindsley is a man of taste and means and where Bamburger will be persuaded into buying Brindsley's art; all is in the interests of creating the conditions that will enable a further fraud – a loveless but convenient marriage between Brindsley and Carol.

The inherently dishonest nature of this relationship is indicated throughout the play; for a start, Brindsley has lied to Carol about his past relationship with Clea and is lying to himself about his feelings for her which persist despite his engagement to another woman. Further, Brindsley has kept his engagement to Carol secret, this leading a hurt Harold to state, 'you know how to keep things to yourself' (p.173), a remark that is more perceptive than he realizes: in fact, Brindsley goes one stage further and keeps things *from* himself, most notably his feelings towards Carol and Clea. Not only this, Brindsley also has a need to keep *people* from himself, as Clea points out when she decides that darkness is his 'natural element' since it allows him to conceal his true nature and identity (p.198). But if Brindsley's relationship with Carol is inherently dishonest, then so is hers with him since enough hints are provided in the text to suggest that in Brindsley, Carol sees only a stylish marriage to a potentially fashionable artist. Obviously, this network of frauds must be exposed and, this being a farce, it is exposed in progressively chaotic terms where the communication issue motivates the increasingly frenetic stage action.

In one dominant example of this emphasis, the darkness in which the 'magic' room is shrouded (the stage is light, of course) allows for a moment when the uncertain connection between words, communication and truth or meaning is dramatized on several levels simultaneously. Unaware that Carol's father has entered the room during his absence, Brindsley refers to Colonel Melkett as a 'monster' who he has to 'keep happy': this is a rare moment when words and truth connect. Unfortunately, this 'truth' was not something that Brindsley had wanted to communicate to his future father-in-law, and he therefore embarks on a frantic damage limitation exercise:

> BRINDSLEY [*wildly embarrassed*]: Well, well, well, well, well! ... [*Panic*] Good evening, sir. Fancy you being here all the time! I – I'm expecting some dreadful neighbours, some neighbour monsters, monster neighbours, you know ... They rang up and said they might look round ... Well, well, well! ...
> COLONEL [*darkly*]: Well, well.
> MISS FURNIVAL [*nervously*]: Well, well.
> CAROL [*brightly*]: Well!
>
> (p.156)

Here, Brindsley scrambles to replace honesty with lies, using the repeated word 'well' to give him time to muster his forces (he had used the same technique when speaking to Clea on the telephone). However, so discomforted is he that his words become muddled and he is forced to retreat back into his confused refrain. This is then picked up by the other inhabitants of the room who introduce another communication issue by altering the connotations of the word 'well' through their tone of voice. As if the network of lies and deceptions in this play were not evidence enough that the relationship between words and meaning is contingent at best, Shaffer here proves his point beyond all doubt.

In addition, the darkness in the room allows for moments when the gap between words and meaning (and the communication failures that this causes) is illustrated through characters saying one thing and the expression on their faces 'saying' another. In the light, this would not, of course, be possible, but in this situation social convention is obsolete. As a result, when the Colonel states that if Brindsley can prove that he will take care of Carol then he will allow their marriage, rhetorically adding 'I can't say fairer than that, can I?', Brindsley replies, 'No, sir. Most fair, sir. Most fair': his genuine response, however, is revealed in his physical action: '[*He pulls a hideous face one inch from the* COLONEL'*s*]' (p.174).

In the darkness, then, communication becomes increasingly distorted as characters hear words that were not intended for their ears, as Brindsley's lies become wilder and wilder, and as Clea takes advantage of the situation by creating a role in which she is able to create futher havoc. Mistaken identity is added to the chaos as Schuppanzigh the erudite electrician is confused with Bamburger the deaf millionaire, communication again becoming linked to the theme of deceptive appearances when Schuppanzigh's informed appraisal of Brindsley's work is listened to and appreciated only when the inhabitants of the room believe that his fortune gives him the right to speak and to be heard. When the mistake is realized, Schuppanzigh is abused and silenced. In the darkness, Clea comes to believe the words of a character she herself has created and Carol comes to realize through the 'hand' game that Harold knows Brindsley better than she can ever do. In the darkness, Miss Furnival's hysterical monologue converts emotion into words in a way that she has never managed before, and Brindsley is at last shaken out of his verbal passivity. By the end of the play, only Brindsley and Clea have achieved a level of communication where they recognize the meaning behind each other's lies; for the rest, words have been abandoned altogether as they circle the room in silent hostility, thirsting for Brindsley's blood.

In *Black Comedy*, then, as with all the plays examined in this chapter, Shaffer's theme of communication gaps caused by the ambiguous relationship between words and meaning is placed central to the dramatic logic of the stage action. In these five texts, lies and evasions block the possibility of true communication while words distort the expression of emotion and forbid final meaning. With each play focusing on a close-knit social situation in a state of decay and incipient crisis, Shaffer explores the possibilities of alternative forms of communication including music, silence, and intuition. Repeatedly, he suggests that for connection to arise between human beings, words must be relegated to a position of acknowledged insufficiency so that communication and knowledge of oneself and others is accessed through instinct. That this message is delivered in the theatrical medium, the most verbal dramatic environment, is an irony that should not escape us. However, as we saw in the previous chapter, one of Shaffer's most important contributions to contemporary theatre is his dramatic and theatrical realization that words have their limits.

4
Alienation, Identity, Dysfunction

The communication issue discussed in the previous chapter leads to a related emphasis in Shaffer's plays where the inability to connect at a verbal level oftens indicates that a protagonist is experiencing a crushing sense of alienation causing (and caused by) a traumatic crisis of identity. These twin forces subsequently give rise to a range of dysfunctional characteristics, detectable in several Shafferian protagonists including Mark Askelon, Salieri, Dysart and Yonadab. This chapter traces the interplay between these impulses, firstly examining them as general concepts in Shaffer's plays, and secondly applying this analysis to two texts with striking points of connection between them: *Shrivings* and *Yonadab*.

To begin with, it should be stressed that the word 'alienation' is being used here in its non-Brechtian sense; the specifically Brechtian meaning of 'alienation' (*verfremdungseffekt*) is defined in Chapter 2, but in this discussion the word is used to connote estrangement, dis/integration and disconnection. Rodney Simard is one of many critics who note the insistent focus on these negative values in Peter Shaffer's plays; he suggests that 'Shaffer dramatizes people as alienated questers in search of meaning, of both self and existence', this giving rise to their ultimate fragmentation as 'meaning' proves insufficient and as 'existence' becomes untenable as a result.[1] These 'questers' gradually become aware that they are surrounded by barriers erected between themselves and divinity, sensation, man, woman and society, eventually realizing that they exist in a vacuous no-man's-land divorced from contact and experience. Connections have become impossible so they must remain forever stranded in an eternal limbo, literally in the cases of Salieri and Yonadab, and metaphorically in the cases of Mark Askelon and Dysart. All exist in self-constructed hells where they are haunted by a discovery that they had sought but that they had not, fundamentally, wanted.

It is no coincidence that Shaffer invariably selects these alienated individuals as his narrators, characters who interact with both stage action and audience but who belong fully to neither. Part of both and yet finally separate from both, the narrator is suspended between two belongings. Since he is usually learned and articulate, a skilled manipulator and a devious operator, he makes the most of his unique situation (akin to a Prospero-like magician), summoning characters at will and directing response accordingly.[2] It is only at the end of the action that we realize the isolation of his true circumstances, his desire for connection and longing for release from no-man's-land. Such a release, it is implied, has become an impossibility.

Alienation in these plays takes many forms and constructs a network of emphases that the audience can hardly mistake. A persistent situation, for example, involves a character who has abandoned homeland and family in search of integration elsewhere but who now finds himself separate as well from his new surroundings. Lois Neal, David Askelon and his father fall into this category, as do Walter Langer and Sophie, 'Baroness Lemberg'. Of course, as Shaffer is at pains to point out throughout his plays, it is not necessary to leave family and home to feel alienated from them, in which case the entire Harrington family of *Five Finger Exercise* could be added to this category. All of these characters are exiles, all floundering between concepts of self and place, all in varying stages of psychic disintegration, and all unable to locate 'home'.

Another sign of alienation involves a range of characters who are estranged from their contemporary societies, finding themselves out of step with its normative beliefs and value-systems. Dysart falls into this category since, as Una Chaudhuri argues, he is 'the mid-century culture hero, disillusioned with modern civilization, uncomfortable with his role in it'; longing for the primitive, Dysart shares Alan Strang's distaste for the plastic present, but is unable to reject it completely.[3] This, of course, exacerbates his sense of alienation since he realizes that he has neither the courage nor the vision to 'jump clean-hoofed on to a whole new track of being' as Strang (whose name suggests 'estrangement') has done.[4] Where Dysart's patient has indeed become 'a modern citizen for whom society doesn't exist' (p.273), Dysart is trapped in a society which he can neither fully reject nor fully accept. Again, the sense of existing within an unbearable no-man's-land results.

This indicator of alienation is not confined solely to the 'darker' plays but appears frequently in Shaffer's comedies. Miss Furnival in *Black Comedy*, for example, embarks on a drunken tirade against the modern world addressed to the spirit of her dead father: 'Pink stamps, green stamps, free balloons – television dinners – pay as you go out – oh, Daddy, it's *awful!*'.[5] And, of course, their hatred of modern ugliness unites Lettice and Lotte who yearn for the glories embedded in their imaginative visions of the past. All are characters who are out of step with the modern world, forced to live within it, alienated from it and hostile to it; in *Lettice and Lovage*, a solution is provided to the dilemma (this is, after all, a comedy), but in *Equus*, the gap between self and society is not resolved and is left suspended as an insistent question.

Less explicit signs of alienation in these plays involve the recurrence of a chain of metaphors relating to meaninglessness, futility and separation. Firstly there is the idea of limbo noted above where 'questers' such as Yonadab and Salieri haunt the stage in an eternal rendering of their histories, and where men such as Dysart and Mark Askelon are launched at the end of the action into a void of pain and despair which will never cease. Secondly, Shaffer provides us with a network of keywords focusing on notions of nullity and emphasizing the dominant sense of emptiness which so many of these alienated protagonists experience. The chain of negatives at the close of *Shrivings* provides an example of this technique with the word 'no' repeated seven times in swift succession; Yonadab's anguished cry, '*I'm Nobody*' belongs in the same vein,[6] as does Salieri's crucial line (omitted from all performed versions of the play), 'If I cannot be Mozart, I do not wish to be anything'.[7] In each case, Shaffer's emphasis connotes the pain of characters caught in a nightmare realm between being and non-being where the emptiness of alienation defines them.

But the most dominant of these metaphorical strands lies in Shaffer's utilization of the embrace as an emblem of disconnection. Selected for the marketing image of *Amadeus*, the metaphor of the outstretched arms recurs throughout Shaffer's plays and indicates threat, protection, reconciliation or (most frequently) refusal of contact and thus alienation. While the embrace may be accepted (as David finally uses his arms to hold rather than to smash his father in Act 3 of *Shrivings*), its rejection is always a shattering stage moment as when Lois spurns the offer of Gideon's outstretched arms in Act 2 of the same play. The stage directions read: '*GIDEON approaches her, his arms outstretched – but with a stifled cry, she avoids them, and runs into the garden. GIDEON is left standing alone*'.[8] The metaphorical link between the thwarted embrace and estrangement is here made explicit and can be detected throughout Shaffer's work.

The connection between alienation and the crisis of identity is readily definable in these plays; where alienation connotes the unbridgeable gap between 'I' and society, man or God, the crisis of identity connotes the gap between 'I' and 'self' – that is, if 'I' in any complete sense can be known at all. Identity can therefore be read as a form of self-alienation just as alienation can be read as emanating from the crisis in identity. For the purposes of this chapter, the twin impulses have been separated in the interests of coherence, but any attempt to view these emphases as unconnected in the reading of Shaffer's plays will inevitably lead to reductiveness. The two are always related and their 'symptoms' forever intertwined.

Shaffer's concern with the nature of identity, with its mutable and evasive implications, begins as early as the detective novels; *Withered Murder*, in fact, revolves around this entire issue with its cast of characters including actresses (who adopt others' identities professionally) and liars (involved in the constant construction of false identities).[9] In the plays, the preoccupation with identity becomes a dominant emphasis involving the adoption of a wide variety of strategies and metaphors. Many of the protagonists, for example, complain of a sense of invisibility, of not feeling *there* to be accounted for. In a sense, they are correct since the people who surround them constantly resort to labelling them as if in an attempt to register their existence: Louise Harrington aptly names Clive 'Jou-Jou', Ted refers to Bob as 'Tchaik' in *The Private Ear* (notice also that Bob's identity is only half-formed anyway since he is given no surname), and Yonadab's name is constantly linked to a characteristic as in 'The Man of Eyes' (p.110). In each case, identity is registered only via renaming, this avoiding the necessity of having to ask, as Mark does of his son in Act 1 of *Shrivings*, 'Who the hell is he?' (p.126). It is significant that Mark immediately responds to his own question by providing a label for David that partially resolves the issue: 'Master carpenter to Gideon Petrie' (p.126), and significant also that David had earlier stated that all the opposing conflicts within him seem to render him 'invisible', just as 'all colours make up white' (p.109). Renaming also allows for the moulding of identity by another person who recognizes that a character's lack of fixed self-hood renders it 'up for grabs'.

Related to this emphasis is the sense of chameleonism that many of these characters either express or suggest, their lack of fixed identities manifested in constant mutability.[10] For protagonists such as Dysart and Salieri in particular, the crushing knowledge of their own mediocrity simultaneously makes them aware that they are indistinguishable from the crowd, blending in with the background, but never fully at ease within it since they are conscious of their situation as others are not. This process gives rise to a dual sense of self-alienation as a result. In a related emphasis, many characters also envisage themselves as ghosts; Yonadab and Salieri, of course, are literally ghostly presences but Dennis A. Klein notes that this implication spreads wider to include Dysart who 'feels no more than the shadow of a man' and Mark Askelon who 'feels like a ghost separated from the world around him'.[11] The impression of ghostliness largely emanates from the protagonist's fluctuation between states of being and non-being (as noted above) and is connected with invisibility, but it is also involved in the sense of being suspended from historical time. The connection with the alienation issue is clear.

As several critics have pointed out, the crisis of identity which many alienated protagonists experience in Shaffer's plays is revealed in forms of role-playing and role-appropriation. This perception has been overstated in some readings to the extent that spurious connections between characters and situations have been forged, but it is undoubtedly true to state that when a character feels himself to be a 'shadow', a 'ghost', a 'chameleon' or invisible, the desire to create and solidify an identity becomes manifested in terms of mimicry and 'acting'. For example, Alan Strang appropriates the words of his father and of television jingles, while the one characteristic shared by Bob and Doreen in *The Private Ear* is their readiness to speaks words not their own (Doreen rehearsing those of her father, and Bob those of Ted). But in all cases, the attempt to poach an identity ironically backfires since these characters succeed only in drawing attention to the fact that their own is semi-formed, indistinct, or in crisis. Similarly, those protagonists who 'act' a role (Mark Askelon, Salieri and Yonadab among them) cause the audience to wonder just what exactly they are trying to hide.

The recurrent idea of role-playing can also be related to a further metaphor involved in the exploration of mutable or concealed identity, this being the preponderance of masks on the Shafferian stage.

In an echo of Greek theatre, masks (in the physical sense) are frequently adopted to obliterate personal or human identity as in the case of the six helpers of *Yonadab* whose *'individual features are obliterated by white stocking masks'* (p.83). Masks also effect the creation of 'a stable of Superhorses to stalk through the mind' in *Equus*,[12] forge links between Mozart's operas (where masks recur as a motif in *Seraglio* and *Don Giovanni*) and the action of *Amadeus*, and are used to enormous emotional and psychological effect in *The Royal Hunt of the Sun* and *The Gift of the Gorgon*. Such masks suggest ceremonies and tragedies of extreme brutality and force the audience to respond to the action in an elemental way. They are, in short, central to the experience of Shaffer's theatre.

But masks in their metaphorical sense are equally important to these plays and, as related to issues of identity, alienation and role-playing, are everywhere apparent. Here we find a series of characters who live their lives behind false faces, concealing their true words, natures and thoughts from all around them. Peter Hall was aware that this gap between public and private faces had to be fully communicated to the audience when he directed Paul Scofield as Salieri in *Amadeus*; as far as Hall was concerned, 'the essential thing is that he should show his brutal self nakedly to the audience, but put on a mask of courtesy and charm to the other characters on stage'.[13] This explains why Salieri has often been described as an Iago-figure, as also has Yonadab, since both protagonists subsume their malign identities in the adoption of a benign mask. In much the same vein, Charles A. Pennell notes that Bob in *The Private Ear*, though not malign in any sense, 'uses pretense to camouflage his real self', while the entire cast of *White Liars* adopt a similar strategy.[14] Meanwhile, Dysart's nightmare in which he feels his ceremonial mask slipping as he disembowels sacrificial victims, fully reveals his crisis of professional and personal identity. Masks, then, conceal and reformulate identity, slipping frequently enough to remind the audience that, for the alienated protagonists, definitions of self and 'being' slide easily through the grasp.

It should be noted in addition that those characters in Shaffer's plays who experience the most intense sense of alienation and crises in identity are also practised voyeurs. This issue will be discussed below, but here it is worth mentioning that voyeurism is, in this context, an attempt to appropriate another's experiences and thus to live vicariously. Because an essential cause of these characters' sense of estrangement and ghostliness is their incapacity to 'feel' in direct terms: all suffer from what Mark Askelon in *Shrivings* calls an 'Incapacity for Immediate Life' (p.174). A sensation of numbness, of void, results, hence the attempt to participate in feeling at second-hand; Dysart, Salieri, Mark Askelon and Yonadab each hope that by witnessing unseen passion, genius, joy or transcendence they can, in some sense, 'catch' what they long to possess.[15] Each necessarily fails and their sense of void is rendered yet more extreme in the light of this failure.

By far the most crucial metaphorical indicator of problems circulating around the concept of identity is Shaffer's connection between 'I' and 'eye'. Those characters whose identities are most mutable, most hidden behind masks, most alienated, are those around whom 'sight' and 'blindness' imagery accumulates. It is as if those who cannot adequately formulate a concrete notion of 'I' cannot also 'see' the truth of a situation, of others or of themselves. In *Equus* and *Black Comedy*, two plays where questions of identity constitute a motivating force, the interplay between light and darkness (or blindness) is transformed into a plot and a visual conceit respectively. In both cases, the plays hinge entirely on the mutualities of seeing and blindness. However, *Black Comedy* (in a shared emphasis with *King Lear*) complicates the issue by demonstrating the fact that only when 'blind' can characters actually 'see' themselves or each other as they really are whereas, when 'sighted', characters may be as 'blind as a baby' as Yonadab finally (and ironically, given his talent for voyeurism) realizes himself to be (p.319).

The connection between the 'I' of identity and the 'eye' of vision is made explicit by Shaffer in a number of ways. Given its plot and theme, *Equus* is liberally scattered with references to eyes as they relate to knowledge; the 'blink game' which Dysart persuades Alan to play is motivated by Dysart's desire to penetrate his patient's experience in a voyeuristic manoeuvre, while the eyes of Equus stare from the walls of Alan's room, insisting on the roles of worshipped and worshipper.[16] In *Lettice and Lovage* too, images of blindness alert us to true identities as when Lotte states that her perceptive eyes are a curse since they register the ugliness that surrounds and oppresses her. The notion of the 'communal eye' also pervades this play. The thematic and metaphorical centrality of sight and blindness imagery in *Yonadab* is too clear and persistent to mistake, but the connection between 'I' and 'eye' is forged through Yonadab's role as voyeur and through his subsequent label as 'The Man of Eyes' (p.110); David's naming of him discomforts Yonadab reducing him to a state of humble confusion – what shakes him is the realization that David has offered an all too accurate assessment of his identity in one concise phrase that has linked his 'I' with his 'eye'.

The emphasis on the white gum 'clouding' Gideon's eyes in *Shrivings* is another example of the same idea since a vital component of Gideon's identity is that he 'sees' the truth neither about himself nor others. Further instances of this pattern appear throughout the plays. As a result, this connection between 'I' and 'eye', as it relates to ideas of identity and alienation, becomes crucial to the audience's interpretation of what it witnesses on stage. Only when this connection is fully 'recognized' do the notions of being/non-being, sight/blindness and connection/estrangement, as communicated via this intricate metaphorical scheme, achieve their full resonance.

The interdependent emphases on forms of alienation and on crises of identity result in marked signs of dysfunction that each of the 'questing' protagonists display. Linked with the role-playing mentioned above, many lie and plot apparently instinctively, as was noted in Chapter 3 in relation to the communication debate. Gene A. Plunka links this emphasis with the identity issue, stating that 'those individuals who lack a strong sense of identity find themselves living not only in a world of illusion and artifice but also in a world of lies and hypocrisies'.[17] While we may naturally refer to *Amadeus* and *Yonadab* here, we should not forget that *White Liars*, *Black Comedy* and *Lettice and Lovage* ('lighter' plays) all revolve around the weaving of enormous lies. Critics such as Dennis A. Klein interpret these lies as elements of game-playing, a description which may obscure the darker connotations implied here.

Another signifier of dysfunction is the range of sexual problematics that we encounter in these plays. Dysart, for example, is sterile, his wife is passionless, Lois is 'frigid', Salieri subsumes sexual desire by gorging on confectionery, Pizarro only feels able to have sex with prostitutes, and several critics suggest that Oedipal relations are in evidence in *Five Finger Exercise*. Further, much has been written on patterns of homosexual desire in these plays, and though homosexuality can hardly be labelled a 'dysfunction' (as many critics have inadvertently implied in the course of their analyses), it becomes related to this dynamic when it is seen to involve lying, concomitant role-playing, and a denial of identity.

However, while some arguments suggesting hidden homosexual motivation in Shaffer's plays are valid and clearly supported by textual evidence, others are sabotaged by internal contradictions. The argument, for example, that Pizarro experiences homosexual desire for Atahuallpa is totally undermined by the fact that Shaffer has woven into this play numerous indications that the two men, being mirror images of each other, are connected fraternally and not erotically;[18] similarly, any suggestion of homosexual attraction between Gideon and David in *Shrivings* is cast into doubt by Lois' statement that Gideon's profoundest wish is that 'David Askelon was his own son' (p.193), and by her realization that, far from being 'Quadri. Quinti. Sexi-sexual' (p.166), Gideon has, in fact, never experienced genuine sexual desire at all. And while homosexual impulses may well explain Clive's attraction to Walter in *Five Finger Exercise*, accepting Charles R. Lyons' suggestion that Clive's invitation to Walter to visit Wells Cathedral with him contains an 'implicit eroticism' (since entering the Cathedral connotes 'the penetration of a womb') is to push the argument to an unacceptable extreme which cannot be corroborated textually.[19]

If hidden, repressed or absent sexuality is a sure sign of dysfunction emanating from alienation and the crisis of identity in these plays, a clearer indication still is the 'Incapacity for Immediate Life' (*Shrivings*, p.173) from which so many of Shaffer's protagonists suffer. His very name suggesting 'dysfunction', Dysart spends innumerable evenings reading 'cultural' books and watching his wife knitting (he tells us that he has not kissed her for years) while Alan 'stands in the dark for an hour, sucking the sweat off his God's hairy cheek' (p.275). Dysart realizes that his patient 'has known a passion more ferocious than I have felt in any second of my life' (p.274), but he also realizes that, while he envies it, he can never experience that passion for himself. Like Yonadab and Mark Askelon he is condemned to spiritual, emotional and sexual numbness, a metaphor rendered literal in *Shrivings* and *Yonadab* where numbness becomes physically manifested in an emphasis on paralysis (as discussed below). Of all the dysfunctional signifiers in these plays, this is the most lethal since it creates a void somewhere between life and death where direct sensation and experience can never be achieved.

Alienation, identity and dysfunction, then, are inextricably connected emphases in Shaffer's plays and any attempt to regard one as separate from the others will always give rise to reductive interpretation. Taking the ideas and impulses outlined above, we need next to trace the workings of these patterns in the texts themselves.

Shrivings is a play with a 'battle-scarred' past, rejected by critics and audiences upon its first appearance as *The Battle of Shrivings*, and extensively rewritten subsequently. The text titled *Shrivings* published by Penguin in 1976 has not, to date, been performed on the professional stage; it is a 'reading' text, untested and therefore unmodified by theatrical performance. However, despite the un-staged nature of this play, *Shrivings* offers us a dominant example of the metaphorical network described in this chapter and provides us with a clear demonstration of its emotional and psychological effect.

Shrivings dramatizes the clash between two creeds; Mark Askelon, a famous (or infamous) poet, unwillingly believes that man is unimprovable and that atrocities will always be committed at his hand. Mark has seen the evidence of this during a violent 'Peace' demonstration in America and has observed the patterns of brutality enacted in the name of belief throughout history and in the clinical setting of university laboratories where he has seen a man killed 17 times 'by hand'. Gideon, a philosopher and peace activist, denies Mark's theories and believes that violence can be driven out of man through an act of will, the hand being used to embrace, comfort and caress. In this, he is supported by his secretary-acolyte, Lois Neal, and by Mark's estranged son, David. The 'battle' of the original title refers to the struggle between the two men as they argue their creeds and as a tortured Mark attempts to prove his by forcing Gideon to eject him from the house of confession and reconciliation. Throughout the whole runs an insistent emphasis on the interconnections between alienation, identity and dysfunction outlined above forcing us towards an acknowledgement of void by the end of the play.

Alienation is connoted in this play not only through the protagonists' situations and conditions, but also through the architectural characteristics of the environment described. While whiteness dominates the imagined stage set (suggesting not only purity but also 'frigidity' in the true sense of the word), we are told in addition that Mark's bedroom is separated off from the others, this indicating his incipient separateness from this household: further, the main living area is divided into two levels. The moment that Mark arrives, he senses that this house of reconciliation, confession and 'retreat', far from welcoming all-comers, in fact actually resists them, insisting on its external and internal separation and disconnection. Apparently with no desire to cause offence, he notes that the tunnel of elm trees ending in a stone porch shouts 'Stop!', and though Gideon corrects him asserting that, on the contrary, it shouts 'come!', Mark remains unconvinced (p.115). Certainly, Mark's own sense of alienation may cause him to interpret any sign of welcome as a sign of rejection, but the stark whiteness of this environment, the division of the house into 'levels' and areas (this mimicked in the two stools parked in front of Gideon's desk where only one chair nestles behind), suggest that Mark's instincts are accurate. Further, we may have noticed that images of solitude and separation characterize our introduction to this environment with David sitting alone on stage carving a table-leg, refusing to respond to a ringing telephone, and with Lois informing a reporter that Gideon always spends the hour after tea 'completely alone' (p.105). Shrivings is, as Mark suspects, a place of isolation and alienation where all those who dwell within it believe they have found 'home' only because they recognize within themselves its pervasive sense of estrangement.

Once the alienating characteristics of the environment have been established, Shaffer begins to construct a history of alienation within his characters. David is in exile from his home, forbidden to return by his father's infrequent telegrams: 'Regret still not convenient you return' (p.110). Lois is similarly exiled, repelled by her Catholic upbringing, the limitations of her home, and the violence of the American Peace Movement. But where David's long years of alienation have left him unsure as to the location of 'the real world' (p.105), so long has he been estranged from it, Lois is sure that she knows exactly where it is though since she points towards the desk when asked to indicate its co-ordinates, we tend to doubt her. David's envy for the old woman he had encountered one day on a walk in the country stems from the fact that she was 'absolutely *there*' (p.147); David is not referring to place alone, but to the woman's sense of who she was, where she belonged and what she belonged to: in short, David envies that sense of self that neither he nor Lois can ever acquire. Both are wanderers seeking definition and meaning; neither belong to place and neither belong to, or even know, them*selves*.

Like his son, Mark is also an exile. Of Jewish origins (he has changed his name from Ashkenazy), Mark states that his father bequeathed him 'no home on earth; only envy of home in others' (p.134). Neither he nor his son can ever identify themselves as true 'Englishmen' nor true 'Greeks' nor 'Americans' since some indefinable trait within them forbids identification with place. Further, neither are able to claim solid identities for themselves, David a temporary carpenter defining himself in terms of invisibility, Mark the 'relic of an enormous man' (p.111) whose shrunken frame connotes mutability and decay, and whose role-appropriation as 'the arriving lecturer', 'the Fabergé Prince', 'the traveller in undies' similarly suggests the masking and metamorphosis of a chaotic identity (p.173). Perceiving himself to be a murderer, he repels and rejects contact with others, particularly those like David who probe him with their searching eyes penetrating the hidden man beneath the carefully constructed façade. Fearing his true identity, he evades connection and psychic dis/integration results.

Nor is Gideon exempt from this emphasis on hidden identity: masquerading as a Western Ghandi, fashioning himself as the 'Pope of Reason' in Lois' words (p.191), Gideon is a false construction, a 'phoney' (p.192), a hypocrite preaching the creed of alienation (non-attachment) because it is the only means of converting his essential lack into a virtue. By the end of the play, Gideon's false identity has been shattered by his striking of Lois and we realize that, like his acolyte, we believe his word on nothing. Enid, whose eyes are said to have been 'like two pebbles in a January stream' (p.133) had quickly seen what Lois' 'unique' eyes, 'blue as the jeans of innocence' (p.150) had failed to see until forced to confront the truth.

The connection between the 'I' of identity and the 'eye' of sight or blindness is forged early in this play and its presence does not relent throughout. As noted above, the gum clogging Gideon's eyes converts his metaphorical blindness into a physically repellent characteristic, made explicit in the following exchange when Gideon, oblivious to Mark's anguish (his eyes, after all, are never really *on* anyone, as Lois points out) suggests that Mark's confession to the murder of his wife is simply the 'warping' work of grief – Mark begins by refusing and mocking the role that Gideon assigns him, a role that Mark would once have appropriated for himself:

MARK: The great poet, grieving for his love! Sagging Jesus!…Look at you. What can you see? [*Viciously.*] Gummy worried old eyes.

What can you really see, Giddy, through all that white gum? [...]
Twelve years ago, you couldn't see. Even when you were in
Corfu, I'd already started to kill her. You couldn't see it.

(p.137)

David, on the other hand, had 'seen' perfectly, Mark raging at him
in Act 3: 'You were never fooled. You saw him only too clear: the
killer in me' (p.188). But Guilia, with her amazing eyes complete
with sun-ring, had been blind to Mark's true nature because, to her,
he was 'literally invisible'. Again, the connection between 'I' and
'eye' is unmistakeable, Guilia's metaphorical blindness later replicated in her physical paralysis, Mark's sense of invisibility causing
him to watch others with fear and loathing, and ways of 'seeing'
and 'not-seeing' passing fundamental judgement on the identity of
the perceiver.

The emphasis on eyes and sight is manifested in this play in
many forms. Shaffer's characteristic delight in word-play is evident
in a number of exchanges which solidify the pervasiveness of this
metaphor. For example, when Mark considers whether he should
attempt the seduction of Lois to 'see' what would happen, the
cliché suddenly acquires unexpected resonance: 'One could always
see. The most anyone can say in the end, to God or Man, is "Let us
see!"' (p.170). Further, in an image later to be echoed in *Yonadab*,
the idea of blocked or distorted sight is wielded in Mark's memory
of the scalped boy looking up at him through a curtain of pollen
while Yonadab's voyeurism is replicated in David's memory of Mark
watching him for hours as a child, his eyes frightened, assessing,
and envious.

As noted earlier, this voyeurism is linked with an attempt to appropriate experience, to connect self with sensation. With his articulate self-awareness, Mark realizes that he is diseased with a
metaphorical 'cancer' which he names 'an incapacity for Immediate
Life' (p.173). He describes how the communal frenzy at football
matches would fail to communicate itself to him, and how, at
student dances, music would leave him unmoved and unexcited.
But words were another matter; words could always reach him,
particularly when they were expressing the 'clear thought of
Gideon Petrie' (p.173). Mark's words could contain and express his
hatred, they could elevate him to the heroic and temporarily make
him feel alive. But when the words ran out and became hollow, his
'hell began' (p.173). In retrospect, Mark finally realizes that even

words had never truly plugged the emptiness, causing him to never live *'now'*; the dysfunctional characteristics of envy, jealousy and vicarious life ('the endless living through others' p.174) originate entirely from this essential lack.

Mark instinctively recognizes this lack in Lois, she of the 'blind eye'. Apparently free from blood-ties and nationalistic loyalties, Lois cultivates an image of herself as liberated and progressive, but the tension manifest in her earliest movements and speeches belies her apparent ease. Familiar with masks, Mark swiftly penetrates Lois' shallow pretence, revealing her recognition of her own numbness and her terror of it. Finally, she offers a parallel 'confession' to Mark's admission that he has never lived *'now'* when she states *'with absolute frankness'*, 'I don't know what enjoy means' (p.156). The confession annihilates her self-deluding frauds and she can at last admit that her alienation from self and place is total: 'I don't know who I am, David' (p.195), 'I'm no place, David. No place at all' (p.196).

Mark and Lois find this an unbearable discovery, but Gideon appears fully accommodated within emotional and sexual numbness and the creed of non-attachment. At several points in the text, he advocates embracing that form of paralysis which Mark and Lois so fear in themselves, suggesting the desirability of a 'true passiveness' which creates 'an immense Nothing inside you' (p.190). Mark knows this is insufficient and his entire 'battle' with Gideon is fought in an effort to prove it, but it is left to Lois to puncture the philosopher's sham 'religion' in decisive terms. Picking up on Gideon's use of the word 'nothing', she tells Gideon that he had felt 'nothing' when she had sex with Mark because 'nothing' is all he is capable of feeling; she adds that the creed of non-attachment is simply a way of 'making a great Cause out of not caring. A way of life, yeah, a whole religion – out of not feeling anything personal at all!' (p.192). When Gideon strikes her *twice* (the second time is deliberate and cannot thus be excused as an uncontrollable flash of sudden fury), he reveals that his creed is a double hypocrisy since he is prepared to use violence if it will silence truth.

Where Mark and Lois share an absence of joy, an incapacity for direct feeling, Gideon and Lois share a dysfunctional sexuality since both are 'frigid', deep-frozen, and incapable of passion. This is the reason why, as Mark so perceptively suggests, Lois has 'selected' Gideon: his celibacy and her chastity guarantee mutual evasion allowing Lois to play the roles she most enjoys, earth-mother and acolyte, and allowing Gideon to play the roles he is most suited to, object of worship and pseudo-saint. Mark's sexuality is also dysfunctional, his confession that he had made love to a woman in front of his paralysed wife seeming perverse and cruel. Now, even the sex act connotes only emptiness for him. David too shows signs of sexual anxiety, doggedly pursuing without hope of eventual success the icy Lois whose devotion lies elsewhere. Whether homosexual desire is involved in David's affection for Gideon is a tenuous area of debate since it is clear from the reversal of father-son roles at the end of the play that what is at stake here is not sexual affiliation.

The web of hypocrisies and lies spun by Gideon and Mark together with the self-deceptions practised by Lois, all contribute to the sense of dysfunction which shrouds these characters. All are alienated in some way having retreated to an environment that itself shrieks estrangement, and all are desperate to construct false selves so as to conceal fractured identities. Hence the emphasis on paralysis in this play since the protagonists are all in a state of emotional, psychological or sexual deep-freeze. Mark perceives his frozen state to be another form of his cancer, but this is more deadly still since it is contagious and kills by proxy. He is convinced that his hatred for Guilia crept steadily up her legs until she was totally paralysed, a literal manifestation of his emotional immobility. Making love to a prostitute in front of her, he feels he has at last beaten her, has reversed the situation whereby Guilia would dance and he would look on, where she would live and he would 'watch and turn it all into literature' (p.169). With Guilia paralysed, Mark flaunts his mobility and mimics life in front of her, but now *her* 'fixed' eyes watch *him* in a 'stare of unbelievable pain' and it is this which haunts him (p.162).

The embrace, and the rejection of it, can be interpreted as an extension of the paralysis metaphor as it relates to alienation. Several examples of the rejected embrace appear in this text with David, at the end of the play, offering his extended arms to Lois who can only stand 'motionless' in response (p.196), and with Lois' earlier flight from Gideon's arms in Act 2. By expressing the essential difference between Mark and Gideon's creeds in terms of hand imagery (the hand that kills and maims can also caress and comfort), Shaffer extends the idea of disconnection further. The dual images are finally conjoined in two crucial moments which follow consecutively: in the first, the hands formerly offered in a gesture of embrace to Lois are converted into weapons by Gideon when he strikes her; but in the second, the image is reversed when David's violent hands are converted into an embrace of ultimate acceptance:

> 'DAVID *moves, quickly. His hands fly up, join violently above his head. For a long moment they stay up there, poised to smash his father down. Then he begins to tremble. Slowly his arms are lowered over his father's head. He pulls* MARK *to him, and kisses him on the face. They stay still'*.
> (p.194)

Shrivings has not rejected Mark as he had predicted it would, but his presence has catalysed the painful process of confronting anxieties circulating around crises of alienation and identity which have frozen each of the protagonists. Throughout has run the network of metaphors accumulating around invisibility/presence, 'being' and 'non-being', the thwarted embrace (disconnnection) and sight/ blindness, each involved in the interconnected dialectic of alienation, identity and dysfunction. These same impulses, manifested in a range of alternative forms are also present in *Yonadab*, to which this discussion turns next.

Like *Shrivings*, *Yonadab* was not successful in theatrical or critical terms when the original play was first performed at the National Theatre in December 1985. Shaffer rewrote the play extensively and the resulting text was staged by the Oxford University Dramatic Society in 1995 to great acclaim. The context of the play is the blood-soaked biblical world of dreams and visions, revelations and brutality. Yonadab, the eponymous 'hero', is a man born out of his historical time being possessed of a modern cynicism and rationality but existing in a world of contingent bloodshed and, to him, irrational faith. In effect, he represents what Edward Damson in *The Gift of the Gorgon* defines as the 'abstract mind' which is pitched in eternal hostility against the 'concrete mind'; the latter believes that 'God is always invisible' where the former requires '*illustration*' of divinity before it can perceive its existence.[20]

Yonadab longs to believe what those who surround him accept unthinkingly: he needs to know that there is a God who orders the universe and a creed which connotes value and truth. The only problem is that Yonadab, being possessed of the 'abstract mind', requires proof of divinity before he can commit himself to it since his intellect blocks faith. Further, he finds it difficult to believe in a God who seems to require a commitment to constant genocide. As a result, Yonadab aches for belief but can never acquire it, this alienating him from those who surround him, from divinity, and from himself. He exists in a void, aware only of a profound emptiness, an 'anguished figure forever caught between the impossibility of religious credo and the equal impossibility of perpetual credulity'.[21]

Recalling Salieri, Yonadab enters into a 'duel' with God in order to prove his non-existence ('praying', as he does so, that God intervenes thus proving the opposite). These two protagonists have much in common, both being likened to Iago by several critics, both orchestrating the events around them, both part of, yet separate from, action and audience, both imagining a wrathful, punishing God (if he exists at all), both sardonic and erudite, and both longing for immortality. It should also be noted that both finally achieve eternal life-in-death and death-in-life in an ironic over-fulfilment of their desires: they do indeed achieve immortality, but only as ghosts 'attached to the Tree of Unattachment' (p.182).

From the beginning of the play, Yonadab's alienation and hidden (or dual) identity is emphasized by Shaffer, eager to establish a vital chain of meaning. His introductory address to the audience stresses the idea of dual identity and simultaneously the notion of invisibility in an echo of David Askelon: Yonadab tells us that he merits two mentions in the Second Book of Samuel, 'one as cunning, one as kind – creating between them a kind of invisibility. Highly appropriate for me as a matter of fact' (p.87). This emphasis is continued in the information that he is 'son of Shimeah the Ignored' (p.87), and the opening scene at David's court certainly suggests that Yonadab has inherited his father's opaqueness since his bows and greetings to David's son pass unnoticed and unreturned.

Similarly, his sense of alienation is communicated by Shaffer as early in the text as possible with Yonadab announcing at the beginning of his opening monologue that he lives 'in limbo for eternity'. The sense of unbelonging, of standing apart from society/God/man, is stressed whenever possible throughout the play and is communicated in a variety of ways. His sardonic erudition has, from the first, identified him as a man out of step with his primitive context who professes religious conformity in order to avoid a stoning (the gap between 'seeming' and 'being' inherent in this construction of a false identity again becomes involved in issues of alienation). Retreating to the comparative safety of his estate at strategic points throughout the text (and ultimately banished there by David), Yonadab frequently draws apart from his fellow humans while his role of 'watcher' recalls Mark Askelon's estrangement from direct experience. When Amnon begs Yonadab to accompany him to Absalom's estate, brushing aside Yonadab's objections that he 'wouldn't belong', and telling him that, on the contrary, he belongs *'any*where' (p.168), Amnon is absolutely correct: Yonadab does indeed belong 'anywhere' because he belongs 'nowhere'. This pattern of alienation is a replica of that found in *Shrivings*.

Belonging simultaneously nowhere and therefore 'anywhere' requires developed survival skills and, specifically, a talent for camouflage. The chameleonism mentioned earlier reaches its most extreme form in the character of Yonadab who finds it relatively effortless to adopt the roles of friend, servant, spy and confidant at will. He gains most enjoyment, however, from his role as a 'Mini-Samuel' and modestly explains the 'acting' techniques required for it: 'It's actually a fairly easy role to play if you have been starved for attention all your life. All it takes is a taste for theatrics and the right tremble in the vocal cords' (pp.163–4). Having no fixed identity of his own, Yonadab, like Mark Askelon, is accomplished in the donning of masks to mimic one.

But always the sense of himself as a ghost remains, this exacerbated by his habit of watching unseen. Like Mark Askelon, Yonadab's voyeurism is not sexual in origin: both men desire knowledge and experience which they are blocked from gaining directly. Voyeurism is, of course, a dysfunctional sign, linking as it does with the 'I-eye' of identity and with the attempt to appropriate feeling which is inherent to the experience of alienation.[22] But here, voyeurism is only one of many dysfunctional signs since we also find in this play the sexual deviations of rape and incest, the peculiar nature of Absalom's virginity, Tamar's fanatical quest for vengeance which incorporates fratricide, her paralysis of spirit, and, of course, the destructive lying and spying in which field Yonadab is not the worst offender. All attests as much to deceptive identities and to dis/integration as to the nature of this terrifying context.

In Shaffer's imagination, this brutal world is characterized by a series of curtains 'hiding what must not be looked on'.[23] Such curtains not only suggest the emphasis on voyeurism in this play, but also links with the motif of barriers which similarly connects with the alienation issue.[24] For the original London production, John

Bury designed a set of opaque drapes adorned with the Hebraic alphabet which suggested the heat, light and breezes of biblical Jerusalem and which simultaneously obscured vision and retranslated the shadows into sinister images. The idea of curtains is woven into the play in a number of alternative ways, these enforcing the ideas of forbidden vision and distorted sight, and providing a series of verbal and visual metaphors for the thematic emphasis on voyeurism. Yonadab, for example, is amazed when Amnon drops the curtains around the rape-bed in his face, is equally amazed when Absalom releases the astonishing 'curtain' of his hair (p.149), and is destroyed by David's curse on him which is to see life 'as through a veil drawn before your eyes' (p.172).

But it is Tamar, the victim turned victimizer, who is the character most closely connected with the curtain metaphor. The first time we meet her she is veiled; she is subsequently described riding in a curtained litter, and her removal of her veil in front of Yonadab constitutes a transfiguring stage moment. It is no coincidence that she is also the character most connected with deception and false identity (more so even than Yonadab), and no coincidence that the source of her vengeance is communicated in the dreadful shadows her body throws onto Amnon's bed-curtains during her rape. Also closely connected with eye imagery, Tamar's true identity and her alienating 'quest' for revenge are revealed in this system of signification.

While vision is impeded in this play (literally by curtains, or metaphorically in terms of failing to 'see' the truth), so too is movement. As in *Shrivings*, we find a pattern of images and situations that suggest paralysis and immobility, but here these impulses are contained within the staging of the play as much as in the events and emphases of the text. Central to the simultaneous representation of 'past', 'present' and 'future' (in addresses to the theatre audience or in forward projections in time) is the technique of 'freezing' characters to allow space for Yonadab's narration and commentary and to indicate when he is involved in the action or is temporarily leaving it. Characters are frequently caught mid-pose, as when Amnon is said to *adopt a "prophetic" posture and freezes* (p.142), or when Absalom stands before David, *his hand flung out in a frozen attitude of demand*; a series of tableaux is thus formed throughout the play, each suggestive of the biblical context, and each related to the metaphor of paralysis. Only Yonadab is never at rest, participating in each scene and even appearing in past, present and future simultaneously. Constantly in movement, Yonadab's frenetic activity (psychologically as well as physically) itself suggests the restless limbo in which he finds himself trapped for eternity and the ceaseless quest for divinity which had prevented him from rest in life.

The idea of paralysis, offering a physical equivalent to the emotional and spiritual immobility connected to alienation and identity, finds numerous alternative expressions in this play with various forms of impeded movement incorporated into the action. Trances (frozen moments of altered consciousness) belong in this category. Tamar, for example, does not fight Amnon who has trapped her in his arms prior to the rape because she is said to be 'hypnotized' (p.125), and her search for Absalom following the violence is conducted in an apparently mysterious, even miraculous, trance (though this later proves to have a perfectly rational explanation). Later, when Yonadab watches the two 'beauties' kiss, he states: 'In a trance I watched it happen' (p.160). Further references to immobility litter the text as when Amnon raises his hand to strike Tamar *'but remains paralyzed'* (p.128), and as when Absalom recounts his dream of Tamar's rape which involves him witnessing the violence in the role of a helpless voyeur: 'I can't move to help you. I just have to watch' (p.159). Later, when he is rejected by Tamar, immobility strikes Absalom again when he finds himself *'unable to move'* in response to her threatening dismissal (p.177).

But by far the most dangerous form of immobility in this play is paralysis of attitude. David's rigid certainty motivates the wholescale slaughters that he has perpetrated in the name of faith and this unwavering belief in murder in the name of 'righteousness' has been inherited by his daughter. When Amnon imagines erecting a massive statue of Tamar in the desert sands, her eyes staring from the stone for miles, he little realizes how accurate his perception of her truly is. The image he creates of 'Tamar the praying statue! One of the wonders of the world!' (p.122) is horrifyingly apt by the end of the play when the woman's legend 'hardens' into an attitude of vengeance. Unwavering, unresponsive and 'fixed', Tamar defines the negative values of emotional paralysis finding more joy in the memory of murder than in the possibility of creation.

The metaphor of paralysis that gathers around Tamar, connecting with the interrelated emphases on alienation, identity and dysfunction, is complemented by two other vital signifiers; firstly, her eyes are consistently centralized, interpreted as a prophetic sign of divinity and also imagined as 'chips of crystal' by Amnon, for example (p.122). Like Yonadab, she is an unseen watcher and a born spy, but unlike Yonadab, she is able to interpret what she sees with murderous accuracy. The eye-imagery with which she is associated connects her with her father who is said to have 'anointed eyes', but what distinguishes her from him is the fact that David, though wary always of 'the watching man' (p.171), has been blind to Yonadab's treachery: Tamar, on the other hand, has successfully watched 'the watcher' and rendered him 'blind as a baby' in relation to hers (p.156).

Secondly, Tamar is closely associated with the network of hand, arm and 'embrace' motifs which run through the text. Theatrically, this chain of visual reference contributes to the evocation of the biblical context since the gestures of prophesy, blessing and wrath are central to any audience's collective image of an Old Testament context. Dramatically, the gestures fulfil several functions indicating the dual signs of oath and blessing, threat and protection, acceptance and rejection. Hands become subject to grim irony when Tamar has Absalom literally 'eating out of her hand' as he eats pancakes from her outstretched palm, and also to Shafferian word-play when Yonadab, surprised that his destructive plans are progressing so smoothly, states of a card-sharp Godhead: 'Surely Yaveh must show His hand now and stop it!' (p.111). Further, arms and the embrace feature heavily in Yonadab's dreams of Absalom and Tamar who he sees seated on horses, their arms outstretched in a gesture of benevolent peace and acceptance, an image in stark and deliberate contrast to the later embrace we witness between them following Amnon's gory murder: where the embrace of the dream had connoted harmony and reconciliation, that of reality suggests only grim triumph and the inverted values of revenge. The connection between the embrace and violence is further enforced when we realize that an embrace had preceded Tamar's rape. In addition, she had called on God to 'stretch forth Thy arm' in protection which never came (p.124), so that when she next invokes the arm of God it is as an image of ferocious retribution: 'I am [God's] right hand, Yonadab. I am His arm' (p.176). The embrace, then, that potential image of connection and reconciliation, has been converted through this emphasis into an image finally implying only violence and estrangement.

The eye-imagery so marked in this text connects closely with the complex notion of identity outlined throughout this chapter, since here eyes reveal and conceal, see and are 'blind', define identity (Yonadab as the 'man of eyes') and disguise it. What is obvious may not be seen, and what is seen may be obscured either by a physical barrier such as curtains, or by a metaphorical barrier such as an anxiety to believe only a desired interpretation. Curtains also relate to the sense of estrangement in this play since they form barriers and contribute to the separation between man and man, as when Yonadab mourns, 'Always between me and men that curtain of separation' (p.181). As in *Shrivings*, this intense network of imagery is profoundly involved in the fundamental impulses of alienation, identity and dysfunction, the emphases on which both plays conclude.

Like Mark Askelon, Yonadab has revealed a 'truth' that he had not wanted to believe. Where Mark had proved that humankind is 'totally and forever unimprovable' (p.138), Yonadab has proved the absence of divinity and the ultimate rationality of a vicious universe. These are joyless triumphs for both men. Increasingly frantic, a distressed Yonadab shrieks at David: 'everything was bearable if you were *true* [...] *Why could you not have seen? Stopped me? Struck me down?* SHOWN ME HE *IS*' (p.173). In a sense, the fulfilment of David's curse does suggest a form of proof but this proof destroys Yonadab. Like Mark Askelon, Yonadab is now condemned to hang alone in his own world, forever unattached in death as he had been when alive, an eternal watcher robbed always of 'Immediate Life'. The final unanswered question, 'who will cut me down?' (p.182) offers as complete an image of alienation as any we have been offered in the play.

From a brief examination of these two plays, then, we can see that the constant emphasis in Shaffer's work on the interrelated impulses of alienation, identity and dysfunction involves a network of recurrent metaphors and images which are communicated theatrically and dramatically, visually and verbally. *Yonadab* and *Shrivings* offer two particularly clear examples of this network of signification and have several characteristics in common, hence their selection for this chapter (it is, perhaps, significant, that they both 'failed' on stage in their original forms, a rare event for Shaffer). But it should be stressed that the patterns and impulses detected here are equally applicable to much of this playwright's work and to *Amadeus* and *Equus* in particular. For Shaffer, the questions relating to alienation, identity and dysfunction, as expressed through this synthesized metaphorical scheme, return to haunt his stage compulsively.

5
Murdering Divinities

Of his best-known plays, *The Royal Hunt of the Sun, Equus* and *Amadeus*, Peter Shaffer comments: 'all three pieces share a common preoccupation with worship and man's attempts to acquire or murder a special divinity'.[1] This vital thematic link between these dramas (manifested as well in several others) is the subject of this chapter. Here Shaffer's dramatic and theatrical obsession with the idea of worship is examined from two central points of view: firstly, what 'worship' as a concept means to this playwright and to the protagonists he creates will be discussed; this emphasis feeds directly from the focus on alienation (its causes and effects) outlined in the previous chapter; secondly, Shaffer's constant return to meditations on the nature of religion will be assessed, this involving a brief consideration of his use of myth. These emphases will then be applied to *The Royal Hunt of the Sun, Equus* and *Amadeus*, immensely popular plays in which gods in various guises are created, hunted, and ultimately destroyed.

Associated predominantly with religious credo, 'worship' most often refers to faith in a divine being and to unquestioning adoration of that divinity: Dora Strang worships her Christian god just as Atahuallpa worships his pagan god. Both religions are organized structures which help to give meaning to a chaotic universe and which lend order to the social environment since obedience to doctrine involves adherence to a set of rules predicated on civic peace. However, 'worship' need not be a group experience and may militate against social order as Alan Strang discovers when he invents his own object of worship. Equus is the result of a fusion between Christian, pagan and mythological elements: as such, it represents an anarchic display of individualism which eventually threatens normative society. But Alan's worship nevertheless suggests that the most valuable forms of transcendental experience are individually acquired since organized belief necessarily involves a subjugation of subjective response and experience. Each form of worship, though, revolves around a god-figure and satisfies needs in the individual that cannot be satisfied by the rational, tangible world of daily experience. Worship, in short, satisfies these protagonists' spiritual hunger.

Other forms of worship also exist in Shaffer's plays, these revolving only indirectly around a godhead. Of these, the most common form we find is the worship of pure beauty. This type of worship subdivides into two impulses in Shaffer's work: firstly, knowledge of divinity *through* aesthetic experience and, secondly, worship of the aesthetic *in and for itself* (notions of a godhead being redundant here). The former impulse is clearly familiar to the playwright himself who states: 'My own apprehension of the divine is very largely aesthetic…The creation of the C minor Mass or the final act of *Antony and Cleopatra* seem to me to give a point to evolution; most human activities do not'.[2] In this, Salieri is a character written in Shaffer's image since the 'Absolute Beauty' of Mozart's music allows him to know that God exists.[3]

But where Salieri approaches the divine through aesthetic experience, protagonists such as Bob in *The Private Ear* fall into the second category and worship the aesthetic simply for its beauty and for the levels of experience triggered by it. Bob's passion for music amounts to worship since it is the only thing that lends meaning to his physical and metaphysical existence (notice also how he 'feeds' records to Behemoth, a biblical monster, in a reversed communion ritual); similarly, Lotte in *Lettice and Lovage* kneels at the altar of beauty since, worshipless in religious terms, this is the sole sphere in which she can detect goodness. Both are elevated and released by the 'sacred' experience of pure beauty, but 'god' in any formal sense is irrelevant to their worship: here, as always in Shaffer's plays, it is the capacity for worship (whether 'religious' or aesthetic) that is the point at stake.

Where a character has no capacity for worship, he or she is swamped by a sense of alienation, is cut off from the life-affirming extremities of instinct and passion, and is depicted as only half-alive, drifting like a ghost towards a point of spiritual crisis. Dysart is typical of these worshipless characters; an intellectual caught in a Hamlet-like dilemma of thought versus action, he knows himself to be spiritually stranded (if not permanently disabled) to the extent that he envies a frightened boy committed to a mental institution because he has at least known and experienced passion. Dysart longs for worship emotionally but his access to it is blocked intellectually and an overwhelming sense of futility and meaninglessness engulfs him as a result.

This is the sickness, Shaffer potentially suggests, of modern man. Joan Fitzpatrick Dean argues that Shaffer's creation of men such as Dysart reveals that his 'target is the basic structure of modern life and its diminished capacity to channel constructively man's spiritual impulses';[4] this 'structure' inevitably leads to a 'multi-lane' wasteland of 'plastic' emotion, reaction and capacity.[5] Certainly, in *Equus*, this emphasis is woven into the text, but it does not account for the spiritual angst of men such as Yonadab and Pizarro who, despairing of their own contemporary contexts, reach towards worship of a divine entity. 'Modern life' with all its insufficiencies militates against the spiritual, but that historical figures also suffer from similar despairs suggests that Shaffer's 'target' is wider and deeper than a condemnation of modernity alone. What is at stake here is man's capacity for worship and whether 'man' is of the Renaissance, the Enlightenment or the contemporary context is as irrelevant to this debate as is his nationality.

It would appear, then, that Shaffer's attitude towards worship in his work is fairly straightforward – the capacity for worship is equated with the capacity for life, instinct and passion; the absence of worship is equated with half-life, alienation and despair. But when we notice that a causal relationship between worship and destruction is consistently presented in these plays, we become aware that Shaffer's attitude is not as simple as it initially seems. Whether the form of worship centralized is communal or individual, 'religious' or aesthetic, its negative connotations are dramatized in terms as stark as the implications of its absence. Christian fundamentalism leads to the 'rape' of Peru and to physical or spiritual death in *The Royal Hunt of the Sun*; it equally contributes to Alan's chaos in *Equus*. Sun-worship enslaves its people as surely as does Catholicism in the former play, horse-worship leads to mutilation in the latter, and worship through aestheticism catalyses treachery and murder in *Amadeus*. Releasing elemental, natural man, worship is seen to liberate passions which circulate beyond the margins of surveillance – passions which destroy as surely as they create.

So while the capacity for worship is presented as wholly admirable in these plays, the consequences of it are presented as highly problematic. The main reason for this emphasis on the destructive consequences of worship is that Shaffer's 'sense of the divine' is deeply ambiguous.[6] On the one hand, an individual with the spiritual capacity to perceive the divine is a creature of imagination and instinct; unfortunately, the divinity that he or she worships is a creature of pitiless judgement, always presented by Shaffer as mocking, harsh and brutal. Atahuallpa's sun will blind anyone who attempts to look too closely at it; Salieri's God strikes bargains and displays a malevolent sense of ironic judgement; Alan's Equus is jealous and all-seeing; Valverde's Jesus blesses bloodshed and torture. Each godhead implies a vengeful lust for retribution and the disciple (who is created in its image) has no choice but to destroy in its name.

In Shaffer's plays, the destruction following inevitably from worship finds vindication and organization in normative religious structures such as Christianity. Here we find that the ambiguity surrounding this playwright's concept of worship disappears as an attack is launched on institutional religion which relies for its perpetuation on an image of a wrathful, judgemental God. Though several critics have denied that it is Shaffer's intention to assault 'religion' in this sense, the impulses in these plays speak for themselves; King David's genocidal enforcement of Judaic principles, Atahuallpa's pagan fratricide, Valverde's Catholic brutality, and Dora's lethal Anglicanism all clearly indicate that organized 'faith' (which for Shaffer is a contradiction in terms) has 'blood on its hands'.[7]

It is clear from his own comments that Shaffer's attitude towards organized, institutional religion is unequivocally hostile. In 1965 he told a reporter: 'I resent deeply all churches. I despise them. No church or synagogue has ever failed to misuse its power'.[8] In the same year, he stated: 'To me the greatest tragic factor in History is man's apparent need to mark the intensity of his reaction to life by joining a band. For a band, to give definition, must find a rival or an enemy'.[9] This attitude is expressed in several of his plays, most notably in the three focused upon in this chapter. Here, organized religion becomes a form of neurosis as in Dora's Anglicanism which, because it is normative, is a type of insanity which passes unnoticed. Her husband's Socialism provides another demonstration of limiting, 'blind' allegiance to a 'band' that involves the selection of 'a rival or an enemy' in his wife's Christianity which then retaliates in kind. Here we see that 'religion' for Shaffer (as in the case of worship) need not necessarily involve a church though it must necessarily involve false idols. Repeatedly, the aspects of any religion that Shaffer finds most destructive and most horrifying are the organization of faith (which is by nature an individual

emotion), the standardization of belief into narrow and hating precepts, and the hypocrisy attendant on the entire package.

Not only does organized, institutional religion involve for Shaffer
the blind, limiting worship of false, vindictive idols, it also fails to
meet man's spiritual needs; if the playwright could forgive the
hatred implicit in religious credo, he could not forgive this.
Christianity in particular is envisaged as a weak, pallid faith predicated upon 'Thou Shall Not' rather than 'Thou Shall'; its ceremonies and belief-systems are presented by Shaffer as being
encoded with repression of human and spiritual instinct. As a
result, Shaffer reaches in his plays towards older, darker and more
primitive faiths (which are often individually constructed and perceived) in a constant search for a form of worship that satisfies a
side of human nature that Christianity actually erodes. Of particular relevance to the plays discussed in this chapter is his reach
towards myth.

Christianity, of course, is itself a myth and Shaffer frequently in-
tersects its forms and systems with those of primitive or more
ancient equivalents. The term 'mythology' derives from 'the Greek
mythos, a tale, and *logos*, an account', so that, as Alexander S.
Murray explains, the word literally means '"an account of tales",
the tales in this case being confined to the origin, character, and
functions of the ancient gods, to the origin of mankind, and the
primitive condition of the visible world'.[10] Robert Graves adds to
this definition by stating that myths involve 'archaic magic-
making', this forging a clear link between Shaffer's use of myth and
the principles of Artaudian theatre as discussed in Chapter 2: in
both imaginative visions of myth we find a preoccupation with
darkness (physical and metaphorical) while a mood of 'slaughter,
torture and bloodshed' dominates.[11]

Direct references to primitive or ancient mythology abound in
Shaffer's dramas: *Equus, Amadeus* and *The Gift of the Gorgon* alone
provide too many mythic names and legends to catalogue here. But
in addition to these references we can also detect a number of emphases which suggest that mythic elements are woven into these
plays at less explicit levels. To take one example (which is expanded upon later in this chapter) we find that the deities worshipped in *The Royal Hunt of the Sun* and *Equus* (the sun and the
horse respectively) are among the earliest gods worshipped by man;
in addition, they both display characteristics attributed to ancient
gods including omniscient sight and the ability to transcend time.[12]

For Pizarro and Alan, these deities trigger a response that cannot be explained or expressed in rational terms because a form of archetypal memory (as identified in the work of Carl Jung) has been released in them: the audience witnessing the on-stage events is likely to respond in a similar way since its 'collective unconscious', defined as 'that part of the psyche which retains and transmits the common psychological inheritance of mankind', also recognizes (in the forms of the sun and the horse) the symbols central to its archaic memory.[13]

So where Christianity in its passionless conformity is portrayed by Shaffer as an insufficient answer to man's spiritual needs, more primitive and darker faiths are explored in an attempt to approach the ecstasy of pure worship: paganism and ancient myth potentially hold the keys to such transcendence. But it is too easy to lose sight of the fact that while these prehistoric modes of belief are seen to reach corners of the psyche that more modern faiths evade, and are 'positive' in this respect, they are also, like all forms of worship and deity, portrayed by Shaffer as implying destruction at their core. We cannot, as a result, concoct a neat equation whereby Christian faith equals spiritual paucity and moral hypocrisy in these plays, and pagan myth equals spiritual liberation and moral purity. This would be a serious misreading of Shaffer's use of mythic impulses. Irrational forces satisfying unnameable corners of man's being, Shaffer's mythic creatures destroy their worshippers as easily as they destroy their enemies; they set up camp in dark regions of the mind and cause psychic chaos; they appal at the same time as they awe. This is, needless to say, their fascination.

The preoccupation with the ambiguous connotations of worship, the anti-individualistic nature of organized religion and the potency of primitive myth finds its earliest dramatic outing in Shaffer's work in *The Royal Hunt of the Sun*. In this stunning piece of theatre we find that those impulses outlined above find direct expression in a drama that clearly anticipates *Equus* and *Amadeus*: in each play, a man who longs for worship seeks to destroy a divinity and is himself destroyed in turn.

Pizarro is haunted by an awareness of death that has spiritually and emotionally incapacitated him. From the moment he first realized that 'everything we feel is made of time', life seemed futile to him because he had become aware that transience characterizes the human condition;[14] he sees no point in joy because it will inevitably fade as will all beauty and experience; in the context of inevitable destruction through time, everything becomes trivial to him, even (perhaps especially) concepts such as 'Pain. Good. God...' (p.75). Awareness of death, not as an abstract concept but as an absolute fact, has robbed Pizarro of the capacity for 'Immediate Life' since, like Mark Askelon and Yonadab, he is forced to exist behind a curtain of non-attachment. In Atahuallpa, an apparently immortal man, Pizarro believes he has found 'an answer for Time' (p.56), and the idea of death that has 'for years rotted everything for me, all simple joy in life' begins to retreat (p.75).

The appeal of Atahuallpa and the Inca religion to Pizarro is clear; not only is the 'son' of the sun a 33 year-old former shepherd (in a direct parallel with Jesus Christ), but the religion he leads revolves around a physical, natural object that enshrines the idea of immortality.[15] Day after day, year after year, potentially forever, the sun rises in the sky ordering man's life, feeding him and warming him. Human intervention in the sun's life is impossible – it cannot be destroyed. So blazing above Pizarro in the Peruvian world is a physical symbol of immortality, a visible proof that transcendence of time is possible and, through Atahuallpa, achievable. Beginning the play worshipless, proceeding through it mimicking a god on earth, Pizarro finally comes to believe in a deity that gives meaning to existence on both physical and spiritual levels. His tragedy, however, is that he is finally betrayed by it just as he has always been betrayed by all faith.

As in the later case of Alan's horse-worship, Shaffer makes clear connections in this play between Christianity and the primitive religion: the apparent disjunction between rival forms of worship finally dissolves as we realize that the two faiths share common ground. For example, both Christianity and sun-worship are seen to involve the act of confession, Atahuallpa taking the Catholic priest's role of 'shriving' Pizarro in a ceremony of purgation, forgiveness and reconciliation. In addition, both religions have as their core the concepts of resurrection and immortality. Less positively, both are also connected with bloodshed (Atahuallpa has killed his brother), both subjugate their followers through conformity and through terror of an all-seeing god, and both are revealed to be a fraud as Christian hypocrisy plunders a country and as Atahuallpa's resurrection fails to materialize.

Nevertheless, for the duration of the play, Pizarro's rejection of violent Christianity and his gradual acceptance of sun-worship is presented in terms that awaken the reader to the grossness of the former and the spiritual (and logical) potentialities of the latter. Nowhere in Shaffer's work does his condemnation of 'the Church' reach a more sustained and unambiguous pitch than in this play. Pizarro has little Christian faith as the play begins; he defines himself as a soldier who has seen too much death and bloodshed to accept the myth-making of a corrupt religion; in addition, as Shaffer states, he can only envisage the Christian God as 'something right outside the universe and essentially irrelevent to it and to everyday dealings in the world'.[16] But since militarism and Catholicism are mutually-involved concepts in this sixteenth-century Spanish context, Pizarro has little choice but to accept the Church's presence on his mission since this is his country's means of justifying the plunder enacted in its name: under the guise of converting pagans to Catholicism, Spain robs the 'New World' of its treasures.

The Christian faith of Young Martin is solid as the play begins, his brand of worship being a combination of the laws of chivalry and Catholic belief. By the end of the play, however, now an old man, he has become as worshipless as Pizarro was in Act 1. His descriptions of the rituals performed in the blessing of Pizarro's soldiers clearly reveal his retrospective disgust at the sordidness of Catholic hypocrisy; he recalls, for example, that 'on the day of St John the Evangelist, our weapons were consecrated in the Cathedral Church of Panama' (p.20) – Shaffer's point is too clear to require more direct comment. Besides, we have staring at us from the back wall of the stage a visual symbol of Christian/Catholic brutality in the *'huge metal medallion, quartered by four black crucifixes, sharpened to resemble swords'* (p.13). That Pizarro has no faith in this debased and savage form of worship, and that Martin finally loses it, is a result of an insufficiency in the Christian faith that is expressed verbally and visually, dramatically and theatrically.

So Christianity, with its 'shackles and stakes' (p.26), is portrayed in this play as hypocritical and savage: it is a faith, Shaffer insists, that must be rejected. But there still remains the question of how man's need for a form of worship that will lend meaning to his existence can be achieved. There is no doubt that Pizarro's 'hunt' for gold in Peru is, from the beginning of the play, a 'hunt' for something altogether less tangible. As Shaffer states of the bond between Pizarro and Atahuallpa: 'the theme which lies behind their relationship is the search for god – that is why it is called "The Royal *Hunt* of the Sun"'.[17] Tortured by the approach of death (Pizarro is

63 years old), existing in a 'frostbitten' state of half-life (p.42), the soldier lives between 'two hates' of faith and non-committal (p.90). Much like the later Yonadab, neither 'belief' nor 'none' can satisfy Pizarro since adherence to the former involves faith in a corrupt religion (Catholicism is the only 'belief' he has encountered before he meets Atahuallpa), and refuge in the latter leads to physical and metaphysical despair. When he enters Peru, then, Pizarro is indeed 'hunting' for a god who can release him from the shackles of time and from the 'prison' of himself (p.61).

Peru is an environment where, to a sixteenth-century mind, gods could easily exist. This newly-discovered world, uncharted and unexplored, is known to contain riches beyond European dreams while its geographical splendour complete with glaciers and mountains, verdant valleys and pastures, suggests a semi-mythical (or even ambrosial) realm. Pizarro recognizes that in this magical place, divinity may actually walk upon the earth. As he tells Young Martin in Act 2: 'What if it's possible, here in a land beyond all maps and scholars, guarded by mountains up to the sky, that there were true gods on earth, creators of true peace?' (p.86). In this wildly unfamiliar physical territory, wildly unfamiliar metaphysical territory infiltrates Pizarro's psyche. It is, above all, the concept of 'gods on earth' that thrills him so completely and he returns to the idea of living gods, 'free of time' (p.86), compulsively throughout the play. The phrase is introduced early, upon the soldiers' first entry into Peru, and the following extract clearly reveals the impact it has on Pizarro. The Indian chief is explaining to the invaders the nature of Inca worship:

> PIZARRO: God?
> CHIEF: God!
> PIZARRO: God on earth?
> VALVERDE: Christ defend us!
> DO SOTO: Do you believe this?
> CHIEF: It is true. The sun is God. Atahuallpa is his child, sent to shine on us for a few years of life. Then he will return to his father's palace and live for ever.
> PIZARRO: God on earth!
>
> (p.25)

Initially, Pizarro's questions are incredulous and are separated by two brands of worshippers (the Chief and Valverde) proposing their deities as the true godhead. But as the Spaniards enquire further, and as the Chief explains the informing concepts of Inca credo, Pizarro silently digests the implications of what he is hearing; finally, he can contain himself no longer and the half-oath, half-statement, 'God on earth!', bursts from him. The idea of 'God on earth' is no longer a question lingering in his mind – it is an increasingly plausible reality.

At this stage, however, it is little more than a fascinating notion for Pizarro to dwell upon; it also leads to his idea that his men should mimic gods in their hunt for Atahuallpa who awaits them beyond the mountains. Realizing that, like any god worth his salt, Atahuallpa has eyes everywhere, Pizarro correctly perceives that his army's survival depends upon this impersonation; Atahuallpa waits in the meantime for the white gods foretold in prophecy who, he believes, will ratify his usurpation of his brother's throne.

It is when the two men finally meet and begin their intimate relationship that Pizarro's shadowy attraction to the idea of 'gods on earth' becomes concrete. Pizarro has dreamed of Atahuallpa several nights in succession prior to their first encounter, this suggesting the mythic portent of vision where gods were 'believed to communicate their will to men in dreams':[18] following these dreams, he expects something 'tremendous' (p.44) and he is not disappointed. The relationship between the two men subsequently develops swiftly though most of this development is significantly placed offstage with reports delivered by Young Martin or Diego detailing the growing attachment between the two men. This removal of Pizarro from the increasingly ugly stage action attests to the increasing distance between him, his native culture and its values.

Having slaughtered thousands of Indians and taken Atahuallpa hostage until treasures are delivered into the hands of the invading army, Pizarro begins to explore the precepts of the primitive faith which appears to offer the solution to his spiritual numbness. Spending all his time with his prisoner, Pizarro becomes an 'altered man' (p.68) and rejects the hollow ideology of 'gang-love' (p.84) more surely than he has ever done before. Slowly, his 'frostbitten soul' melts, but the institutional forces of Church and State have begun to close in upon him and his spiritual 'brother'. Having 'raped' the country, Spain now demands blood to protect its gain and Pizarro is forced to renege on his word that Atahuallpa would not be harmed if he delivered gold into Spanish hands.

Here we find a situation that will be repeated in *Equus*: a man who comes to admire a 'transgressive' form of worship and to reject normative values which insist on its annihilation is forced through a network of complicated forces to destroy the divinity that has begun to give his life meaning. Abstract words such as 'worship' and 'god' have been transferred into concrete territories of emotion and experience but, as always in Shaffer's plays, with worship comes destruction. Transgression cannot be tolerated and the god must be driven out and made extinct. All that Pizarro can do is ensure that Atahuallpa's body is not burnt so that the sun can resurrect it: he must then watch and wait for a supernatural proof of divinity. When this proof is not forthcoming, Pizarro is a broken man.

However, as in the cases of Salieri and Yonadab, whilst 'god' does not provide the 'proof' for which the would-be worshipper is seeking, his presence is registered in the alternative means by which he manifests his existence. For Pizarro, the 'miracle' of Atahuallpa's resurrection in the beams of the sun fails to happen, but another 'miracle' occurs as the soldier's soul melts and as sobs rack his body. Pizarro recognizes the enormity of the moment by holding a tear-drop to Atahuallpa's lifeless face and stating: 'In all your life you never made one of these, I know, and I not till this minute' (p.90). But this 'miracle' destroys Pizarro who, according to Old Martin, 'sat down that morning and never really got up again' (p.91). At last, though, he has come to escape the terror of time in an acceptance of death, promising the dead Atahuallpa, 'I'm coming after you. There's nothing but peace to come' (p.90).

Pizarro has, in short, been resurrected. The capacities for emotion, direct experience and worship have been 're-born' in him and though this contact destroys him in a mortal sense, he finally achieves spiritual transcendence which renders the question of immortality obsolete. Imperialist Spanish Catholicism gorges, retches and dwindles as Old Martin hastily concludes the chronicle with words that bring us face to face once again with the persistent Shafferian dilemma implied in the notion of 'worship': 'no joy in the world' can match its ecstasies, but when the destruction implicit at the heart of it is revealed, 'no pain' can match its loss (p.91). Ultimately, though, in a final insistence on the possibility of an eternal, harsh god, oblivious to men's needs and actions, '*The sun glares at the audience*' (p.91).

The Royal Hunt of the Sun is a vivid introduction to the various levels of debate circulating around the concept of 'worship' in Shaffer's plays. Here, paganism is offered as an alternative route to the divine, but when its ethos is revealed to be predicated on grounds that, like Christianity, imply destruction and conformity, its belief-system is challenged. Worship cannot be organized as a group experience whether the religion is based on Christian or pagan myth, but is an individual instinct capable of rescuing man from spiritual stagnation. Finally, though, worship destroys all who partake in it as 'god' turns a 'blind eye' to the sufferings of mortal ·man.

'Without worship you shrink, it's as brutal as that', says Dysart in *Equus*, verbalizing Pizarro's perception prior to his encounter with the Inca king (p.274). Living in a modern world of prefabricated feeling and practising a profession which involves moulding individuals into a contingent but unquestioned concept of 'normality', Dysart's unconscious doubts about his numb existence and professional purpose have been building for years. When Alan Strang enters his world, these doubts are dragged into his conscious life in dramatic and shattering style: the catalyst for this process is Dysart's direct encounter with myth.

Trapped in an impoverished contemporary context, and caught between the warring ideologies of his mother's Christianity and his father's atheistic Socialism, Alan has sought escape in a unique form of self-created worship. Gazing at an 'extreme' picture of Jesus journeying to Calvary which his mother had placed on his bedroom wall, Alan as a boy had been fixated on the associations the image set up in his mind. In the face of his father's protests, the picture was removed and in an effort to stem the boy's tears (he had become hysterical when faced with its loss), a second image was substituted – a horse's head staring frontwards, its eyes bulging out to the sides. The replacement picture had been positioned in exactly the same place as the image of Jesus: it is the last thing Alan sees before sleep and the first thing he sees upon waking. Meanwhile, his zealous mother drums into him mythic stories such as the pagan belief that horse and rider were believed to be one creature, and thus a type of god, whilst simultaneously reminding him (in her Christian, guilt-imposing way) that 'God sees you, Alan. God's got eyes everywhere' (p.241). Myth, pagan belief, and Christian dogma imprint themselves on the mind of the susceptible, anxious boy until their complementary impulses 'snap together like magnets, forging a chain of shackles' (p.268). Equus is born. Years later, Alan apparently unaccountably blinds six horses one night in a stables and is then delivered to Dysart for 'cure'.

Dysart's encounter with Alan Strang is not the first time that he has acknowledged the extraordinary power of myth; the psychiatrist habitually escapes from the rigours of his profession by absorbing himself in books on Ancient Greece, fondly believing himself to be in some way connected with that primitive culture in contrast to his antiseptic wife. Dysart is therefore familiar with the mythological on an intellectual level having absorbed its stories, rituals and traditions. But when he meets Alan, he realizes that knowledge and experience are entirely different propositions and that while he worships the *idea* of primitive forces, he has never truly approached these forces at a fundamental, 'concrete', level: Alan, devoid of intellectual knowledge, has, on the other hand, penetrated mythic territory at an elemental level. As such, Dysart is forced to acknowledge the fact that stories of gods and centaurs are not merely diverting, 'abstract', cultural relics but are projections of the dark figures of the unconscious that stalk man's collective psyche; he must thus finally accept that contemporary man, like his ancient forebears, and despite his 'rationality and efficiency', is 'possessed by "powers" that are beyond his control'.[19] Once he has confronted the proof of this Jungian perception for himself, glimpsed in the 'black cave of the Psyche' (p.267), the 'sharp chain' of Equus can never be removed from his own mouth (p.301).

That Dysart's encounter with Equus is an encounter with a mythological archetype is indicated in the variety of connotations that Shaffer's choice of the horse as an object of worship suggests. The horse occupies a privileged position in a variety of ancient religions and is identified by Carl Jung as an 'archetypal paradigm' which informs the unconscious psyches of diverse human cultures. Una Chaudhuri reminds us that in his book *Symbols of Transformation*, Jung details the range of horse-myths that existed in primitive belief-systems where 'clairvoyant and clairaudient horses, path-finding horses who show the way when the wanderer is lost, horses with mantic powers' regularly appear: further, Jung notes that the horse was frequently regarded as 'a symbol of the animal component in man' which explains its 'numerous connections with the devil' who has 'a horse's hoof and sometimes a horse's form' – Chaudhuri adds that 'this Christian version of the archetype appears in *Equus* [...] through Dora'.[20]

Several of these emphases find their way into Shaffer's portrayal of Equus. When, for example, the horses are blinded by Alan, we are told in the stage-notes that the three horses which appear in the arena are not 'naturalistic' like the first creatures, but are terrifying, vengeful *archetypal images* (p.298); in addition, frequent references to centaurs appear throughout the play while the devil's presence is indicated not only in direct references to him, but also in the emphasis on the number '6' which Gene A. Plunka notes recurs persistently during the course of the action.[21] Further details are also taken from ancient and primitive horse-mythologies and imprinted by Shaffer onto the notion of Equus: Bettina L. Knapp, for example, notes that the horse represents 'unbridled instinct, night (the mare as in "nightmare"), and terror [...] in psychological terms, the horse symbolizes the unconscious world: imagination, impetuosity, desire, creative power, youth, energy and sensuality'.[22] A creature of terror and instinct, darkness and passion, Equus is an amalgamation of mythic material designed to trigger the audience's archetypal memory: and like all Shaffer's 'gods', its dual aspect means that it creates as easily as it destroys.

That Equus is potentially a malign figure is emphasized by another intersection with mythic belief in this play. Alan's rituals take place at night and, while this is a practical necessity, it also suggests a further link with sinister territories of pagan experience. Alexander S. Murray notes that ancient religious ceremonies were conducted 'in the morning in the case of the gods of heaven, the evening in the case of the gods of the lower world'; when we place Equus in this context, his associations with malevolent, unaccountable territories become yet more concrete.[23] And since Dysart states that if the god can be driven out of Alan at all, it will only be 'with your intestines in its teeth', the 'nightmare' representation becomes a threatening, parasitical invader.

Dysart's dream in which he appears as a priest had also involved the removal of intestines from sacrificial victims so that both the object of worship and the 'cure' designed to remove it are aligned in their destructive capacities. That the profession of psychiatry is aligned in many of its aspects in this play with the rituals and belief-systems of ancient myth becomes increasingly clear as the drama progresses. In order to fully understand this connection, it is necessary firstly to examine one of the central debates in this text, that focusing on the definitions (and purposes) of 'normality', 'sanity' and their opposites.

In *Equus* we are confronted with the ideas expounded by the eminent psychiatrist R.D. Laing. Shaffer's interest in Laing's work was first expressed in his drama in 1967 when he produced an un-performed television play, written in stream-of-consciousness style, focusing on a middle-aged Professor of English in the throes of a Dysartian crisis induced by LSD. Ten years later, *Equus* vividly continued the exploration into societal perceptions of normality and 'reality' (at the root of all definitions of 'sanity' and 'insanity') leaning directly on Laing's theories.

Very briefly, Laing argued that definitions of 'normality', 'sanity' and their opposites are societal labels based on contingent precepts designed to maintain social order: the application of such labels thus constitutes a political act. So, by labelling a person 'insane' because they behave in a manner that lies beyond the reaches of normative practice, society can avoid having to question itself (what 'lack' in societal structure has given rise to this 'behaviour'?) by consigning the 'mad' to its margins: the status quo is therefore maintained, society having insisted upon, and enforced, its standards of conformity. Words such as 'normal' subsequently come to delineate acceptability where a word such as 'hysterical' comes to delineate transgression and thus unacceptability. It is the psychiatrist's task to convert the latter into the former, to 'adjust' the citizen to what society accepts as 'sanity' (it is no coincidence that Dysart refers to the 'adjustment business' on page 213). In this definition, Laing is identifying the construction of a modern myth.[24] He does not go so far as to suggest that 'insanity' involves 'truth' where what we would normally define as 'sanity' involves 'madness', but he does question the validity of such labels and asks us to re-examine the principles on which they are based. Laing calls, then, for an analysis of the myths that psychiatry is propagating.

As John Russell Taylor notes, *Equus* 'does not expound Laing's theories, it inexorably shows them worked out in practice';[25] the play, he continues, suggests that 'Alan's particular brand of insanity [is] a legitimate and valuable response to experience which brings its own benefits and has to be emasculated by society in the cause of self-preservation'.[26] As the man charged with the 'emasculation' of the transgressor, Dysart defines himself as psychiatry's 'Priest' in his key speech assessing the precepts of 'normality' (p.257); his use of the word draws our attention to the extent to which ancient religion and modern clinical practice have been aligned here. Both are predicated on the principle of civic order and both are relied upon by the community for its preservation.[27] In addition, the citizens of both cultures have only the vaguest awareness of what 'rituals' are involved in their respective 'religions' and are unsure of the precise details of what they are intended to achieve (each also has a specialized language to preserve these mysteries): they have, though, been inculcated with the idea that these rituals are vital. Both 'religions' are, in addition, revealed as deeply flawed, Dysart's dream questioning the ancient 'use' of mass sacrifice and his encounter with Equus presenting 'fundamental' questions which are wrongly assumed to have 'no place in a consulting room' (p.268). Hence Dysart's juxtaposition of 'Sacrifices to Zeus' and 'Sacrifices to the Normal' (p.257): both revolve around destruction in the dubious interests of social control.

The myths inherent in ancient religions and those inherent in modern psychiatry are therefore aligned and explored in this play through a dramatization of Laingian thought. The contemporary world is shown to be spiritually bankrupt, rigorously conformist and destructive of human instinct since a conceivably 'sane' response to this context is labelled 'abnormal' and intolerable. As a result, the ambiguity associated with Equus is duplicated in Dysart's recognition of the difficulties implied by the word 'Normal'. But as the 'priest' of a religion which he no longer worships (if he ever did unreservedly), Dysart has no choice but to conform to its demands; after all, as his dream suggests, if his distress is glimpsed, together with 'the implied doubt that this repetitive and smelly work is doing any social good at all', he will be 'next across' the sacrificial stone of 'normative' society (p.217).[28]

Dysart's relationship with Alan triggers this 'doubt' because he is forced to confront the fact that his own existence is pale and meaningless in comparison with that of the frightened, damaged boy he is required to 'treat'. Having convinced himself that he is at heart a 'primitive' because he enjoys annual fortnights wandering around Mediterranean ruins, he eventually has to realize that, when faced with Alan's version of 'primitive' experience, his own is a sick joke. In an ironic comparison of his and his patient's nocturnal activities, Dysart examines the nature of this joke in terms that again lead us back to Laingian theory: while Dysart sits 'looking at pages of centaurs trampling the soil of Argos', Alan tries 'to *become one*'; Dysart watches his wife knitting while Alan 'stands in the dark for an hour, sucking the sweat off his God's hairy cheek! [*Pause.*] Then in the morning, I put away my books on the cultural shelf […] and go off to hospital to treat him for insanity' (p.275). Alan's passion and his capacity for worship have been designated by society as clear signals of 'insanity' while spiritual numbness and an absence of 'extremity' have been posited as characteristics of 'normality'. But here, the 'sane' man envies his patient for the route to direct feeling that he has achieved and for the life-affirming extremity of response that it has made possible. Dysart despairs of a situation in which, in the interests of individual and civic 'health', he must render Alan as numb as he knows himself to be.

Of all the forms of worship that we see in this play, Alan's is depicted as the most rational response to instinctive religious desire. Dora's Christianity is, as argued above, based on fear and neurosis; Frank's pornography (he is a member of a 'congregation' which suggests a form of worship) is furtive and suggestive of the 'bad sex' by which he defines religious impulse (p.296); his regressive brand of Socialism, a non-religious rationalism, evades 'now' and focuses on 'then'. But Alan, like the Incas, has selected a tangible, physical object to worship, an object which, according to Jung, has been archetypally recognized by his unconscious. The dark, terrifying realm he creates where *'extremity* is the point' (p.210) is an antidote to an antiseptic context where inanimate electrical appliances such as the television are worshipped and where this absurd situation is considered perfectly 'normal'. It is Dysart's task to murder Alan's replacement deity and return Alan to the 'normal world' from which Dysart himself longs to escape, and which, finally, he no longer believes in. He will exorcize Alan's 'passion' and he will 'shrink' his worship (since Dysart colloquially refers to himself as a 'shrink' on page 253, the negative implications of psychiatry are again made explicit). Mocking, pitiless Equus, however, leaves its 'sharp chain' in Dysart's mouth and there it will remain (p.301): Dysart has learned to his cost (or perhaps gain) that gods do not die as easily as he had assumed. Staring into the Jungian 'black cave of the Psyche' (p.267), he comes face to face with an archetypal, mythological image which he can never account for and which he can never escape.

Equus abounds with issues, connotations and debates which continue Shaffer's dramatic obsession with the nature of worship and with the dark power of myth. Related manifestations of this emphasis can be detected in the staging and design of the play where choral humming suggests both eerie levels of experience and the techniques of ancient theatre, and where an arena is created wherein the audience is placed (physically and dramatically) in the position of witnessing mythic ritual (ancient and modern or, more accurately, ancient *as* modern given the alignment here between mythic ceremony and psychiatry). The intersection between Christianity and paganism is also, of course, central here: the fusion of myths involves the transposition of biblical passages (for example, from the Book of Revelations) onto prehistoric iconography, just as Christian rituals such as the Last Supper intersect with Pagan night-time ceremonies designed to summon the gods of darkness. In short, every level of debate, of action and of 'theatre' in this play contributes to Shaffer's examination of the nature of worship and of the capacities it creates (and destroys) in man. Definitions of 'god' are at stake in this play as also are definitions of man's relationship with him/it: the emphasis began in *The Royal Hunt of the Sun*, continued in sharpened form through *Equus*, and appears again in *Amadeus* where the battle between man and 'god' leads once again to annihilation.

In Shaffer's most commercially successful play, the image of a vindictive, mocking god stands central to the stage action. Salieri is introduced to the audience in terms that suggest satanic presence with a hissing sound heralding his arrival and with the shedding of his shawl reminiscent of the sloughing of a serpent's skin: gifted in the art of rhetoric, deceitful and sly, Salieri is indeed God's fallen angel. From an early age, he had been aware that 'music is God's art' (p.20) and had made a bargain with his tradesman God (who is not necessarily 'Christ') where he would live in virtue all his days and honour him through his art in return for musical fame. Salieri's deity is based on images staring at him from the walls of Lombardy churches, 'an old candle-smoked God' complete with 'dealer's eyes' which 'made bargains real and irreversible' (p.20); from these sinister, calculating representations, Salieri should perhaps always have been aware that this God is not to be trusted.

By the 1780s, however, he seems to have stuck as rigidly to his side of the bargain as has Salieri; living a virtuous life of public works and extreme repression, Salieri is comfortably embedded in the Viennese Court where his mediocre music is revered. His position is apparently unassailable. His average music is a perfect expression of the context in which he writes and his slick rhetoric and public virtue make him socially indispensable. But when Wolfgang Amadeus Mozart bursts onto the scene, it seems as though God has simply been toying with Salieri, waiting for the opportunity to reveal the flaw in the bargain which his servant had struck with him so many years before. Salieri had begged for the opportunity to be a composer and had pleaded for fame: both pleas have been granted. What he had omitted from the transaction, however, was the request for true talent, if not genius, through which he could express divine worship.

Before he encounters Mozart, Salieri appears to have little idea of his own essential mediocrity; he basks complacently in the worldly success he has been granted and is unaware of its (and his own) limits. But when he first hears Mozart's music, Salieri is forced to confront the fact that his own work falls far short of divinity where Mozart's art fully expresses the voice of God; and the voice manifested in this music is not that of a calculating dealer but is that of a redeeming, magnificent Christ. Salieri's anguish in the light of this revelation is crushing. He calls *'in agony'* to his 'sharp old God', *'What?! What is this? Tell me, Signore!* What is this *pain*? What is this *need* in the sound? Forever unfulfillable yet fulfilling him who hears it, utterly. Is it *Your* need? Can it be yours?...' (p.31). Salieri, the worshipper of a trader God, longs to express the divine in his work, but when he hears Mozart's music, he knows that this capacity has been denied him. The injustice of this situation torments him; living an honourable life full of charitable works, pious in his own vision of religion, the gifts he believes should by rights be his have been bestowed upon 'an obscene child' who is spiteful, selfish and infantile (p.31). Little wonder, then, that in the divine beauty Salieri hears in Mozart's music, he also detects a divine snigger.

For Salieri, and for the audience, the connection between moral virtue and genius has been shattered since God is seen to bestow his gifts with a total lack of discrimination.[29] As Salieri bitterly notes, 'Goodness is nothing in the furnace of art' (p.62). Feeling betrayed by a mocking, unjust God, Salieri then embarks upon a duel with him in which Mozart is to be the battleground; his quarrel, he insists, is not *with* Mozart but *through* him, though he is honest enough to admit that 'the satisfaction of obstructing a disliked human rival' adds an incentive to the contest (p.62). Nevertheless, critics who state that *Amadeus* is a 'drama' about professional rivalry are absolutely incorrect since Salieri is 'envious' of Mozart in one way alone: it is not his genius in itself that he envies, but the love that God has for the significantly named 'Amadeus' that has led to the bestowing of that genius upon him. Salieri, in short, envies the 'love of God'.

Despite the necessity of having to destroy Mozart in order to block God's presence in the world, Salieri's admiration of Mozart's work grows steadily until it reaches the level of worship. Inspecting his original manuscripts which bear no trace of corrections, Salieri acknowledges that he is 'staring through the cage of those meticulous ink strokes at an Absolute Beauty!' (p.58): meanwhile, the music he reads echoes around the theatre involving the audience in Salieri's recognition of divinity. Again we find the concept of an aesthetic version of worship mentioned earlier as the depths of Salieri's soul are moved by the notes he hears: towards the end of the play he states, 'It is only through hearing music that I know God exists' (p.107). Similarly, in a speech sadly cut from all performed versions of the play for reasons of length, Salieri's knowledge of the divine is expressed in unambiguously aesthetic terms: 'The God I acknowledge lives, for example, in bars 34 to 44 of Mozart's *Masonic Funeral Music*'.[30] Having previously worshipped a calculating God who enters into fraudulent pacts with man, Salieri now transfers his worship to the music in which a more magnificent God is expressed. This worship is demonstrated most clearly when Salieri reads Mozart's Requiem Mass and then '*elevates it in the manner of the Communion Service, places it on his tongue and eats it*' (p.100). The implications of this action speak for themselves. A less explicit but equally significant moment occurs when Salieri, at the end of Act 1, hears unmistakeably for the first time the divinity implicit in Mozart's music; as Salieri attempts to come to terms with what he has experienced, a clock is heard to strike nine – the hour traditionally associated with Jesus' death. Connotations of the divine, as expressed in and represented by Mozart's music, are thus signified on multiple levels throughout the play.

Salieri has, like Dysart and Pizarro, been forced into a position where he must murder the god in whom his passion and belief can at last be focused. A man of intellect like the psychiatrist, an Establishment representative like both Pizarro and Dysart, Salieri follows in the Shafferian line of worldy 'winners' who are required to destroy transgressive, disempowered individuals. Atahuallpa, Alan Strang and Mozart are to a greater or lesser extent the prisoners of societal agents who, in order to maintain their positions in the hierarchy, must drive out the destabilizing force. Devoid of genuine worship, men such as Salieri come to an understanding of the true nature of divine passion and then become the unwilling annihilators of it. But as with his predecessors, this annihilation destroys the destroyer and simultaneously suggests the continued existence of the divinity that has supposedly been extinguished.

At first, Salieri (like the later Yonadab) cannot understand why God takes no action against him when his plots against Mozart are set into motion. Not only does he remain unpunished, but he actually seems to be being driven from 'success' to 'success'. Salieri's charitable works are suspended, his house is filled with golden objects and his bed with a mistress, Mozart is marginalized from court circles and gradually starved out, but divine wrath is still not visited upon the sinner. It is only by the end of the play that Salieri understands the nature of God's punishment and recognizes fully its bitter irony; here, he concisely summarizes his fate:

> I was to be bricked up in fame! Embalmed in fame! Buried in fame – but for work I knew to be *absolutely worthless*!...This was my sentence: – I must endure thirty years of being called 'distinguished' by people incapable of distinguishing!...and finally – his Masterstroke! When my nose had been rubbed in fame to vomiting – it would all be taken away from me. Every scrap.
>
> (p.105)

God has over-fulfilled his side of the bargain and has simultaneously exposed the flaws in it: fame without merit is a taunt, not a reward. And when that fame is withdrawn and bestowed on a more worthy subject (Mozart, whose 'music sounded louder and louder through the world', p.106), that taunt becomes more vicious still.

Salieri's tragedy has been that he is able to hear in Mozart's music the voice of God: had he been denied this perception, his own work would not have sounded worthless in his ears. He is therefore caught in a desperate no-man's-land where he can hear an *'Absolute'* (p.107) but cannot achieve it himself: he can approach it but cannot attain it. Hence his meditations on 'mediocrity'. If Salieri did not know himself to be mediocre, he would not be a tortured man and could achieve contentment, but the awareness of his own ordinariness becomes an endless torment. Salieri here summarizes his own position, addressing his dealer God in tones of bitter reproach: 'You put into me perception of the Incomparable – which most men never know! – then ensured that I would know myself forever mediocre' (p.59). Salieri's laughing, manipulative God could hardly have bestowed a more vindictive fate on the fallen angel.

Finally even the reach towards infamy fails when his false confession that he poisoned Mozart with arsenic is not believed and is dismissed as the insane ramblings of a senile and bitter rival. Salieri is then stranded in a state of limbo, a 'ghost' pleading his case to the future. We refer back to Act 1 when Salieri, stating his intention to write a 'huge tragic opera', cites the Legend of Danaius, 'who for a monstrous crime was chained to a rock for eternity' (p.39): at the time, he had imagined Mozart in that position but as the play closes we realize that ultimately this is Salieri's own fate. At the end of *Amadeus*, Mozart's Masonic Funeral Music fills the theatre and the final emphasis therefore falls, as it did in *The Royal Hunt of the Sun* and *Equus* on the continued existence of the divine. Man's attempts to annihilate the sun, the horse and the music have failed and each survive to confront the audience with the certainty of an absolute.

Shaffer's continuing debate on the nature of worship, religion and myth has covered much ground in the three plays centralized here and has incorporated a range of metaphysical questions related to the nature of man's essential being and to the nature of his relationship with a viable godhead. In all three plays, worship is seen to be a subjective experience; attempts to organize it institutionally inevitably lead to conformity and to the extinction of passion and instinct; in each, worship is inextricably linked with violence and destruction, particularly when it is related to pillars of the social apparatus such as Church and State (as it invariably is); in each, the god in man dies, but divinity survives regardless; and in each, 'god' is regarded as a potential monster, ambiguous in all its aspects.

But at the end of *The Royal Hunt of the Sun*, *Equus* and *Amadeus*, the audience has been brought to a point where it must concede that life without worship, and without the levels of experience that it is capable of triggering, is finally meaningless. We are reminded again of Dysart's vital statement: 'without worship you shrink, it's as brutal as that' (*Equus*, p.274). Worship and destruction may go hand-in-hand in these three plays, but to dwindle away into a passionless half-life is, Shaffer insists, the most bitter annihilation of all.

6
The Clash between Two Kinds of Right

The previous chapter suggested that a series of clashes inform Shaffer's representation of 'god' and worship in his three central dramas: opposition was identified as central to the notion of divinity itself with the benign and the malign implied in its ambiguous representation. This second chapter focusing on Peter Shaffer's most popular and best-known plays, *The Royal Hunt of the Sun*, *Equus*, and *Amadeus*, extends the debate by expanding upon the systems of oppositions and disjunctions lying at the heart of these texts. In this discussion it will be argued that the clashes detected in the playwright's representation of divinity and worship are related to a network of competing impulses that motivate Shaffer's theatre at every level.

Every dramatist knows, and every audience unconsciously realizes, that conflict is vital to drama. Usually, conflict is conducted through opposing individuals whose confrontation provides dramatic stimulus: drama is, after all, invariably centred on people, certainly in the theatrical context. Shaffer accepts these precepts and consistently presents his audiences with a situation where characters occupying two defined and apparently absolute positions dramatically collide. Both 'camps' are aware that there can only be one victor and victory thus becomes an urgent imperative. What is usually at stake in Shaffer's plays (and in starker terms than ever in the three texts discussed here) is not simply a tenuous and ultimately meaningless triumph where one vague and abstract belief-system defeats another: what is at stake in these conflicts is the meaning of existence itself.

Even the most cursory glance at Shaffer's plays suggests that basic systems of opposition and conflict are located at the core of his dramas. Leaving aside the three plays that most concern us in this chapter, we can see that in every text a divisive disjunction can be identified. In *White Liars* we find Sophie Lemberg's distinction between 'givers' and 'takers'; *The Public Eye* contrasts 'spirit' with 'letter'; *Black Comedy* pitches 'light' against 'dark'; *Yonadab* sets 'belief' against 'none'; *Lettice and Lovage* presents 'fact' versus 'fantasy'; *Shrivings* opposes 'faith' and 'disbelief'; *The Gift of the Gorgon* pitches the 'abstract mind' and the 'concrete mind' into contestation. The list seems to be endless and the more we look, the more conflicts, oppositions and collisions we find.

However, when these oppositions are examined more closely, it becomes clear that Shaffer is taking the idea of conflict and using it in an entirely original way. While the disjunctions which lead to subsequent dramatic collisions are presented in the earlier stretches of the dramas as being well-defined, fundamental differences between characters, ideologies or belief-systems, it becomes evident that these differences are gradually eroded as the plays progress. One of the reasons why conflation between apparently oppositional forces occurs in these plays is that Shaffer is emphasizing the fact that the most powerful drama emerges not from a clash between 'right' and 'wrong' (where oppositions would be unambiguous) but from a clash, in his words, 'between two kinds of Right'.[1] The audience, as Rodney Simard notes, is forced into 'the position of moral arbiters between the oppositions', often frequently concluding that, by the end of the play, these 'oppositions' have become little more than different facets of the same impulse, argument or personality.[2] Conflicts have been waged in which one 'side' is always defeated or eradicated, but that the 'victor' often comes to occupy the vanquished's position attests to the symbiosis between oppositional forces that has been effected.

The plays focused upon in this chapter, while each operating through a strategy of disjunction and opposition, show significant variations in the way in which the clash between 'two kinds of Right' is presented. In *The Royal Hunt of the Sun* and *Equus*, for example, we find that the erosion of difference between initially clear-cut oppositional forces is at its most apparent. *Amadeus*, on the other hand, refuses such fusion. Similarly, where oppositions such as the fundamental conflict between reason and instinct are common to all three plays, we can detect a difference of degree in their representation and configuration: it is only in the later play, for example, that this conflict is presented in terms that suggest an unambiguous archetypal clash which is often considered to be central to Shaffer's theatre: this clash is frequently referred to as the Apollonian-Dionysian dialectic.

The clash between Apollonian and Dionysian impulses motivates many of Shaffer's best-known plays where an Apollonian representative is pitched against the darker, more passionate forces of Dionysian man. As Doyle W. Walls informs us, the terms derive from Nietzsche's *The Birth of Tragedy* where a fusion between the two impulses is detected, but, for Shaffer, fusion only occurs (when it occurs at all) after a bloody conflict.[3] The playwright admits that he uses the terms 'loosely' to describe the oppositional impulses that he feels battling within himself:

> There is in me a continuous tension between what I suppose I could loosely call the Apollonian and the Dionysiac sides of interpreting life [...] I just feel in myself that there is a constant debate going on between the violence of instinct on the one hand and the desire in my mind for order and restraint.[4]

Shaffer plants this awareness of oppositional instincts at the heart of his dramas, focusing each impulse onto two conflicting protagonists. Apollonian man represents conscious forces of logic and rationality, order and control. He is a creature of intellect, frequently given to Hamlet-like philosophizing, and is sophisticated in his attitudes and way of life. Dionysian man represents contrasting unconscious forces of instinct and passion, individualism and excess. His intellect is not developed and he relies on direct experience, or contact with 'Immediate Life', for his empirical knowledge; a creature of extremes, his 'behaviour' falls outside the boundaries of 'normative' values. In short, Dionysian and Apollonian impulses are initially presented as being alien to each other, their representatives apparently inhabiting separate universes.[5]

From this springs the Shafferian pattern of 'duelling protagonists' which, as C.J. Gianakaris notes, dominates *Equus* and *Amadeus* in particular.[6] This is, of course, one of the reasons for their remarkable success in front of audiences: as before, the most effective drama centres on conflict. However, in *The Royal Hunt of the Sun* and *Equus*, conflict which is intitially configured as a clash between two protagonists (this motivating the early action of the drama), is gradually resolved into a clash between rival impulses within the individual himself. In *Equus*, this process is traced within the Apollonian representative through whose logical mind the audience's access into Dionysian levels of experience and response has been achieved.[7] As Dysart wades further and further into unconscious levels of impulse that have previously lain unacknowledged within him, Apollonian man is, as Christopher Innes notes, 'forced to abandon [his] logical position' and recognize that his own instincts are not as unequivocally rational or clear-cut as he had always supposed.[8]

In these dramas, the audience comes to realize that not only is the Dionysian experience expressive of vital needs and human impulses, but also that its presence cannot be repressed out of existence in any individual without incurring enormous penalties. Apollonian rationality can go too far. Similarly, the fate of the Dionysian representatives in these plays suggests that their vision can also easily get out of hand. Its ethos is, after all, summed up in Dysart's observation, '*Extremity* is the point'.[9] Again, we find Shaffer's emphasis on 'two kinds of Right' where Apollonianism ensures civilization, order and survival (but implies spiritual incapacitation and removal from 'Immediate Life'), and where Dionysianism ensures primitive passion and the life-affirming values of direct experience and extremity (but implies destruction and self-destruction). The audience realizes that these conflicting impulses contained within man's nature must be conjoined. It is significant, however, that only in a comedy such as *Lettice and Lovage* does symbiosis between them finally occur; in the darker visions presented by the plays discussed in this chapter, Dionysian impulses are annihilated to the ultimate extermination of the Apollonian force. Symbiosis here occurs solely at the level of mutual destruction.

This pattern, which recurs persistently in Shaffer's best-known plays, can be related to the theories of Carl Jung, a writer and thinker whose ideas the playwright deeply admires. Drawing on Jungian theory, Shaffer weaves opposition into the heart of his protagonists and plays in order to illustrate the potentially hostile relationship between man's conscious and unconscious. Central to Jung's theory of the human psyche is the idea that 'man becomes whole, integrated, calm, fertile, and happy when (and only when) [...] the conscious and the unconscious have learned to live at peace and to complement one another'.[10] This theory itself connects with Shaffer's constant return to the idea of 'two kinds of Right' since, as Joseph Henderson notes, the unconscious mind is no more the repository of 'dark' or 'nefarious' impulses than the conscious mind is of 'good qualities, normal instincts and creative impulses': rather, just as the conscious mind can contain destructive qualities, so too can the unconscious mind imply positivity.[11] The two levels of 'being', then, each propose a 'kind of Right', are not fundamentally opposed, and are theoretically capable of reconciliation, harmonization and mutual accommodation.

However, effecting fusion between the conscious and the unconscious is a tricky business, as Shaffer's dramas demonstrate. Jung himself indicates that a state of eternal conflict exists between the two realms when he connects man's psychic condition with the system of disjunctions and oppositions which characterize his being: 'The sad truth is that man's real life consists of a complex of inexorable opposites – day and night, birth and death, happiness and misery, good and evil [...] Life is a battleground. It always has been, and always will be; and if it were not so, existence would come to an end'.[12] As such, the conflict between the conscious and the unconscious replicates the condition of man's physical and metaphysical universe, constituting a 'battle for deliverance'.[13] This is a 'battle' that men such as Pizarro, Dysart and Salieri would surely recognize.

When Shaffer presents and dissolves stark disjunctions, then (and he does not always choose to do so, of course), he is potentially indicating the internal war between the conscious and the unconscious (and between all levels of existence) which characterizes the human condition, and reaching towards a negotiated settlement. But the fact that the Apollonian 'camp' representing the conscious mind is persistently seen to be responsible for the destruction of the Dionysian 'camp' of the unconscious (whether willingly or otherwise) perhaps suggests that such settlement can never be possible given the complexities of the human psyche. Oppositions have been transformed into dualities, into twinned and potentially complementary impulses (mimicking the internal relationship between the conscious and unconscious realms within man), but the individual's inability to assimilate them fully leads to the disintegration of protagonists such as Pizarro and Dysart. The clash between 'two kinds of Right' thus becomes a clash between versions of 'Right' proposed by the conscious and the unconscious minds: but the reach towards symbiosis between them in these dramas invariably resolves into a lethal impossibility indicating the ongoing 'battle' of the human psyche.

Having briefly outlined the theories that motivate the system of disjunctions, oppositions and clashes at work in these dramas, this discussion now turns towards an analysis of these patterns in Shaffer's three best-known plays. Beginning with *The Royal Hunt of the Sun*, the earliest of the three, we find that Shaffer builds a complex structure of oppositions in the first Act only to melt 'difference' into 'likeness' in the second.

The various levels of disjunction we encounter in this play begin to accumulate the moment the action begins. Listening to the cynicism and defeat inherent in Old Martin's narration and watching his youthful hope and optimism enacted before us, the audience is presented with a physical representation of two 'selves' within the single individual. The boy and the man bear no resemblance to each other psychologically or emotionally and the audience is immediately engaged in the chronicle which promises to reveal how a youth's spirit was shattered so conclusively. When Old Martin introduces Pizarro to us, it becomes clear that this ruptured man (physically and spiritually) will be central to his retrospective drama.

Pizarro signifies 'difference' at every level of representation. Described upon introduction as *'secret'*, he continues in the long line of Shafferian protagonists who are alienated from their native land and from all that this implies[14]: as he informs De Soto, 'Spain and I have been strangers since I was a boy' (p.19). Willing to use the cant of the Catholic Church to attract soldiers to his army, he nevertheless refuses to engage in its ruthless hypocrisies; similarly, he can barely veil his contempt for the Court representative Estete and for the Imperialistic greed that he embodies. Though he is more at ease with his soldiers, Pizarro even so suggests distance, non-contact and non-attachment at the beginning of the play. Alienated and self-alienated, suspended between 'two hates' ('belief' and 'none'), Pizarro's internal battle leads us to realize that it is less gold that he is seeking in the 'New World' than self-conciliation and meaning.

The oppositions within Pizarro have led to spiritual fragmentation and it is only through the unification of his conflicting fears, desires and impulses (which he can barely even identify) that his 'salvation' can occur. As discussed in Chapter 5, the vital opposition between death and immortality he perceives must, for him, be resolved. As the idea of the man-god Atahuallpa takes root in his mind, Pizarro's obsession with this opposition becomes increasingly marked but by this stage of the action, alternative clashes and disjunctions have also begun to claim our attention.

Central to the drama in socio-political terms is the conflict Shaffer presents between rival organizational systems: Peru is modelled on

Communist principles where 'equality and authoritarian regimentation' produce 'material plenty' and a highly disciplined society.[15] Spain, by contrast, accords with Capitalist principles where 'competitive individualism' produces enormous personal wealth, but also poverty, greed and indiscipline.[16] This structural difference between the two societies becomes manifested in a number of ways throughout the play, notably in the contrast between the perpetual movement of the Spanish (marauding, destructive, potentially anarchic) and the serene stillness of the Incas (peaceful, obedient, controlled).

But where in Act 1, the two socio-political systems are placed in sharp opposition to each other, by Act 2 crucial similarities between them have been drawn. As Shaffer notes, the point of connection occurs when we realize that 'the conquistadors deified personal will; the Incas shunned it. Both in a deep sense denied man'.[17] With Spanish individualism and capitalism comes greed, inequality and poverty. Man must fight, destroy and steal to survive; meanwhile, through a combination of fear and superstition, he is held in obeisance to authoritarian and corrupt institutions such as Church and State. With Inca conformity comes material plenty, equality and order but citizens are equally subjected to authoritarian rule as indicated by the fact that Atahuallpa is said to have 'eyes everywhere', this wholly suggestive of a totalitarian context (p.32). In addition, as the reasoned De Nizza argues, 'man' is 'denied' in Atahuallpa's Peru because his access to human instincts and emotions is institutionally blocked so that, eventually, human identity itself is questioned:

> happiness has no feel for men here since they are forbidden unhappiness. They have everything in common so they have nothing to give each other. They are part of the seasons, no more; as indistinguishable as mules, as predictable as trees.
>
> (p.63)

So on one side we find the 'unhappy, hating men' (p.82) of Spanish Christianity and individualism, while on the other we find 'a population of eunuchs living entirely without choice' (p.82). Here, in other words, the 'denial of man' produces a 'clash between two kinds of *wrong*'. But the gap between the two, which in the first act had seemed so immense, has now become negligible. Finally, both systems, in perfect counterpoint, destroy each other, a symmetry that is indicated through the repetition in Old Martin's phrasing as the play closes: 'So fell Peru [...] So fell Spain' (p.90). The 'New Worlds' which had initially seemed so alien to each other (being forged on apparently conflicting principles) ultimately tear each other apart in a final statement of likeness. The disjunction dissolves.

The connections between pagan sun-worship and Christianity were explored in Chapter 5 where it was argued that though the two religions differ in terms of form, the basic tenets of each belief have several elements in common. Like Jesus, Atahuallpa's status as the son of a godhead unites the opposition between man and divinity since he is both a man-god and a god amongst men: this is, of course, his appeal to Atahuallpa since, in him, the death-immortality disjunction is apparently resolved. But Pizarro's fascination for, and attraction to, Atahuallpa, though focused on his tortured preoccupation with the inescapable fact of time, is based on more than this alone. It is based, in fact, on a recognition of likeness.

Our first introductions to Pizarro and Atahuallpa do not prepare us for the similarities between them that will subsequently evolve. Pizarro is a tough, internally wrecked man of action: he is an elderly, worshipless commander who has clawed his way up from peasant stock. Atahuallpa, on the other hand, is an impressive, serene, bird-like vision; he is youthful, elegant and aristocratic in his bearing and manner. Above all, he has unquestioned faith in a credo he interprets as 'fact' rather than 'belief', a capacity Pizarro profoundly envies. No two men, it seems, could be placed in more direct opposition, each embodying one aspect of man's psychic life – the conscious and the unconscious.

However, as the play develops, Pizarro and Atahuallpa become connected through a chain of similarities implying that the two men are effectively projections of mutual yet antagonistic impulses within the individual psyche. On an explicit level, we learn that both men are illegitimate, illiterate, former herdsmen; both are also 'robber birds', Atahuallpa stealing the kingdom from his brother whom he murdered, Pizarro stealing the kingdom from Atahuallpa whom he will murder (albeit unwillingly) in turn. The connections between the two then multiply through less obvious emphases; both are objects of worship, Atahuallpa enjoying this privilege by virtue of his status as son of god, Pizarro being for Young Martin an 'altar' and a 'bright image of salvation' (p.13). Both men also share an Absolutist attitude towards rule, Atahuallpa exerting iron control over his people and Pizarro, when he has usurped this power, stating, 'this is my kingdom. In Peru I am absolute' (p.80). Neither man sets much store by 'mercy', Atahuallpa declaring, 'It is not my way. It is not your way' (p.73). In addition, as Atahuallpa points out, neither man believes a word that the Catholic priests say and both are eventually aligned in terms of divine belief. The final, vital connection between them occurs following Atahuallpa's death when tears issue from both men's eyes: a dead man and his murderer weep together and their tears constitute a mutual miracle.

Critics who argue that the relationship that develops between these two men suggests an element of homosexual desire are not only detecting connotations which are simply not available textually but are also guilty of dismissing or misreading this chain of likenesses and its significance. This significance is focused on two levels; the first involves the point that in Atahuallpa, Pizarro finds a type of long-lost spiritual son: following the failed resurrection, Pizarro comments that he will soon, like Atahuallpa, be 'put into the earth, father and son in our own land' (p.90). The second significance, more relevant to this discussion, is that Pizarro finds in Atahuallpa a projection of unconscious impulses lying dormant, or at war, within him. In Pizarro lies a deep well of worship waiting to be channelled: Atahuallpa is a living embodiment of this impulse. Within Pizarro lies a longing for direct life but an incapacity for it because he constantly feels the shadow of death around him: Atahuallpa represents the life-force through his status as son of the sun which both gives life and is immortal. In short, the connections made between the two men suggest that the conflicting impulses raging within Pizarro are, in Atahuallpa, both externalized and reconciled. And as the oppositions between the two men fade away, the oppositions between the conscious mind and the unconscious within the individual man (in this case, Pizarro) melt.

The archetypal opposition between Apollonian and Dionysian man with which we become so familiar in *Equus* and *Amadeus* is not central to any significant degree in the relationship between Pizarro and Atahuallpa in this play. In one area alone does this disjunction intrude here, and that is at the level of Dionysian man's capacity for worship.[18] Clearly, Atahuallpa could be defined as 'Dionysian' in this respect. However, Atahuallpa's connection with the sun aligns him with the mythological sun-God, Apollo, while in his pursuit of authoritarian order he is as 'Apollonian' as Pizarro: further, both men are as rational or as 'irrational' as each other.

Pizarro may be a thinker and a philosopher, but he is clearly no 'Apollonian' intellectual and his introspective nature has not eliminated the capacity for action as it has in Dysart. Applying these labels to protagonists in this play is, therefore, a tricky business and critics who attempt it are falling into the trap of interpreting the text in accordance with their knowledge of the Apollonian-Dionysian dialectic centralized in Shaffer's later plays. The pattern is certainly here in embryonic form, but it will not take us very far in understanding the system of disjunctions, and their various reconciliations, in this play.

This system, as we have seen, revolves around the oppositions implied in the socio-political organization of Spain and Peru and in the apparently contrasting natures of Pizarro and Atahuallpa. In both cases, disjunction dissolved into likeness. However, not every disjunction in this play involves unambiguous reconciliation with its opposite and one example of potentially unresolved conflict involves the warring principles of masculinity and femininity that Christopher Innes suggests lie at the heart of the text. Shaffer's comment, 'I saw the active iron of Spain against the passive feathers of Peru', is used by Innes to argue that the Spanish faction is here aligned with 'masculine' activity while the Inca contingent is aligned with 'feminine' passivity: the Spanish 'rape' of Peru is obviously involved in this equation. But while this disjunction is left apparently unresolved, it could be argued that the 'masculine' and 'feminine' principles are harmonized within Atahuallpa whose androgynous quality characterizes him.[19] The man-God's positioning between gender identities can, in addition, be linked with the Jungian concept of the 'anima', the 'female element in the male unconscious' representing an 'inner duality' that is often 'symbolized by a hermaphroditic figure'.[20] In Atahuallpa, then, the apparent disjunction between warring gender principles is potentially reconciled.

However, in this case, Shaffer does not unite the disjunction in unequivocal terms and it remains a matter of debate whether the conflicting forces of 'masculine' and 'feminine' impulses in this play, as represented by Spain and Peru, are ever brought to a point of connection. Certain oppositions are, in addition, left in stark and deliberate contrast, one notable example being the clash between 'the bleak picture of total devastation' contained at the level of plot and the 'positive vitality' involved in its 'theatrical presentation'.[21] The pattern of disjunctions that this strategic clash represents multiplies throughout the text, but where opposition frequently dissolves into likeness, unresolved confrontation may still remain: the 'battle' raging within the psyche is, after all, eternal and ongoing, as is illustrated by the fact that Pizarro must kill a man who has come to represent and embody his own unconscious.

The clash between 'two kinds of Right' and the confrontation between conflicting embodiments of human impulse are emphases continued through from *The Royal Hunt of the Sun* into *Equus*. A play where disjunction melts into alignment at every level, the clash between rival instincts here becomes distilled into a confrontation between Apollonian and Dionysian archetypes as developed through Jungian theory. Here, Apollonian man wages a war against Dionysian forces but simultaneously perceives that these forces cannot, at a fundamental level, be eradicated. In Alan Strang, Martin Dysart discovers a projection of his own vital lack and the audience recognizes that, in the tortured, stunted patient and in the sophisticated, learned psychiatrist, Shaffer has created mirror images which represent conflicting impulses within man's psyche.

Before looking more closely at the Apollonian-Dionysian dialectic in this play, it is worth outlining other forms of opposition and disjunction that appear here. Beginning with the staging of *Equus*, we find a marked contrast between the spartan simplicity of the stage set (which suggests a boxing-ring or a clinical amphitheatre) and the dark complexity of the experiences played against it. Further, the analytical connotations of the lecture-hall atmosphere are in conscious opposition to the unknowable passions that circulate within Alan's psyche. We can, however, argue that this brutally sparse stage set actually complements the play's action in that the suggestion of a boxing-ring proves an apt arena for the 'vigorous contest for control of modern man's soul', while the design also recalls ancient theatre and thus aligns the brutalities of ancient ritual with the brutalities of modern psychiatric practice.[22] Here, the oppositions implied in the clash between the simple stage set and the intricacies of the experiences revealed within it condition the play in both theatrical and dramatic terms.

As the play develops, the audience becomes aware of a number of head-on clashes between individuals and ideologies which are seen to be at least partially responsible for Alan's chaotic state. The first of these involves Frank's Socialism as pitched against Dora's Christianity; Alan's parents are engaged in a hostile battle of belief and each seeks to persuade their son of the rightness of their cause.

Within Dora's Christianity, another opposition appears – that between judgemental, punishing God and wayward, sinful man. As we have already seen, this vengeful vision of the divine becomes incorporated into Alan's individual creation of godhead when all-seeing Equus proves merciless. In addition, the Christian idea of a multi-faceted God is also carried into Equus and both gods are perceived as simultaneously wrathful and gentle, malign and benign as a result. Both imply gentle majesty and savage darkness, a potentially irresolvable disjunction which is projected in Christianity onto two separate and opposing forces which, as we are reminded by Dora, are known as 'God' and 'The Devil'.

These oppositions are each seen to contribute to Alan's need to create Equus, to be manifested in the notion of Equus itself, and to be involved in Alan's fragmentation. However, as the play develops, it seems that the oppositions outlined here fail to hold their clearly-defined ground: as in *The Royal Hunt of the Sun*, they begin to dissolve into likeness. Frank's Socialism and Dora's Christianity are seen not to be warring beliefs so much as different facets of the same authoritarian principle: each propose the values of individual discipline, communal conscience and civic order. Both suppress personal desire and look to the past in their hopes for the future; both deny the validity of the present and find in it only shabby morality and disillusion. Finally, both propose 'two kinds of Right' but in doing so, and in an echo of the earlier play, both 'deny man'.

Another opposition is broken down in Alan's notion of 'oneness' with Equus. Dora's Christianity was seen to involve a radical breach between God and man, but when Alan, seated on the back of his tangible god, states 'two shall be one' (p.259), he creates a fusion between traditionally disparate elements.[23] When horse and rider become one entity, the oppositions between man and animal, man and god dissolve. In addition, the Christian projection of God's double aspect onto two separate forces ('God' and 'The Devil') is again unified in the single notion of Equus who, though gentle and submissive, is also a 'mean bugger' (p.259), mocking and cruel, who will leave Alan only with his 'intestines in his teeth' (p.299). This unified double aspect is then projected again onto his servant, man, and the opposition between God and his creation dissolves into likeness as a result.

Where Alan had, as it seemed in Act 1, been placed in opposition to his parents' world-views and beliefs, by the end of Act 2 we find that the boy has become aware of the points of connection that can exist within apparent conflict. This becomes particularly evident in the case of Alan's relationship with his father. An alert audience may have registered scattered clues sprinkled lightly through the play which align father and son (both have the word 'extreme' applied to them, for example), but it is only following the cinema fiasco that Alan can realize that his father and he, apparently so alien to each other, are in fact cast in the same mould. Both detest the snobbery of Dora, both slide off at night for furtive bouts of 'worship' and sexual self-gratification, both need to do so because of their 'extreme' repression (insisted upon by Dora), both seek passionate experience and have the capacity for it, and both subsequently lie about their activities. When Alan states, 'There's no difference – he's just the same as me' (p.289), father and son cease to be warring factions and become instead connected projections of the same unconscious drives, impulses and desires.

This alignment between supposedly alien forces becomes still more marked in the central relationship of the play. Like Alan's parents, Dysart is another authoritarian figure representing the values of normative society and civic health. Where Dora worships a Christian God and Frank worships a Socialist creed (and naked actresses, of course), Dysart is employed to worship the god of the 'normal'. Alan's anarchic individualism is again pitched against the forces of authoritarianism; his 'religious mind' is again set in conflict with 'the abstract and scientific mind' of normative society and its agent, Dysart.[24] But as in the case of his father, both Alan and the audience quickly perceive that these oppositions melt upon analysis and finally generate likeness rather than degenerate further into insuperable difference.

At the beginning of the play, Dysart's Apollonian characteristics (aligning him with the conscious mind) seem to be as marked as the Dionysian forces which are projected onto Alan. A scientist concerned with converting the irrational into the rational, Dysart's forte is the logical analysis of experience and the neutralization of unconscious terrors. Eloquent and self-controlled, educated and urbane, he is a successful modern man, respected within his community and profession. However, where Apollonian forces governed him in his younger days (he was, as he tells us, 'Doctor MacBrisk' defined by 'Antiseptic proficiency', p.253), these forces declined when maturity brought doubt and a questioning of absolutes. In Apollonian cure, he begins to perceive a form of destruction: he becomes aware that the 'God of medicine' is also the 'God of death', and this duality increasingly haunts him. By the time we meet the middle-aged psychiatrist, in fact, it is entirely a matter of debate whether we can truly describe him as Apollonian man at all, particularly as the statue of Dionysus which he touches daily for 'luck' suggests an alternative affiliation (p.275). Rationality and logic diminish as soon as he realizes that '*Extremity* is the point' (p.210), while his professional and social doubts question his status as a representative of normative order. Further, his glimpse into the 'black cave of the Psyche' (p.267) reveals to him the potentially lethal yet liberating presence of Dionysian impulses squatting unacknowledged within man's unconscious.

Critics who argue that the clash between Dysart and Alan involves a straightforward encounter between Apollonian and Dionysian representatives are, therefore, missing the point that Dysart's alignment with Apollo is hardly unambiguous. If we are looking for Apollonian figures in this play, we find more fertile ground in Hesther and in the absent Margaret. When Dysart states that he sits 'opposite' his wife, he means this in more ways than one; baiting her with pictures of acrobats 'leaping through the horns of running bulls', she responds, 'what an *absurred* thing to be doing! The Highland Games, now there's *norrmal* sport!' (p.253). Though Dysart comes to realize that his own alignment with the primitive is hardly a 'fantastic surrender' to dark regions of experience (p.274), he can at least understand that such a 'surrender' gives meaning to existence. Margaret, the arch-Apollonian, cannot.

Hesther is a more central representative of Apollonian forces in this play, her surname suggestive of reasoned biblical judgement recalling as it does the apocryphal wisdom of Israel's King Solomon. Her priorities are summarized by her as 'children before grown-ups', a simple but precise philosophy which draws from Dysart the exclamation, 'You're really quite splendid' (p.253). Her position is unarguable but it nevertheless evades the complexities that Dysart has been attempting to express. For Hesther, 'worship isn't destructive', and her certainty is emphasized in her following statement: 'I know that' (p.273); Dysart, on the other hand, having come face-to-face with the Dionysian unconscious, cannot be so sure. That Dysart can take away Alan's pain is 'enough' for Hesther where Dysart understands that this amputation is both destructive and should not be demanded (p.273). When Dysart talks of 'worship', Hesther suggests he is being 'extreme' (in an echo of Dora's charge against Frank) (p.273); when he states that he envies that worship, she labels the sentiment 'absurd' (in an echo of Margaret) (p.274). Dysart questions his role as societal agent: Hesther questions only her fitness to fulfil it, not the role itself.

So where Dysart is stranded in an uncomfortable position between Apollonian and Dionysian mind-sets, recognizing the co-existence of both within his psyche, Hesther's alignment with Apollonian forces is clear. She, not Dysart, is the 'God of the Normal' in this play.[25] But Dysart's problem is that he can see in Hesther's philosophy and in Alan's psyche 'two kinds of Right'. Hesther's version of 'normality' leads to 'the good smile in a child's eyes' (p.257); Alan's extremity indicates the liberating, 'ferocious' passion of worship (p.274). He simultaneously sees 'two kinds of wrong' when 'the good smile' turns into 'the dead stare in a million adults' (p.257), and when 'ferocious' passion is seen to imply pain, destruction and self-destruction. Like Pizarro torn between 'two hates', and like Yonadab caught between 'belief and none', Dysart is also suspended between two belongings, but this time Shaffer's protagonist is caught between Apollonian and Dionysian visions of 'Right'. Their representatives, Hesther and Alan, are merely physical projections of warring impulses within Dysart's own mind.

That these rival impulses co-exist in Dysart becomes clear when his encounter with Alan reveals levels of likeness between them. Through these similarities, Shaffer indicates the presence in Dysart of the Dionysian impulse as embodied in Alan and brings the psychiatrist into confrontation with his own unconscious. To begin with, Dysart's infertility is matched by Alan's impotence: neither man is sexually enabled. That Dysart has 'the lowest sperm count you could find' (p.274) attests to his inability to 'create' worship, passion or extremity while it also suggests physical incapacitation as a result of intellectual overactivity. Alan's impotence derives from his worship of Equus which he also associates with sexual excitement and ejaculation so that sexual experience with another partner becomes a form of sacrilegious infidelity which must be punished. Both men are furtive about their sexual failures, Dysart keeping his low sperm count a secret from his wife and Alan lying that he had successfully completed the sex act with Jill.

In addition, Dysart and Alan are aligned when they become each other's inquisitors, Alan insisting that he will only answer the psychiatrist's questions if he is allowed to question the psychiatrist in turn. This is an exercise at which the partially educated patient proves far more expert than the learned doctor. Each probes the other's darkest secrets and reaches conclusions about each other's 'conditions'. The most significant moment in these encounters occurs when Alan, believing himself to be under the influence of a truth drug, draws himself and his psychiatrist into unmistakeable alignment. Dysart tells Alan that, if he could, he would live by the Mediterranean and abandon his profession:

> DYSART: I don't actually enjoy being a Nosey Parker, you know.
> ALAN: Then why do it?
> DYSART: Because you're unhappy.
> ALAN: So are you.
> [DYSART *looks at him sharply.*]

(p.280)

Alan is, as Dysart has previously recognized, 'aware' of him 'in an absolutely specific way' (p.252), and what he is 'aware' of is Dysart's agonizing internal battle between conscious reason and unconscious instinct. Exploiting his perception that Dysart longs to share his capacities, his stare telepathically asks, '*At least I galloped! When did you?*' (p.274): connection between them is assumed. Similarly, he instinctively realizes that Dysart is, like himself, sexually incapacitated, but when he goes too far and touches Dysart's sorest point (his lack of sexual contact with his wife), Dysart rejects him and labels him 'wicked' (p.252). But even in this, a further connection between the two is made when Hesther, listening to the tale, comments, 'It's *you* who are wicked, you know!' (p.253).

As in *The Royal Hunt of the Sun*, it is in a concluding image that the most complete alignment between oppositional forces occurs. Where miraculous tears had unified Pizarro and Atahuallpa, here Dysart's perception that he, like Alan, metaphorically 'stand[s] in the dark with a pick in my hand, striking at heads!' connects the two in absolute terms (p.300). The 'sharp chain' of the Dionysian psyche has been beckoned from its 'black cave' and has set up camp in the psychiatrist's head: it will 'never come out' (p.301). As the disjunctions between 'two kinds of Right' have dissolved, and as Dysart is forced to extinguish in his patient a human impulse that he now acknowledges exists within himself, Shaffer's dramatic strategy becomes clear. The oppositions between belief-systems, world-views and visions, each embodied in an individual protagonist, have become projections of the opposition between the conscious and the unconscious within the individual psyche, a condition described by Jung as 'the undeniable common inheritance of all mankind'.[26] Warring they may be, but these oppositions are aspects of any individual being, hence their dissolution into likeness. However, given that these oppositions are resolved into dualities (twin impulses), they essentially remain in conflict and the individual cannot survive the internal battle between the conscious and unconscious realms that this conflict connotes. Dysartian disintegration results.

As Dysart's journey into uncharted territories of experience reveals, and as *Equus* as a whole suggests, 'rationality and irrationality are always articulated together'.[27] Nowhere is this Freudian insight more concentrated than in Salieri's narrative in *Amadeus*, a play which differs radically from *The Royal Hunt of the Sun* and *Equus* in terms of its pattern of oppositions and clashes. Here, the Apollonian-Dionysian dialectic sharpens into a head-on confrontation where disjunction, far from melting into likeness, is never resolved. In this play, oppositions do not achieve fusion and annihilation results.

Amadeus is a play structured upon disjunction: Werner Huber and Walter Zapf draw our attention to the 'dualisms sobriety versus passion [and] mediocrity versus genius', while the battle between man and God wages more fiercely than ever before.[28] A range of additional conflicts appear here, all of which are linked to the Apollonianism of Salieri as pitched against the Dionysianism of Mozart. The 'clash between two kinds of Right' becomes a fight to the death and, as usual in Shaffer's plays, the Apollonian destroys the Dionysian in wordly terms: in doing so, he is himself destroyed. In order to trace the pattern of oppositions which lead to mutual destruction in this play, it is necessary to examine the Apollonian-Dionysian disjunction centralized here in some detail.

It has been argued that Salieri is not rational enough to be labelled a true Apollonian, Christopher Innes suggesting that, unlike the 'rational Dysart, the eighteenth-century court-composer is warped by jealousy, even insane'.[29] However, as noted above, Dysart is rather less 'rational' then he seems, 'irrationality' can never be divorced from its 'opposite' in psychoanalytical terms, and 'irrationality' and 'insanity' are no more inextricably connected than are 'rationality' and 'sanity' (the problems involved in defining 'insanity' in the first place are examined in Chapter 5). Salieri is certainly 'warped' and the audience must constantly analyse his words in search of objective 'truth', but that Salieri represents Apollonian forces of the conscious mind, and that these forces are in conflict with Mozart's Dionysianism (representing the unconscious mind) is, in *Amadeus*, indicated at every level of signification.

To begin with, Salieri is firmly aligned with Establishment forces of Court and State. Moving easily in the world of Emperor Joseph's Vienna, he is a smooth courtier upholding the standards of good taste and hierarchical order. His clothes are subtle and elegant, his speech measured and eloquent. Nothing he says or writes disturbs the dull waters of the Court: on the contrary, everything he says or writes perfectly reflects its staid mediocrity. Into Salieri's orderly world bursts Mozart, noisy, indiscreet, and vulgar in conversation and dress. He is an outsider, initially accepted warily into Court circles but gradually edged out of them as the play progresses. As he seeks refuge in working-class vaudeville theatre, we realize that he is essentially an anti-establishment figure who represents an anarchic individualism that militates against any form of authority. As his father tells him, he should 'be more obedient' and '*Know my place!*', but Dionysian man cannot tow the line as his Apollonian counterpart can (p.376): his instincts cannot be assimilated by the Establishment since they are alien to its principles and a mutual rejection results.[30]

Salieri's understated elegance as opposed to Mozart's flamboyant vulgarity suggests further characteristics of both men that are associated with the Apollonian-Dionysian dialectic. Salieri's Apollonian control involves a suppression of his sexual drive and (in an echo of Dysart) his marriage to the worthy but absent Teresa is sexually sterile. His vow of chastity made in a bargain with his trader God forbids extra-marital liaisons and, given the repression we detect in him, it seems unlikely that he would seek such gratification anyway. His sexual drive seems to be as absent as his wife, and his desires are easily satiated in his displacement activity of guzzling confectionery (his sole region of excess): 'Nipples of Venus' are as close as Salieri comes to the real thing but he seems content with this situation. When he steps into the realm of sexual sin and attempts to seduce Constanze (not because he desires her but because she is another pawn), his unfittedness for this task is indicated in the degeneration of the escapade into 'fiasco' (p.57). And when he describes the encounter in terms of 'sheer sweating sordidness', we feel that he is actually expressing his attitude towards the sexual act itself. Little wonder, then, that Mozart hears in Salieri's music, 'the sound of someone who *can't get it up!*' (p.49).

Mozart, on the other hand, carries the idea of excess through from his manner and clothes and into the realms of debauchery and sexuality. Uncontrolled in his drinking and language, Mozart is similarly uncontrolled when it comes to seducing his students in the Bacchanalian manner. At ease within the sexual sphere, he sees nothing inappropriate in setting an opera in a harem and writing of manly love; for Mozart, sex is not an anxiety, a sin, or a 'fiasco' but is a human drive which he (often injudiciously) satisfies as regularly as possible. Just as *'extremity'* was 'the point' of Alan's Dioynisianism, the 'excessive' is the point of Mozart's (p.41).

The Apollonian-Dionysian conflict in this play, then, is clearly marked at every level. There is, however, a significant difference between the formulation of this conflict in Shaffer's other plays and its dramatization in *Amadeus*. As C.J. Gianakaris points out, this difference lies in the fact that where 'Apollonians' such as Pizarro and Dysart (as before, this label is arguable here) envied the Dionysians, in this play, Salieri 'in no way wishes to "become" his antagonist [...] Quite the opposite: Salieri sees Mozart as an aberration in the universal order, and thus as something that must be destroyed'.[31] This is a vital point because it helps us to understand why the oppositions and disjunctions that are dissolved into likeness in the previous plays remain resolutely divided here.

The answer lies in the fact that since Salieri does not find himself torn between conflicting impulses, the Apollonian being firmly ascendant in him in a way that it is not in his predecessors, he cannot detect points of connection between himself and Mozart because none appear to exist. Alan was a projection of Dysart's unconscious impulses, but Salieri can see no likeness between himself and Mozart because the former is not willing (or able) to recognize his unconscious instincts. As such, Mozart remains absolutely 'other' and totally alien to Salieri who cannot accept that the oppositional world-view he represents constitutes any 'kind of Right' at all. He may envy Mozart for having the love of God bestowed upon him, but since Salieri only knows this God as a mocking, vindictive force, this only hardens his belief that the 'creature' represents a 'kind of wrong' ('an aberration') that must be destroyed.[32]

However, we could argue that what Salieri fails to realize is that Mozart is a projection of his own unconscious which he has ruthlessly suppressed. Salieri does not register this recognition at a conscious level, but his antagonism towards Mozart clearly suggests that the 'aberration' he defines as Mozart is actually the 'aberration' of drives and impulses he refuses to acknowledge within himself. The 'battle for deliverance' between the conscious and the unconscious realms raging within Salieri therefore becomes externalized in the fight to the death that he initiates with Mozart. Salieri cannot accept Mozart because he cannot accept the duality which exists within himself and he strives to suppress both with lethal determination.

As a result, the connection between oppositions that we detect in *The Royal Hunt of the Sun* and *Equus* not only fails to materialize in *Amadeus* but actually becomes less and less possible as the play develops: the breach between the two men and between what they represent grows ever wider. In creative terms, this breach is signalled when Mozart transforms Salieri's *'extremely banal'* March of Welcome into the joyful strains of *Non Più Andrai*, remaining oblivious to the offence this necessarily causes (p.38). This incident, which Shaffer describes as 'the most effective scene in the play' since 'the whole theme of the drama is there', sets the tone for the artistic breach between the two men.[33] It is encapsulated in Salieri's statement: 'We were both ordinary men, he and I. Yet he from the ordinary created legends – and I from legends created only the ordinary' (p.82). This is, of course, a reversal of previous Shafferian situations, since here likeness ('we were both ordinary men') results in irresolvable difference. The breach between mediocrity and genius is similarly charted when Salieri notes that Mozart can 'put on paper, without actually setting down his billiard cue, casual notes which turn my most considered ones into lifeless scratches' (p.59). In essence, Salieri's conscious mind produces the steady, measured tones of 'considered' music while from Mozart's unconscious spring apparently 'casual notes' of splendid and almost irrational beauty. This is an opposition that Salieri can neither understand nor tolerate.

For Huber and Zapf, this creative breach indicates further levels of disjunction in *Amadeus*, notably the clash between 'two opposing concepts of the artist: the craftsmanlike composer [...] and the (divinely) inspired genius'.[34] In addition, they argue that Salieri and Mozart 'come to personify two different modes of opera-writing and everything these stand for: Italian versus German, the heroic (mythological matter) versus the everyday, tragedy versus comedy, grand opera versus *Singspiel*': equally useful is Huber and Zapf's observation that this creative disjunction springs from the clash between Salieri's overly dominant super-ego and Mozart's controlling id.[35] The point is clear: opposition builds upon opposition in this play and each disjunction is seen to be related in some way to the archetypal conflict between Apollonian and Dionysian forces, and thus to the confrontation between the conscious and the unconscious mind. Everywhere we look, a breach develops between their representatives while, looming over the entire play, the conflict between man and God rages. The dualisms multiply to the end of the drama and connections between them are resolutely refused.

Despite Shaffer's reluctance to fuse oppositions in this play, he is nevertheless keen to forge systems of parallel which hold the oppositions together in antagonism. Simultaneously, these parallels suggest the hostile relationship between the conscious and the unconscious within the individual mind since they suggest mutuality yet also, at the same time, fundamental hostility. Salieri is aware of the irony implicit in a situation where he and his enemy seem mutually involved. The year that Salieri leaves Italy to begin his musical training, Mozart, 'a miraculous virtuoso', is touring Europe (p.21): their careers begin in the same year though Mozart is, of course, younger than Salieri. Later, as Salieri's career flourishes, Mozart's declines: later still, as Salieri's music slides into oblivion, Mozart's 'sound[s] louder and louder through the world!' (p.106). In short, careers that begin in parallel end in sharp and bitter contrast. The ironic patterning continues as we realize that Mozart's infantilism is matched by Salieri's eventual senility, and that both seduce (or attempt to seduce) the same women in Constanze and Katherina. Their fates seem intertwined, connected in some malicious way, but this connection is not based on likeness but on murderous psychic difference.

This is indicated when Salieri states: 'We are both poisoned, Amadeus. I with you: you with me' (p.100). The phrasing here suggests the level of antagonistic mutuality in operation with the repeated words and syntax drawing the two forces together in final hostility – they have, after all, 'poisoned' each other. This mutuality has been expressed syntactically earlier in the play when Salieri verbally mimicked the ironic patterning inherent in his relationship with Mozart by stating that 'he from the ordinary created legends – and I from legends created only the ordinary' (p.82). Similarly, at the end of the play, patterning is evident again in Salieri's promise that 'whenever men say Mozart with love, they will say Salieri with loathing!' (p.107). Such connection between oppositions suggests not likeness emerging from difference as it had done in Shaffer's earlier plays, but bitterly ironic juxtaposition confirming unresolved, archetypal antagonism. In short, it suggests an interlocking of the conscious and the unconscious realms but a refusal (if not the impossibility) of symbiosis between them.

In *Amadeus*, then, we find less alignment between conflicting principles than we have previously found in Shaffer's work: Salieri refuses to accept the existence and validity of the unconscious realm, repressed in him, and projected onto the hyperactive, manic and 'aberrant' Mozart. The conflict, however, results in the familiar destruction of both warring parties with the tragedy perhaps sharpened here by the fact that reconciliation between them is never achieved. Paradoxically, Salieri's contemptible actions arguably cause an audience to respond to his tragedy more acutely than to that of either Pizarro or Dysart who, in effect, do little 'wrong'.[36] We can perhaps account for this by arguing that not only is the audience acknowledging its alignment with Salieri's mediocrity (and can thus share his pain), but is also responding to the 'kind of Right' that he represents. Particularly in the first Act, we can have little sympathy with the 'all-farting, all-shrieking', spiteful, arrogant and infantile Mozart that Shaffer presents us with;[37] at the same time, Salieri who lives honestly and charitably, and who behaves with consideration and restraint, seems to have been dealt a needlessly cruel hand. He is a victim of 'the injustice of life' (which Shaffer posits as the central theme of the play) and is the carrier of the drama's motivating proposition that 'there is an unfairness in the inequality with which talent is distributed'.[38] Where Mozart's genius represents a divine gift with which few (if any) audience members can identify, Salieri's craftsmanship represents the values of hard work and dedication – a 'kind of Right' with which we are all more familiar. Mozart's music, of course, symbolizes another 'kind of Right' which is divine in origin, but its human manifestation in Mozart suggests, to the audience as to Salieri, a 'kind of wrong'. It is this conflict that generates Salieri's tragedy as much as it does Mozart's: Salieri's descent into sin is the most 'rational' response possible to an apparently 'irrational' situation.

Amadeus therefore offers us an important variation on Shaffer's consistent use of oppositions and disjunctions in his drama. *The Royal Hunt of the Sun* and *Equus* had dissolved difference into likeness in order to indicate the clash between 'two kinds of Right': simultaneously, as difference melted, it became clear that conflicts *between* protagonists and ideologies were, in fact, projections of warring impulses *within* the individual. While it is arguable whether the Apollonian-Dionysian disjunction can accurately be applied to Pizarro and Atahuallpa respectively, and given that Dysart's Apollonian characteristics are rather less well defined than is often assumed, it is nevertheless true that Pizarro and Dysart detect in their 'adversaries' physical manifestations of impulses they detect and long to release within themselves. Their final disintegration attests to the ultimate inability to negotiate the resulting dualism. Salieri's situation is rather different; he unconsciously views Mozart as a projection of repressed impulses within himself, impulses he cannot and will not acknowledge. Meanwhile, on the conscious level, he regards Mozart as a manifestation of divine malice. The Apollonian-Dionysian opposition is clearer in this play than it has ever been in an illustration of this psychic activity, just as alignment between conflicting forces is more absent than it has ever been in an illustration of the ongoing and lethal 'battle for deliverance' between the conscious and the unconscious minds. In all three plays, however, conflict between representatives of opposing impulses results in the destruction of them both. In this, Shaffer is staging the eternal tragedy of the human condition.

As has been suggested throughout this discussion, Shaffer's theatre relies for its meaning on the dramatic requisite of conflict. It is significant, however, that seven years after the writing of *Amadeus*, alignment between oppositional forces is again offered in *Lettice and Lovage*. But unlike the situation we find in *The Royal Hunt of the Sun* and *Equus* where connection between oppositions resulted in irreconcilable dualisms and thus in mutual destruction, in *Lettice and Lovage*, connection results not in annihilation but in assimilation, survival and positive value. It is to this drama, and to the issues raised by it, that the next chapter turns.

7

The Problem with Women...

As readers will have noticed, Peter Shaffer's best-known plays are male-dominated zones. Where women appear at all in the spiritual or metaphysical tussles discussed in the two previous chapters, they are a subsidiary focus only, weak-voiced, marginalized to the edge of the action, and finally unimportant to the central debate. The purpose of this chapter is to investigate this situation, to examine Shaffer's representation of women in his dramas, and to trace the development of female presence in his work from the crude stereotypes of the early comedies to the powerful, developed protagonists presented in recent plays such as *Lettice & Lovage* and *Whom Do I Have the Honour of Addressing?* A previously ignored area of debate, this focus is important not only to patterns inherent in Shaffer's work itself, but also to wider issues concerning the positioning of the female spectator, and the articulation of 'femaleness' within theatre and drama.[1]

Tracing patterns is, as always, difficult in Shaffer's work: as soon as one paradigm apparently emerges, a character or situation will inevitably question it. His drama is, after all, characterized by mutability and by a constant search for new theatrical forms and dramatic directions. Despite this hazard, we can identify certain broad trends in Shaffer's work that suggest notions of femaleness and gendered assumptions that hold their ground until we reach the most recent plays. For example, a cursory examination of the female protagonists in his drama reveals that Shaffer has usually associated gender with genre, placing his most developed and credible women in comedies where the emotional territory traditionally ascribed to this form appears to suit female presence. The 'harder', more intellectual territories of tragedy, meanwhile, have remained solidly male zones, this again in line with traditional connections between gender and genre. As a result, the contests that we associate with Shaffer's drama have, until recently, always involved male 'doubles': Pizarro/Atahuallpa, Dysart/Strang, Salieri/Mozart. Similarly, the protagonists we associate with comedic spirit and/or emotional life include Clea from *Black Comedy*, Sophie from *White Liars* and Belinda from *The Public Eye*.

This distinction between male and female dramatic roles has held fast until very recently; though Lois in *Shrivings*, and possibly Sophie, potentially anticipate a tragic female protagonist, it is only when we encounter Tamar in *Yonadab* and Helen in *The Gift of the Gorgon* that we find ourselves presented with an articulation of femaleness that refuses traditional definitions of gendered activity and response. It is, of course, possible to argue (as some critics have done) that since Shaffer's dramatic project involves an investigation of the human condition, gender becomes irrelevant – the issues he raises forbid such localized enquiry. However, not only may gender be very much an issue for a female audience in particular (especially when contests are consistently fought out between male protagonists), but also Shaffer himself has made gender an issue by presenting his audience with characters who are encoded with notions connoting 'maleness' and 'femaleness'. Since the former has, necessarily given Shaffer's work, been implicitly discussed in previous chapters, it is the latter impulse that concerns us here.

Before looking at the development of Shaffer's presentation of 'femaleness' in his work, it is necessary to outline certain issues that must be considered as this discussion progresses. Firstly, we need to constantly ask ourselves whether Shaffer's female protagonists are credible *as women*; some critics, particularly in reference to *Lettice & Lovage*, have argued that they are not, and have suggested that they are simply male characters from earlier plays reappearing in unconvincing female guise. There is no simple way of deciding this issue since every individual will differ as to their own definitions of what constitutes a developed 'female voice'; in addition, it is easy to fall into cliché, preconception and stereotype when attempting to isolate 'female traits'. However, when asking whether Sophie, Lettice, Angela, Helen, and so on, are convincing as women, it is useful to apply a strategy known as the commutation test; frequently used to identify prejudices such as racism and sexism, the test operates through a simple reversal which, in this case, involves imagining the words spoken by a female character in the mouth of a male equivalent. Could Lettice, in other words, be played by a male actor? If the answer is 'no', we have asserted that there is something about the character as written that is specifically and *only* 'female', that there is something about the words and/or the situation that connotes 'femaleness'. The charge, then, that Shaffer's female characters are simply men in disguise can be assessed by stripping away the 'disguise' via the commutation test: in doing so, we find that the charge is rarely valid, though we may be no nearer to deciding what precisely has gendered the voice in such unambiguous terms.

A second issue that must be considered throughout this discussion concerns the positioning of the female spectator in relation to Shaffer's drama. If it is accepted that characters such as Lettice and Lotte, Angela and Helen, accurately and unmistakeably connote qualities of 'femaleness', do they, in the course of their dramas, articulate the female experience as the female audience recognizes it? Again, we are entering into subjective territory at this point, since what one audience member will recognize and respond to, another audience member will not: individual experience and perception is at work here. Nevertheless, certain broad impulses in Shaffer's drama seem designed to express as fully as possible female experience, particularly the female experience within patriarchy (literally, the 'law of the father'). We find, for example, a string of female protagonists who are constrained and contained by their roles as wives or daughters, women who are pressurized into repressive and limiting role-playing and who yield to (or fight against) male domination. We find potential that has been wasted or that is in the process of being wasted, women marginalized by a society that is organized on lines that are alien to female perception, and women stifled by rigid, narrow, male representatives of it. All is contained in dramas that (at their finest) re-place women as equal, if 'different', human subjects and which seem to express the experience of the female spectator. The 'success' of this articulation together with the means of achieving it are matters that must be considered throughout this chapter.

The issues and impulses outlined above provide the framework for an analysis of the way in which Peter Shaffer uses and presents female presence in his drama. Before turning to a detailed investigation of *Lettice & Lovage* and *Whom Do I Have the Honour of Addressing?*, two plays in which these ideas become central, it is useful firstly to trace the development of 'femaleness' in Shaffer's work as a whole. This not only reveals a number of forerunners to characters and experiences in the recent female-focused drama, but also suggests certain traits here associated with female being.

Beginning with the earliest full-length drama, *Five Finger Exercise*, we find that female presence is registered solely in stereotype, in clichés that will recur throughout Shaffer's work. This play is, in addition, 'male-dominated' in a double sense. Firstly, its most consistent focus involves the relationships between Clive and his father, and Clive and Walter; secondly, and following from this, it is a play heavily concerned with fathers and the struggle against them – both Clive and Walter reject the roles, behaviour, standards and attitudes demanded of them by men they fear, love, despise, and potentially mirror. *Five Finger Exercise*, then, is, in the truest sense, a play about patriarchy, but in its 1958 context, this motivating impulse excludes women from its dramatic discourse.

These women, outnumbered by men, are easily categorized emblems of femaleness: they are, in short, ciphers. As John Russell Taylor notes, here we find standard images of middle-class womanhood with a 'fussy, scatterbrained mother' and a 'bossy, tomboy daughter'.[2] Further, Louise is a snob through and through, prone to constructing a personal history of European grandeur, a trait that will recur in Sophie Lemberg and Dora Strang. In line with other female protagonists in Shaffer's drama, she is also unintellectual and more easily accommodated within emotional territories and fantasy than within logic and reality. It is, in fact, true to state that, until his most recent plays, 'woman' and 'intellect' have often constituted a contradiction in terms for Shaffer, a point that takes us back to the earlier connection between gender and genre in his work. While, as we have seen, the capacity for intellectual enquiry as associated with the Apollonian mind can go too far in his drama, and the capacity for instinctive response and 'spirit' (as in *The Public Eye*) may frequently be more highly valued by Shaffer, it is also the case that several of this playwright's women are conspicuously devoid of *either* intellect *or* instinct/'spirit'. Louise is perhaps the first in this line, and Carol and Dora will follow in her wake.

Louise indicates a further dimension of Shaffer's attitude towards 'femaleness' that will become manifested in the later plays: Louise's contribution to the drama revolves around her sexuality which is located as a problematic force. Her romantic yearnings for Walter, which do not involve the desire for sexual consummation, are presented in such a way as to suggest that these yearnings duplicate her feelings towards her own son: an Oedipal paradigm is subtly forged. Her sexuality is therefore conceived as a transgressive and destabilizing force while her development as a character beyond the region of her sexuality is, as before, limited. In later dramas, Shaffer will often similarly define women in terms of their role as sexual subjects and will refuse investigation of them beyond that realm: nowhere is this tendency more clearly marked than in this early social drama where the female voice, submerged by the male voices that surround it, emerges solely as a plaintive, sexualized problem. The audience may recognize Louise as a 'type', and respond to her accordingly, but the audience may not recognize Louise as a fully-developed *woman*: in 1958, however, it may not have expected to.

Turning next to the one-act plays where comedic impulses are frequently manifested, we find that genre traps Shaffer into further stereotype and gendered cliché.[3] In addition, we again find that wider societal attitudes towards woman and her role are reflected in the action (and conception) of these dramas, particularly in the assumption that the female finds existence on stage solely in relation to her attachment to a male force. As a result, women here are included as identifiable, labelled functions: girlfriend, fiancée, wife, spinster, virgin, daughter. All, of course, are roles defined in relation to, and circulating around, notions of maleness. As a result, men again dominate these plays while women operate within them as protagonists dependent upon male presence.

Given this, however, and given also the social climate within which these plays were written and presented, Shaffer manages to surprise us by providing glimpses here of impulses that will eventually culminate in the creation of powerful, fully-developed female protagonists who control and motivate the dramatic action. He accepts stereotype in these one-act plays, works within it, but produces something new from it. For example, Doreen in *The Private Ear* is, again, a sexual pawn – the 'quarry' which the dominating male protagonists pursue; she is unintellectual, unimaginative and uninformed, but by the end of the play, Shaffer has conveyed the fact that her powers of perception are sharp and that, in resisting the temptation to expose Bob's lies, a capacity for kindness and mercy render her rather more admirable than the audience had previously suspected. The cipher has emerged as a character we must take seriously, a situation we could not have imagined during the course of the action.

Similarly, in *Black Comedy* (a farce where stereotype necessarily dominates), a jilted and vengeful girlfriend comes to represent almost supernatural dimensions. Clea, using the darkness to create malicious havoc in the manner of a hyperactive poltergeist, personifies the values of perception so that, as Gene A. Plunka suggests, she 'perhaps needs an *r* on the end of her name to describe her function as a seer in the play'.[4] Further, Clea is, as Shaffer notes, the only character in the 'farce pack of cards' to emerge as 'a real person', a person, moreover, who becomes the 'moral re-agent of the play'.[5] Meanwhile, Miss Furnival (a traditional stage spinster) potentially anticipates characters such as Lettice and Lotte in her role as a 'ghostly' bridge between past values and present aesthetic and spiritual decay, and moves from a figure of amusement to a protagonist capable of expressing genuine despair.

This is a characteristic she shares with Sophie Lemberg, Shaffer's first female protagonist to emerge as a fully-developed, centralized dramatic force. Occupying a subterranean lair like Lettice, demonstrating a propensity to fantasize about her family history like Louise, and sharing with Lotte a conflicting attitude divided between love and scorn for her dead father, Sophie emerges from *White Liars* as by far the most admirable character of the trio gathered on stage. She at least has recognized 'truth', has moved from misperception to clear perception, and has arrived at a position whereby she can forge her own destiny as an autonomous human subject. The charlatan fortune-teller subverts all audience expectations of her and provides yet another example of Shaffer's ability to both work within and extend the limits of generic and gender stereotype.

The Public Eye similarly extends the limits of stereotype through its portrayal of three characters, an accountant, a private detective, and a wife, of whom the audience thinks it knows what to expect. In terms of role, however, all preconceptions are confounded as each protagonist proceeds to question the bases of functions which have been imposed either by themselves or by others. As far as the discussion in this chapter is concerned, Belinda's questioning of the definition of 'wife' and of the arbitrary and thus illogical limits this places upon her as a human being *and* as a woman, seems to suggest that Shaffer's desire to articulate the female experience within patriarchy finds its first extended expression here. But while this is certainly a concern within this play, and is communicated forcibly through Charles' ridiculous definitions of 'wifedom', dominant emphases in this play are liable to make contemporary audiences uneasy about the portrayal of femaleness that we find here. That Belinda is a 'free spirit' is located as positive by Shaffer, but that an injection of knowledge, rationality and intellect is required to 'balance' this, and that this injection is administered at male hands (Julian and Charles), may not necessarily be interpreted as positive by a female audience. Belinda is, in fact, paedocratized (made child-like) in this transaction since her knowledge and induction into the world of 'grown-ups' (culture, art, life itself) is at the hands of men. Finally, she is further infantilized (literally, made speechless) when, together with her much older husband, she is removed from the sphere of articulation altogether and is forbidden to speak for a period of weeks. The logic behind this imposition of silence has been outlined in Chapter 3, but it remains true that if Charles is guilty of paedocratizing Belinda, then so too are Julian and Shaffer himself. The female audience may respond to Belinda's experience within a crushing patriarchy which imposes illogical rules and roles upon womanhood, but it is unlikely to respond fully to the resolution of this situation in this play. In addition, where 'spirit' may be presented here as a positive and specifically 'female' trait, Shaffer implies that it cannot stand alone: and its necessary balance ('letter', rationality, intellect, knowledge) is posited in this surreal comedy as *male*.

The female audience has no opportunity to find the portrayal of femaleness or of the female protagonist disturbingly ambiguous in *The Royal Hunt of the Sun*, the first of Shaffer's 'think-pieces' which, perhaps because of this definition, is a female-free zone.[6] Apart from the tiny role of one of Atahuallpa's wives (whose only function in the drama is to feed one man and to be threatened with rape by another), woman is absent from this 'epic' play. We could perhaps argue that Atahuallpa's androgynous qualities posit female presence within him while, to extend this argument, the 'rape' of Peru possibly locates this entire territory as a female realm. It remains true, however, that in the first of Shaffer's intellectual, metaphysical contests, woman in the flesh becomes noticeably absent: the connection between gender and genre, where comedy is aligned with 'female' territories of emotional experience and where 'epic' or tragedy is aligned with 'male' territories of intellectual and spiritual enquiry, here appears to hold strong.

Where *The Royal Hunt of the Sun* rejects female presence, *Shrivings* simultaneously marginalizes and centralizes it. In this play, we find that woman is more central to the dramatic development of the action in her absence than she is in her on-stage presence. In the revised version of the text, the two forces which haunt the drama and the protagonists engaged in it are the absent wives, Enid and Guilia. Both hold the keys to their ex-husband's hypocrisies and guilt, and both are more important in their ghostly memories than they could ever have been incarnated as stage protagonists (hence the eradication of Enid in revision): it is their *absence* that is the point since both have been either driven away or destroyed by the demons and lies that are, in turn, destroying their surviving husbands.

Given the fact that female absence is a potent form of female presence in this play, absence is also, in a reversed situation, registered in the presence of Lois Neal, a naive, alienated young American who is prone to the worship of false idols.[7] Central to the drama in the sense that she is involved in the development of the contest between Gideon and Mark, she is simultaneously marginalized from it since not only has she no direct part to play in the conflict between the warring men, but also her contribution to it is again connected purely with her sexuality. Her frigidity renders her a natural companion to the equally frigid Gideon, while her problematic sexuality is appropriated by Mark who uses it in his war against his former idol. Lois appears, then, not as a developed protagonist in this play, nor as a credible female focus, but as a sexual subject whose role is defined solely in relation to her sexual function. Woman, in *Shrivings*, is therefore more central in her absence than she is in her presence; in the former she exposes the male problematic, but in the latter, she herself becomes problematic and is marginalized as a result.

Equus, the next play in Shaffer's canon, returns to the male-dominated realm of 'think-piece' drama that was initiated by *The Royal Hunt of the Sun*. Here again we find that the play revolves around the relationship between two men while the female voice oscillates on the edges of the drama. The pattern of absent wives continues in Margaret who becomes little more than the butt of a joke and an extension of what Dysart fears within himself; Jill continues in the line of female sexual catalysts, a middle-class, highly-sexed, horse-crazy teenager whose absent mother (like Alice Evans Douffet) loathes men as a whole untrustworthy gender. Dora Strang, meanwhile, recalls Louise's social snobbery and the war between wife and husband that is staged on the battleground of an only son; in addition, she, like Lois, is sexually problematized via frigidity and is associated, in addition, with a neurotic brand of religious fanaticism which borders on hysteria.

Of the three women in *Equus*, then, only Hesther is worthy of sustained attention in the terms of this discussion. Described by Barbara Lounsberry as the 'ethical authority' of the play, Hesther represents humane and normative social conscience.[8] She is also, however, crucially sexless, as though a female protagonist whose dramatic function is so central cannot be trivialized by the suggestion of sexual activity or affiliation. Significantly, this sexless quality is later transcribed onto the intellectual Helen in *The Gift of the Gorgon* which suggests that, for Shaffer, female mental activity precludes the type of sexual role-playing that we have been accustomed to up to this point. Hesther, then, is a normative benchmark, an unsexed voice which we must respect and respond to, but a voice that is nevertheless drowned out by the passionate male cries of the protagonists who inhabit the spatial, psychological and emotional core of the drama.

She is, nevertheless, a crucial moral and intellectual touchstone in the play, a role that is withheld from the female protagonist in the next great 'think-piece', *Amadeus*. Here, women revert to their positions as absent caricatures (Teresa and Princess Elizabeth), sexual subjects and pawns (Katherina and Constanze), and male-attached roles: nagging mother-in-law (Frau Weber), inconstant wife (Constanze).[9] Further, woman intrudes here only to the extent that her sexuality is used in the cause of a spiritual and metaphysical struggle between males; Salieri's attempted seduction of Constanze and his successful seduction of Katherina are embarked upon solely in the interests of outwitting his enemy (God) and striking against God's instrument (Mozart). As a result, woman appears in this play only by 'virtue' of her sexuality which is used to comment on or further a wider battle; this sexuality is, in addition, used to victimize her, as in the case of Constanze who is blackmailed by Salieri. In the third in the triumvirate of 'thinking plays', then, woman's status as sexual subject, passive victim and marginalized protagonist becomes reaffirmed. Yet again, the intellectual landscapes wherein Shaffer's metaphysical battles are waged appear to be no place for women.

However, the move towards the recent centralization of women on Shaffer's stage, and the removal of them from the realm of sexual subjects hovering on the edge of the action, begins in earnest in the next 'epic', *Yonadab*. Yet again, we find a male-dominated play whose central, most powerful voices are placed in the mouths of men, but here a woman is finally woven into the spiritual and metaphysical action in decisive terms. Finally, a female voice escapes from Shaffer's comedic world and penetrates the weightier territory of investigative tragedy. Her entrance into this realm is, as usual, effected via her sexuality since her rape catalyses the drama in real terms and allows her access into the male context that has been presented up to this point. Discarding the roles of 'daughter', 'sister' and victim, Tamar evolves during the course of the action into a cunning, perceptive manipulator whose careful vengeance is enacted with terrible results. She out-watches Yonadab, out-thinks her father, and out-schemes all who stand in her way. The victim turns victimizer.

For the female audience, this is surely an ambiguous situation. At last, Shaffer presents us with a fully-formed dramatic agent whose intelligence and ability to 'read' character and situation suggest positive female values. In addition, we respond to a female protagonist who refuses to be acted *upon* and who rejects victimized passivity. On the other hand, the audience understands that Shaffer has imbued in Tamar the purely negative values of vengeance, and these 'values' hold no final meaning. So when a female finally breaks into the world of spiritual enquiry and 'epic' encounter, she does so with lethal results. For the female audience, which then is the preferable situation – to be effectively absent from Shaffer's world of dramatic and spiritual enquiry, or to be present but deadly?

In her vengeful crusade, Tamar is markedly different from the four women who precede her in Shaffer's most recent plays: these women all reject vengeance in favour of the positive values of reconciliation, mercy and connection. Suddenly, we find that women dominate Shaffer's stage, marginalizing or completely eradicating male presence; in addition, we find that these women emerge as powerful, autonomous, independent protagonists whose dominant characteristics include sharp perception and, above all, the capacity for survival. Much of the earlier stereotyping disappears as Shaffer's women begin to move easily between comedy, tragicomedy, and tragedy; in addition, their sexuality ceases to define them in problematic terms, and their places within the dramas that they motivate are carved independently of men. Many of the qualities associated with 'femaleness' in the earlier plays are brought into sharper focus here so that protagonists such as Lettice Douffet, Lotte Schoen, Angela Parsons and Helen Damson come to embody the values of positive difference.

These moves towards the development of a powerful female-dominated stage are initiated in *Lettice & Lovage*.[10] In this play, Shaffer dramatizes conflict in comedic terms, journeys through tragi-comedy, teeters on the edge of tragedy, and finally reclaims the comedic spirit in an image of celebratory connection. Here, we witness something that we have never seen before on Shaffer's stage and have not seen since: that is, a positive reconciliation between Apollonian and Dionysian instincts. We could argue that this reconciliation results from genre since comedy insists on satisfactory resolution and Shakespearean comedy in particular (with which this play has strong links) inevitably concludes with union: in addition, Shaffer himself states that to have rejected the values of connection at the end of the play would have constituted 'a betrayal of the genre of comedy'.[11]

This is certainly a persuasive argument, but just as it would be a mistake to omit genre from the matter of connection in this play, so too would it be a mistake to omit the question of gender: the two are, as we have seen, profoundly linked in Shaffer's work. In addition, impulses within *Lettice & Lovage* alert us to the fact that certain characteristics imbued in the protagonists here, characteristics that are for Shaffer closely associated with 'femaleness', allow reconciliation between apparently conflicting instincts to occur. Connection arises in this play not simply because this is a comedy (Shaffer has, after all, written comedies before and connection remained elusive), but because its protagonists are both, for the first time, women.

Lettice and Lotte's Dionysian and Apollonian qualities are as marked as they were in earlier male pairings. Lettice's name means 'gladness', and all who come into contact with her are infected by her spirit. The word 'endores', of which she is so fond, describes not only her nature but also her discursive strategy since, through her life-force and her stories, all that surrounds her is 'made golden'.[12] Her 'watchword', 'Enlarge! Enliven! Enlighten!' has been inherited from her mother, a female Wolfit with a comically literal grasp of the French language from whom Lettice's love of theatre and fantasy derives (p.23).[13] Dedicated to 'lighting up the world' rather than 'dousing it in dust' (p.25) she is a 'compulsive story-teller', a 'romancer', in Lotte's words, fond of embroidered versions of reality when 'fact' fails to live up to the romantic imagination (p.61). Embarrassingly emotional in an echo of Mozart, Lotte's emotions run unchecked, as do her words which form a garrulous, riveting torrent of comment, information and anecdote. A creature of

Dionysian passions and extremes, she despises modern ugliness and its toys (computers, answerphones, dictaphones), loathes the Puritan instinct, worships the arch-Dionysians of history (including Falstaff), and is attracted to colour and richness as manifested in glorious tales of the past. Imbued with witch-like connotations through her magical brew of lovage and through her 'familiar', Felina, and inhabiting a subterranean, unconscious realm, she hovers on the edge of modern existence, refusing its precepts.[14]

This refusal could potentially lead to her destruction or, as she fears, to her incarceration as some historical prisoner. Her basement apartment is a refuge and a place where time stands still, but it is also, as she suggests, a type of 'dungeon' (p.33); hence her identification with a chain of historical victims who are noted for the nobility (and drama) of their executions, her favourites being Marie Antoinette, Mary Queen of Scots and Charles I. She, like them, feels alienated and victimized by a society that she rejects and which in turn rejects her: her resulting separation is thus both enforced and self-enforced. When she first encounters Lotte, this woman of spirit and life (positive forces inherited from her mother) is on the verge of becoming a 'ghost' (p.75): those very Dionysian forces which mark her 'difference' simultaneously mark her for destruction since, as in *Equus*, society will inevitably eradicate any destabilizing, apparently transgressive force.

Lettice is, perhaps, as unlikely a ghost as Lotte is an unlikely rescuer; Lettice's life-force seems so powerful and Lotte's willingness to 'rescue' anyone seems so absent. In fact, in the first of many connections between them, *both* are bordering on ghostliness and *both* will rescue the other from that shadow state. Where Lettice is threatened by her Dionysian instinct, Lotte is threatened by her Apollonian nature, this being particularly pronounced at the beginning of the play in order to characterize her as a natural counterpoint to Lettice. Introduced as '*a severe-looking lady in her late forties, her dark hair and dress aggressively plain*' (p.14), Lotte is said to exude a 'certain grey integrity' (p.29). Despising the theatre, espousing an anti-humanistic philosophy (she states that she cares 'more for buildings than their inhabitants', p.44), she is a repressed mass of anxieties and hostilities when we first meet her in confrontation with Lettice. This confrontation centres on the definition of 'fact' and 'truth', and on the use and abuse of rhetoric; Lotte solidly maintains that 'untruth is untruth' (p.28), and asserts that 'I don't say what I don't mean' (p.49). Lettice's contrasting belief that words decorate, 'endore', and express *imaginative* truth if not necessarily *factual* truth is a philosophy that is indeed 'alien' to Lotte, though she can at least realize that this is 'not at all bad' (p.39).

This admission indicates that connection between the two alien instincts may not be as impossible as we had at first believed, particularly when the two protagonists' relationship with 'words' and 'truth' begins to reveal some degree of overlap. Where Lettice's easy dismissal of factual 'truth' had appalled Lotte who could not understand that more levels of 'truth' exist than the one that she instinctively respects, Lettice's allegiance to 'truth' is revealed to be more solid than either we or Lotte had suspected. It is significant, for example, that Lettice loses her job selling the disgusting cheese because she had refused to lie and had told 'the public not to waste its money' (p.49). Similarly, in a reversed situation, Lotte is not perhaps the strict adherent to factual truth that she would have us believe, telling Lettice that, in order to win her the job as a guide on a tourist boat, 'I did somewhat exceed the limits of veracity' (p.36). Both women being, above all, creatures of perception, they each understand that these moments connote a greater connection between them than their apparent positions in relation to 'words' and 'truth' had initially implied. Both, after all, respect 'words' and 'truth' for their capacity to access alternative levels of beauty and 'reality'.

As the play develops, the connections between Lettice and Lotte multiply. Both women are middle-aged, unmarried, and alone in life; both have been reared by single parents who have moulded them into what they are. Where Lettice had been subject to a liberating matriarchal life-force, Lotte had been subject to a repressive, inhibiting patriarchal ghost, but both have been conditioned by these influences and both live in the shadows of their dead parents. In addition, both are worshippers at the altar of beauty and, though they may define this word in different terms, both feel deeply the eradication of it in the modern world. Finally, both feel themselves to be victims in a victimizing environment and although Lotte's response to this is to attempt to conform to the executioner's role, her slide into 'ghostliness' cannot be long delayed as she herself realizes.

The connections between the two women, then, are many and various and are gradually revealed as the play progresses. But a further, deeper, system of connections is woven into the text by Shaffer as he dramatizes the conjunction between Apollonian and Dionysian instincts (and between the conscious and the unconscious) within the individual mind. That Lotte detests the theatre rather less than she asserts is noted by Lettice in her conversation with Bardolph, and that her allegiance to beauty implies Dionysian instinct, indicates that (in an echo of Dysart) her accommodation within Apollonian territories of order, logic and rationality is less absolute than we at first suspect. The most significant indication of this occurs when, in a historical charade that anticipates the mock-executions she and Lettice will later stage, Lotte is aligned with Elizabeth I; as they leave the basement to dine together, Lettice spreads her cloak on the ground for Lotte in the manner of Sir Walter Raleigh paying homage to the Virgin Queen. Since Lotte has, seconds before, revealed her cropped head in an eerie imitation of Mary Queen of Scots, this strikes us as a peculiar moment since, from her alignment with the victim, she is then immediately aligned with Mary's executioner, Elizabeth. The explanation is that, in Lotte, both roles co-exist in a replica of the division within herself between Apollonian/Dionysian instincts. Similarly, Lettice (always, in her imagination and in her dramas, the victim) is the comic near-executioner of Lotte *in reality*. That the victim and the executioner are combined within the single psyche, with one role dominant, effectively reflects the struggle between the conscious and unconscious mind as developed through the Apollonian/ Dionysian dialectic in this play and in several that precede it.

By the end of the action, both Lettice and Lotte have come to understand that, while the instinct ascendant in them will always remain dominant, absolutes no longer apply. Further, where both instincts can go too far, each has the capacity to balance and complement the other: as a result, possibly the most crucial line in the entire play is Lotte's statement towards the end of Act 3, 'We're a combination' (p.76). Given the discussion of the previous chapter, we can apply this statement not only to the partnership between apparently conflicting instincts as embodied in the two women, but also to the union between conscious and unconscious regions within the individual psyche. Connection, reconciliation and, above all, *meaning* results, values that are communicated via the ritual celebratory toast to the audience as the curtain falls. Shaffer chooses to conclude with a deliberate echo of the image of union that concludes Shakespearean comedy and thus reminds us of the metaphysical union between Apollonian and Dionysian instincts, and thus between the conscious and the unconscious mind, that he has effected in the course of his drama.

As before, this union results not simply from genre but from gender, but the question is, what are the qualities that Shaffer associates with 'femaleness' in this play that make such union possible? Firstly, we notice that woman here is associated with imagination, not only in terms of the ability to weave fantasies, but also in the capacity to enter into another's vision, even when that vision is apparently alien to her. This is one aspect of the dominating sense of acceptance with which the play concludes. Linked to this also is woman's capacity for love, not necessarily in sexual terms, but in the sense of deep and valuable connections forged on the basis of recognition and compassion.[15] As Shaffer notes, *Lettice & Lovage* is 'about love [...] not love in the romantic sense, but [...] love of the spirit'.[16] In a play where women dominate Shaffer's stage for the first time, this form of love permeates the stage action.

Above all, though, the quality most associated with 'femaleness' in this play is a quality that we have seen in less sharp focus in Shaffer's earlier work; here 'woman' and 'perception' become inextricably linked. Lettice is aligned with this quality more obviously than Lotte, though each 'perceives' in the other capacities they both recognize in themselves and/or value.[17] One clear example of this emphasis on perception occurs following Lotte's removal of her wig to reveal her cropped head: Lettice, we are told, '*laughs: a clear bright laugh of perception*' (p.51); similarly, she tells Bardolph that she 'soon perceived' that Lotte protested her aversion to all things theatrical 'altogether too much', thus suggesting an attraction to the power of fantasy that she appears to despise (p.58). In addition, Lettice recognizes that Lotte's desire to forsake her role as executioner and play Charles I instead constitutes a cataclysmic moment; in her words, 'It represented – so much!' (p.61). Lettice has understood that Lotte's desire to swop roles was, in effect, a rejection of Apollonian repression (as embedded in the Puritanism that destroyed Charles) and an acknowledgement of her own duality; it is a moment that Lettice has been leading Lotte towards during the whole of their association. Similarly, Lotte perceives all too clearly the ugliness of the modern world, but perceives also that Lettice's 'uniqueness' potentially offers an antidote to it: she therefore unconsciously understands that connection with this 'alien' can save them both (p.49). Both perceive what each other are; neither attempt to change or alter these forces, and connection arises. The quality of perception that had characterized Clea and Sophie (and which is so frequently and fatally lacking in Shaffer's male protagonists) finds its clearest expression in the developed notion of 'femaleness' that conditions the vision and characters of this play.

The final 'female' value posited in this play involves a departure from the impulses detected above in relation to *Yonadab*, but connects forward with the plays that precede *Lettice & Lovage*. In the revised version of this text, Lettice and Lotte embark on a campaign of terror against ugliness that involves not destruction through violence, but destruction through words. In this fine comic resolution, the women reject the course of vengeance and arrive at a mediated settlement where 'terror' is planned via a more subtle and potentially more 'deadly' route: as Angela notes in *Whom Do I Have the Honour of Addressing?*, 'It's not true about sticks and stones – words hurt much more!'.[18] Passivity is rejected: both Lettice and Lotte refuse to allow themselves to become ghosts and decide to take action against the sights and objects that appal them. But unlike Tamar, this refusal to become passive victims does not involve negative value and instead suggests positive connotations of female power and autonomy because, in rejecting the role of 'victim', Lettice and Lotte do not become victimizers themselves (as Tamar had done). Instead, Shaffer here provides the audience (and the female audience in particular) with an empowering image of femaleness that celebrates the values of connection and which points towards effective female activity.

The move from passive victim to active force continues into Shaffer's next play, *Whom Do I Have the Honour of Addressing?*, where several of the qualities associated with 'femaleness' in *Lettice & Lovage* reappear. In this radio play (adapted for the stage in 1996), woman is now not simply the dominant voice, but is the *only* voice.[19] As in the drama that immediately precedes it, we are initially confronted here with a single, middle-aged woman who is struggling to communicate to a faceless audience whom she can never know (as the title, with its rhetorical enquiry, suggests). By the end of the play, however, communication not simply with others but also with herself has been achieved, and a courageous, autonomous woman evolves from the self-destructive victim we had initially encountered. In Angela we find a woman who survives both a hostile, disappointing world and the false dream of fantasy: in so doing, she emerges as a worthy successor to Lettice and Lotte and represents an image of 'femaleness' that is as credible as it is potent.

Angela, like so many of Shaffer's characters (regardless of gender), is characterized through duality. Shaffer comments that she is 'practical and romantic', both 'clear-eyed' and 'deluded', a creature, in other words, of extreme and apparently conflicting opposites.[20] Although she notes that she is 'an excessive personality', she is also aware that she is the type who has 'always made a Top-and-Two Carbons of everything all my life' (p.11). An apparent Apollonian in her lifestyle and occupation, her Dionysian instincts are barely in control and, following her first encounter with Tom, they begin to dominate her existence. Prior to this, she has successfully displaced them through her addiction to fantasy as indicated by her relationship with cinema, but when fantasy steps into reality, Angela spins out of control.

This 'addiction' (p.9) to cinema is likened by Angela to a type of 'drug' (p.12), a narcotic which numbs her sufficiently to enable her to exist in a flawed world she feels to be meaningless and which has been driving her 'steadily bonkers' with its 'dreariness' for years (p.10). Cinema provides her with psychological release from her narrow life because it produces a parallel world of heightened emotion and romantic encounter. That Angela should have selected cinema as her release is significant since it links with her defining characteristic: disconnection. The glass screen separates event from reception and allows for emotional contact *at second hand* seated in front of an impenetrable barrier (itself an image of alienation as *Yonadab* suggests). Like Shaffer's earlier biblical protagonist, images of separation surround Angela extending from her disconnected voice summoning anonymous addressees, to the ironically named Bud's blocking, mirrored sunglasses. Cinema thus appeals to Angela because, knowing herself to be isolated and alienated, she is attracted to a medium wherein these values are a fact of production: it allows her to simulate contact through voyeurism and to participate without involvement.[21]

As in the case of the earlier Lettice, an essential element of Angela's 'femaleness' in this play is her accommodation within fantasy. This, of course, is a further attraction of cinema which works within, and upon, the escapist imagination: as Shaffer notes, 'films are a very powerful source of fantasy, fantasy that constructs its own reality'.[22] However, when the physical and metaphorical barrier between 'reality' and 'fantasy' begins to break down (as it does when Tom Prance steps from the screen and into Angela's life), Angela's already tenuous grip on herself and her world begins to disintegrate. Her tendency to view herself as a character in a film accelerates: when she first talks to Tom on the telephone, she tells us that, 'When I speak, it's like one of those highly-charged conversations in a classic film thriller – like Barbara Stanwyck and Fred MacMurray in *Double Indemnity*' (p.16). When Tom asks her to go to Los Angeles and work for him at his Drug Rehabilitation Clinic, she comments, 'Time just stopped. The film, which I sometimes imagine as my life, became a freeze' (p.20).

Her habit of viewing herself from a third-person point of view, as if she is not inhabiting her own body but is watching herself on a screen, similarly intensifies, and references to performance and role-playing increase as when Tom refers to her as a 'Margaret Rutherford type' (p.21), and as when Angela comments of her new work, '*I had a role*' (p.27). Finally, her ability to distinguish between 'reality' and 'fantasy' breaks down completely when she storms the film set on which Tom is working, ignores the director, and proceeds to participate in a 'scene' in which she confronts Tom with Bud's activities. In retrospect, she describes the sense she had that she and Tom 'were both in a tremendous film together about tropical passion' (p.32), and then significantly asserts: 'I wasn't acting. It was absolutely real. Real!' (p.33). Angela has discovered 'reality' in the midst of a film set.

The catalyst which disrupts Angela's tenuous relationship with 'fantasy' and 'reality' is Tom Prance. Existing in two apparently separate worlds (the screen and 'real life'), the film star seems to connote a connection between the two; for Angela, Tom has the potential to infuse her drab reality with glamorous fantasy, a chance she eagerly accepts. His appeal to her is also located in two additional areas: firstly, her aesthetic sense is stimulated by Tom's physical beauty which she initially appreciates objectively but to which she increasingly responds sexually; the possibility of physical contact awakens her and her desire for it is triggered by the hug she receives from him. But more than this, Tom's appeal to Angela resides at the imaginative level. His name 'Prance' suggests not only a tendency to posture (as will be revealed towards the end of the play), but also a Prince of Arthurian legend who rescues the damsel in distress. This, of course, coincides with Tom's fantasy of himself and his cultivation of a courtly manner contributes to the image he is keen to project. Hence his careful elocution (the 'whom do I have the honour of addressing?' of the title derives from his opening line to Angela), and his determined self-education. When Angela dubs him 'the Clean Right Fellow' (p.15) she is responding not only to her own needs of him, nor simply to a photograph of Tom dressed in knightly armour campaigning against drug abuse, but to a fantasy he himself has constructed in his search for identity.

If Tom appeals to Angela's romantic imagination, she also appeals to his. In casting her as a 'Margaret Rutherford type' (a label she resents because it wounds her vanity and militates against the idea of what she longs for her role to be), Tom is also guilty of imposing a fantasy on reality. Rutherford was a cinematic construction, type-cast as an elderly spinster or headmistress, capable, brusque, yet fey: Tom projects this persona onto Angela just as she projects the idea of an Arthurian Prince onto him. Neither see each other as they really are, so blinded are they by what their imaginations want the other to be. But we who realize that the boundary between 'reality' and fantasy is solid and must always remain so, recognize that this relationship, fraudulent to its core, is hopelessly doomed.

In Los Angeles, Angela finds herself temporarily seduced by the city of dreams where her actual and imagined needs appear to be satisfied by Tom and by her new 'role'. However, when this world is fragmented by Bud's abuse and by the shattering image (significantly, viewed on screen) of Tom engaged in sado-masochistic, homosexual acts, and when Angela is *accused* in some way of causing this fragmentation, Angela emerges from her self-imposed seclusion (her instinct is to hide) to become a retributive, punishing force. As she herself comments, no one is 'harmless' (p.42). Confronted with the hypocrisy and vanity which is so often associated with 'maleness' in Shaffer's plays, Angela lashes out, wounding Tom physically as she herself has been wounded both emotionally and psychologically. For Angela, as for the audience, this is a powerful, liberating act which constitutes a declaration that she will take no more abuse.

However, upon her return to London, Angela, having refused the role of victim at male hands, prepares to victimize herself in the most final way possible: her recorded message is a suicide statement. Not only does this option connote purely negative value, but the message itself suggests only destructive revenge since it is a 'little time bomb' (p.4), designed to destroy Tom's carefully-constructed image, and thus his lies, life, self-constructed fiction and career. Angela seeks vengeance because she senses that she has, in the terms of her own frame of reference, been 'typecast' (and cast as a 'type' or role, in addition, that she finds unflattering) and, more significantly still, because her fantasy (and thus also her reality) has been shattered.[23] On both counts, she feels that she has been mocked and it is this which she cannot, at this point, forgive. Like the later Helen in *The Gift of the Gorgon*, she plans to destroy Tom through publicity, a more lethal form of wounding than even physical violence can achieve.

As she explains her motives to her anonymous addressees, however, Angela's resolve begins to waver. For some minutes, she oscillates between the desire to wreak revenge and the desire to forgive so that, as Shaffer notes, 'the actress [playing Angela] is like a windscreen wiper moving from one side to the other side, illustrating an interlocking of opposites'.[24] The duality central to the human psyche is again implied. But here, a female quality suggested in *Lettice & Lovage* acquires sharp focus as the capacity for acceptance, reconciliation and mercy deters Angela from her vengeful course. Her perception allows her to realize that, though Tom is a sham, that sham at least holds more value than the 'malice' and 'envy' of 'Bloody Fleet Street Nothings' (p.42). In a reversal of their previous roles, Angela decides to 'protect' Tom as the Damsel in Distress metamorphoses into the Knight in Shining Armour (p.42). In this, however, there is some satisfaction for the audience since, in deciding on survival, Angela relishes the prospect of becoming 'A nasty little Miss Rutherford sitting in Clapham, able to speak at any time! [...] Miss Sword of Damocles!' (p.43). Finally, she imagines herself, for the last time, in a film being pursued by Bud sent to London to eliminate her: 'one of those murdering-lonely-women films' (p.44). But by now, Angela has understood that 'reality' and 'fantasy' are not a continuum and must never become so: in this recognition, her survival is assured.

In *Whom Do I Have the Honour of Addressing?*, then, woman again emerges as finer and more admirable than the men who inhabit her world. Angela has escaped from a marriage to a cold, unimaginative man who had ignored her in favour of his billiard cue, and must escape again from a relationship based on fraudulent fantasy in which she is again marginalized and commodified. Her powerful imagination may get out of hand, but it always represents her capacity to perceive that her world is insufficient and impoverished; she may lack 'rationality', but her 'irrational' addictions, obsessions and furies connote an unconscious logic with which any audience can readily identify. Her voice remains warm and intelligent throughout, and by the end of the play, as Angela hovers on the edge of fragmentation, it communicates also the strength and compassion of the survivor. She ends the play as she had begun it, alone, but her retrospective journey has allowed her (like Sophie) to perceive the truth of her situation and of her being, and this will enable her to forge a way ahead. Through Angela, Shaffer has shown us that, if no one is 'harmless', no one is 'ordinary' either, and from 'a middle-aged woman in a mac' (p.7) locked in a world of fantasy, he creates a complex, powerful life-force.

Shaffer has journeyed a long way in his representation of the female protagonist. From the stereotypes of the early plays and one-act comedies, through the male-dominated zones of his 'think-piece' dramas, he finally creates a theatre where woman emerges as central. The recent female protagonists (culminating in Helen who will be discussed at length in the following chapter) suggest positive images of independence, perception, imagination and survival; moreover, they represent the values of connection, mercy and forgiveness. Repeatedly, these middle-aged women, always alone in life, emerge as finer human beings than the men with whom they deal since not only do they survive victimization at their hands, but they also refuse the option of vengeance against them. Connections with others and with self occur as they have never done before, and Shaffer's stage becomes suffused with a notion of love that is not sexual, nor maternal, but resembles instead a love of the spirit that is based on acceptance. Finally, conflict does not end in destruction in these female-dominated plays, but in mediation and survival: as the male focus retreats, so too does the inevitability of physical, metaphysical and spiritual annihilation.

'The problem with women' in the earlier work is therefore fully resolved in the dramas produced by Shaffer over the last ten years. The question as to whether his female protagonists are fully credible as women remains open and must be left to the reader to decide. However, what cannot be questioned is the fact that in these plays, Shaffer presents us with female characters who articulate, embody and express a gendered perception of the world which, for the female audience, rings true. In so doing, he places both women and an articulation of female experience squarely on the mainstream stage. Critics who argue that gender is irrelevant in Shaffer's work are missing the significance of this point: they are, moreover, denying not only the validity of patterns inherent in the dramas discussed in this chapter, but also the responses of the female audiences who witness them.

8

Myth and Morality: *The Gift of the Gorgon*

The Gift of the Gorgon (1992) is Peter Shaffer's most recent and most controversial play. Dealing with fiercely divisive issues such as the morality of revenge, this drama forces its audiences to think actively about what it sees and hears on stage and rejects the option of passive neutrality. Confrontation is, indeed, the keyword of the play which revolves around two diametrically opposed notions of morality explored through a network of mythological allusions and encounters connecting modern man with his ancient soul. It is this linked emphasis on myth and morality in *The Gift of the Gorgon* that this chapter will explore, examining the way in which mythological elements are integrated into the drama, tracing allusions connected with this, and investigating the nature of the ethical debate presented here. In this play, Shaffer posits fundamental questions about the nature of man's psychic 'memory': in doing so, he presents his audience with a dilemma that is worthy of sustained analysis.

As Shaffer himself comments, his 'Greek Play', involving a 'story of passionate love, achievement and estrangement between a turbulent writer and his wife',[1] is a 'complicated business', and a brief introduction to the dramatic and theatrical techniques employed here may therefore be useful at this point.[2] To begin with, Shaffer is using the term 'Greek Play' in three senses: firstly, as it relates to the play's setting; secondly as its images, subject matter and staging devices recall Classical Theatre, and thirdly as its theme incorporates ancient attitudes, dramas, and mythological figures. In addition, we find here a play that 'somewhat resembles a fugue in that three related "plays" take place simultaneously':[3] the first 'framework' play involves the relationship between Helen and Philip; the second 'retrospective' play involves the story narrated and enacted by Helen which deals with her life with Edward; the third 'play-within-the-play' involves the relationship between Athena and

Perseus, Helen and Edward's dramatic projections. Underlying the whole is the ancient story of Agamemnon, murdered in a bath by Clytemnestra, whose death is revenged by Orestes, their son. Shaffer refers to this as 'the base, lower strata of the play', upon which the Athena/Perseus myth is developed.[4]

Not only does *The Gift of the Gorgon* involve a complicated mythological subtext, it also makes use of a complex staging strategy. Here, Shaffer utilizes a technique with which he had experimented in *Equus* and *Amadeus* where two scenes (often in differing tenses) are presented side-by-side on the stage. This offers, in effect, a theatrical version of the cinematic split screen. In *The Gift of the Gorgon*, Shaffer takes this technique one step further by unfolding the play's action through a continual interplay between past and present, this frequently involving the construction of three-cornered scenes in which characters interact with the past and the present simultaneously and become both narrators and participants in the events described. As a result, a single character may be engaged in dialogue enacted within two simultaneous tenses, as in the following exchange where Helen discusses *Hamlet* with Edward in the past and with Philip in the present:

> EDWARD: The only mistake Shakespeare made is to forget the ghost at the end. We should actually see it stalking away, satisfied at last, daubing the blood of Claudius on its spectral cheeks.
> PHILIP: Well, that's a point, anyway! The ghost *is* forgotten.
> HELEN [*to* PHILIP]: So it should be! The play's more *advanced* than that! [*To* EDWARD.] Hamlet reaches a point where he says, 'Let be.'
>
> (p.16)

Helen acts as a lynchpin not only between the two men (who argue a similar case) but also between two tenses: without missing a beat, she moves from one to the other. This staging calls on actors to participate in a theatrical play which is designed in the manner of 'a fully edited, finished film'.[5] Capitalizing on any contemporary audience's ability to 'read' the electronic media, Shaffer transplants its techniques onto the stage and, in so doing, rewrites theatrical grammar.

It is possible that this innovative staging strategy as allied with a complex subtext caused overcomplication in the play. However, what focused critics' and audiences' attention was neither element because, overshadowing them both, were the powerful ingredients of myth and morality, here inextricably connected.

Shaffer's use of myth and of the dark, violent forces that define it, has been addressed in earlier chapters. However, in *The Gift of the Gorgon*, the gods, heroes and archetypes of ancient legends are incorporated into the drama in an entirely new way. Not only are these figures central to the 'plays' enacted on stage, but they are central as well to the entire logic of the drama. The ancient gods of myth are not remote on this stage, cut off in some absolute way from modern man or society, but are portrayed instead as intrinsic to both; hence the ramp that connects the ancient with the contemporary world – the pathway provides a physical sign of the mental, emotional and psychological connections between the two realms that the play insists upon. Returning once again in this study to Jungian theory, we find here a direct physical projection of Jung's account of ancient memory where 'the inherited shapes of the human mind' survive in the shadowy unconscious of modern man.[6]

To understand fully the way in which Shaffer uses myth in this play, and to understand the play itself, we need to explore the ancient stories incorporated here in some detail. Beginning with the 'base lower strata' of the drama, the tale of Agamemnon provides the touchstone for the play's debate upon the morality of revenge to be expanded upon later in the discussion. Agamemnon, in Greek legend, was the King of Mycenae and leader of the Greeks at the siege of Troy. He married Clytemnestra, a daughter of Tyndarus and Leda, and together they bore three daughters, Iphigenia (or Iphianassa), Laodice (named Electra in later legends), and Chrysothemis; they also bore one son, Orestes.

During the Trojan War, Agamemnon had killed a stag, sacred to Artemis (also known as Diana, Goddess of the moon and of hunting) and had dared to suggest that he could out-hunt Artemis herself. In revenge, Artemis inflicted on Agamemnon and his men a string of misfortunes which caused the King to attempt to appease the angry Goddess by offering as a sacrifice to her his daughter, Iphigenia. Lying to his wife, he instructed her to bring their daughter to Aulis so that she could be married to Achilles: Clytemnestra arrived only to find that their daughter was to be slaughtered instead. Artemis, however, satisfied that Agamemnon's desire to appease her was honest, substituted a goat for Iphigenia and carried the Princess off to a cloud where she thereafter took charge of Artemis' temple. But Clytemnestra could never forgive her husband for what he had been prepared to do and set about planning her revenge upon him.

Returning finally from the Trojan Wars after an absence of ten years, Agamemnon was greeted by Clytemnestra who had secretly taken a new husband, Ægisthos: together they had been organizing his death. Agamemnon had been warned of this by Cassandra, a prophetess, but chose to ignore her visions. Accepting his wife's expressions of joy at his return as genuine, Agamemnon stepped into a bath that she had prepared for him; having washed him, she threw a cloth over his head, rendering him helpless, and stabbed him to death. Agamemnon's murder was later avenged by Orestes who was subsequently pursued by the Furies and finally brought to trial. At the hearing, the Goddess Athena appealed for justice on his behalf while Apollo defended him. Since the decision of the court was divided, the casting vote was given to Athena who found in Orestes' favour and brought peace once more to the land.

The myth of Agamemnon is obviously central to the play that Shaffer presents us with here. Edward Damson raises it as a topic of debate early in his relationship with Helen, declaring the 'rightness of Clytemnestra chopping up her husband in that bath' and celebrating its 'cleansing' potential in his invented rendition of 'Clytemnestra's Stamp'.[7] We also, of course, have an Orestes in Philip and an echo of Agamemnon's death in the revenge that Edward plans and enacts on Helen's behalf. The 'base lower strata' of the drama therefore operates as a framework for the entire play which focuses increasingly on the violence of human instinct that informs brutal action and reaction.

Athena's role in the trial of Orestes introduces the Goddess of wisdom into the Agamemnon myth, and Shaffer centralizes her in his play by aligning her closely with Helen. Faced with the communication problems that afflict so many of Shaffer's alienated heroes, Edward is forced to concoct fictional projections through which he can express the fears that torment him:[8] he selects the Perseus myth where a heroic adventurer presents himself before the Goddess Athena and begs for help, strength and deliverance.[9] Since Helen's affinity with Athena has already been indicated through the former's academic interest in her, the casting of Helen in the role of the Goddess of wisdom is perfect.

The connections between Athena and Helen are both overt and subtle, and are encoded at every level of signification in the play to produce a dense, allusive network of meaning. To begin with, Athena (daughter of Metis, Cleverness) embodies the wisdom of the world and, in one representation, moral and spiritual light: Helen similarly represents these values. Further, Athena was literally 'born of man', since Zeus had swallowed Metis when warned that her child would one day rival him in power, subsequently giving birth to the child that Metis was carrying from his own head: Helen has also, metaphorically, been born of man, her mother (an intellectual) having died young and she having been reared and moulded from that point on by her father. Both are also protectors of those employed in artistic endeavour, and both are defenders of passionate men (Perseus/Edward); they are thus connected with heroes whose stories suggest a mission to slay 'the dread monsters with which the imagination peoples darkness'.[10] Finally, Helen, like Athena, is both worshipped by Edward/Perseus and feared, and she too could also be labelled 'Mother', 'Saviour' and 'Victorious' just as Athena is labelled in various local legends.[11]

The choice of Athena (in Rome she was known as Minerva) as the Goddess represented in and by Helen is therefore not random. In addition, the duality or ambiguity associated with the Goddess becomes vital to our interpretation of the play. The doubleness of her name (Pallas-Athena) comes to represent the terrifying duality of the Goddess's symbolic function since the 'Pallas' of battle and warfare co-exists with the 'Athena' of peace and restraint (Athena is strongly associated with the olive tree and thus, through the olive branch, with a dominant symbol of peace). As Alexander S. Murray, in lyrical mood, comments: 'She is at once fearful and powerful as a storm and, in turn, gentle and pure as the warmth of the sky when a storm has sunk to rest and an air of new life moves over the freshened fields'.[12] In short, Athena becomes a syndrome for the duality that Shaffer perceives at the heart of all concepts of divinity.

The ambiguity implicit in representations of Athena is debated by Edward and Helen during the course of the play. As Edward notes, Athena having sprung fully armed from Zeus's head screaming war-cries, she is aptly described as 'the most aggressive of all the Gods' (p.18): Helen, however, offers an equally valid interpretation when she states that Athena's armour signifies her function which was to 'keep order' and to 'keep man temperate'; her war-cries, she contests, were in fact '*Warning* cries', this linking with her 'most famous actions' which were 'about *restraint*' (p.19). Both

Edward and Helen are essentially correct since both implications lie at the heart of Athena's symbolization.

However, the ambiguity associated with Athena necessarily becomes transplanted onto Helen (at least, in Edward's mind), as the snarl of Athena's thwarted rage when Perseus rejects her transmits itself to our interpretation of Helen's story and actions. Hers, after all, is a purely subjective account of her relationship with Edward and we should perhaps be as wary of accepting her version of events as we are wary of accepting Salieri's distorted vision: in both cases, the histories that we, the audience, see are focused through a point of view. In addition, since Helen is, throughout her account, leading up to persuading Philip to publish a damning indictment of Edward's life, her agenda is finally revealed as hostile and her narrative delivered in this mind-set: Philip had been correct when, in his first encounter with Helen, he had suggested that those who live in Greece too long 'have revenge on the brain' (p.6).

Any audience lured towards a straightforward acceptance of Helen's narrative enactment of her life with Edward should, therefore, exercise caution and should bear the ambiguity associated with Athena firmly in mind: this is a Goddess, after all, who wears a 'double-face' as Perseus reveals when he '*takes off her mask – to reveal another mask underneath, smiling horribly*' (p.66). From Edward's point of view, she is not, therefore, to be trusted and neither, by extension, is Helen. This is not to argue that Helen's story of her life with Edward should be rejected out of hand (there is, after all, no doubting her account of the cruelty implicit in Edward's 'revenge'): it is, however, to argue that the question of Helen's characterization and motivation is potentially rather less clear-cut than it may at first seem.

Where Helen is closely aligned with Athena, Edward is aligned with Perseus. Both 'heroes' are exiles from their own lands, Perseus being encased with his mother Danäe in a closed box and launched upon the waves, finally arriving at the island of Seriphos, Edward being part-Russian and ill at ease in contemporary England or, indeed, in any land where he lives (we find a strong echo here of Mark Askelon and his son).[13] Perseus, like Edward, rashly undertakes to fulfil a heroic deed, promising to acquire the head of the dreaded Gorgon as a pledge of loyalty to his stepfather, King Polydektes: Edward similarly promises Helen that he will complete a masterpiece play. Both require the aid of a benevolent saviour to

fulfil their promise, a saviour who will provide the necessary ma-
terials for the successful accomplishment of the deed. In Perseus'
case, this involves 'the Shoes of Swiftness', 'the Cap of Darkness'
(p.41), 'the Sickle of Adamant' and the 'Shield of Showing' (p.42): in
Edward's case, it involves the provision of emotional and financial
security and the utter devotion of Helen's self to him. Both Perseus
and Edward return to their Goddess initially triumphant and
reborn as 'heroes'.

Though Shaffer suggests that if he ever rewrites this play (as he
would like to do), he would erase the Perseus reference and substitute instead an invented mythological character, Perseus does
suggest interesting symbolic connections within the play and forms
useful parallels with Edward's character.[14] To begin with, both are
connected with darkness and thus with the unconscious realm,
Perseus having been born in a subterranean, lightless chamber,
Edward being associated with forms of 'blackness' recurrently emphasized throughout the play. For example, Edward talks of a
'blinding revelation' (p.81) and of 'worshipping blindly' (p.65),
Helen refers to a 'blackness' that deemed to fill the theatre even
before the action of *I.R.E.* had begun (p.65), and dwells on the
'darkness' that consumed Edward following his exile to Greece
(p.70). Further, she defines Edward as 'a dark man', this unmistakeably enforcing his alignment with threatening and potentially
savage unconscious realms (p.49). This chain of darknesses is
thrown into sharp relief by the references to forms of light which
litter the play, largely gathering around Helen in her alignment
with Athena whose name, in Greek, 'meant originally the light of
the dawn, and finally, moral and intellectual light'.[15] Where Perseus
had been conceived in a shower of gold light sent by his father,
Zeus, Edward is similarly 'born' in the 'glinting' light of Helen's
persona (p.14 and throughout). However, since these references
often imply a menacing quality within the play (for example, in relation to the 'terrible bright' light of Greece, p.29), we should be reminded that the light with which Helen/Athena is connected may
be as ambiguous as the Goddess and her projection themselves.
Similarly, the darkness surrounding Edward may connote more
positive value than we initially suspect: Jungian notions of the conscious and its 'shadow' (neither unequivocally 'positive' or 'negative', as discussed in Chapter 6) are once more in evidence.

A second major connection between Edward and the Perseus
myth (which makes it so suited to this play) is the emphasis on

paralysis which the Gorgon adventure connotes. The Gorgon, Medusa, a mortal who loved Poseidon, was one of the three daughters of Phorkys and Keto; having met once with her lover in the temple of Athena, to the desecration of that building, Medusa had been punished by having her magnificent hair turned into snakes. Her ghastly face, when looked at directly, was said to turn the spectator to stone and the land on which she dwelt therefore became a barren, frozen wasteland – an 'Island of Immobility' (p.84).

As discussed in Chapter 4, Shaffer has used the idea of paralysis before in his work, frequently connecting it with an alienated protagonist whose removal from the sphere of 'Immediate Life' becomes signified through recurrent metaphors relating to immobility. In a play which centralizes the Gorgon myth, this metaphorical network achieves a new centrality. Edward dwells on his recognition of 'a kind of active paralysis' which immobilizes him creatively, preventing him not from writing, but from being able to complete what he is writing. This creative paralysis is subsequently extended into emotional and moral areas when Athena/Helen finally charges Perseus/Edward with himself creating an 'Island of Immobility' (p.84): here, Helen makes use of the Gorgon myth to draw Edward's attention to the fact that his emotional paralysis has stranded them both in a self-created wasteland of frozen psychological attitude and emotion.

The incorporation of the Perseus myth therefore serves several purposes, all of which alert us to dominant currents within the play. Both 'heroes' are exiles and are associated with blackness, paralysis, with a Goddess who must be obeyed, and with the 'dread monsters with which the imagination peoples darkness' (the 'monsters', in Edward's case, being the archaic call of violent instinct). As in all the myths outlined here, Shaffer effects a skilful chain of reference where the characters of Edward and Helen, and the events in which they are involved, are finely integrated with a mythological subtext. The ancient tales of Agamemnon and Clytemnestra, Athena and Perseus are re-enacted through contemporary heroes and the two worlds are drawn into close proximity as a result: the assumed breach between them is thus eradicated.

The integration of these mythological impulses is effected not simply on the dramatic level in this play (plot, characterization, event, and so on), but in the very staging of the drama which moves the audience towards an altered state of experience. The ramp (mentioned above) extends from a wall of lava from the back of the stage set, converting the naturalistic (if abstract) villa into a site of mythological encounter: a *'golden walkway'* springs from the ancient rock to connect *'the imagined mythological world to the middle of Edward's desk'*, this desk being converted from a piece of funiture and into an ancient metaphorical forum (p.40).[16] The ramp is lowered four times during the course of the play, releasing the projections of Athena, Perseus, the Empress Irene and Edward into the contemporary world, each shrouded in masks, their voices amplified around the theatre, and each accompanied by menacing strains of music or chant. Shaffer's mythological network of allusion thus becomes a physical reality enacted within a naturalistic, contemporary world.[17]

Though these scenes are the most obvious examples of mythological encounter enacted in the traditions of Greek theatre in the play, less overt examples of similar devices are everywhere apparent. We find a recurrent 'doubling' of characters, Edward and Helen providing the voices for Perseus and Athena, cooks and maids transforming themselves before our eyes into 'sexy and attractively dressed young girls' (p.53). In addition, we notice that the mental world of a mythological mind-set is created via a range of staging devices which include sharp, sudden changes of light intensity, and sounds moving from muted naturalism to amplified hyper-reality (for example, the sound of Edward cutting paper which gradually becomes so loud and so terrible that Helen must block her ears against it). The wild, sinister choreography of 'Clytemnestra's Stamp', with its rhythmic ferocity and *'high falsetto scream'* (p.31), similarly connects with the violence of the mythological context. In addition, the colour red frequently permeates the stage, usually effected via lighting effects as during Edward's Dance of Rightful Stamping when the tint of an intensifying red *'appears to stain his chest and towel'*, foreshadowing his death (p.31): similarly, the stage set of *Prerogative* involves the projection of a stained-glass window of *'a primitive crucifixion on a blazing red background'* (p.54). All, of course, physically suggests the mental world of ancient bloodshed and recreates the mind-set that produced and gave meaning to it.

These, and similar, techniques are designed with the sole purpose of extending the limits of mythological allusion in the play into the territories of mental, emotional and psychological experience. Through the staging of the drama, Shaffer ensures that the psychic world of ancient instinct is replicated before the contemporary audience to whom such allusion, being buried in the collective unconscious, may otherwise seem remote. Shaffer insists that this audience must understand the meaning of the myths presented here viscerally if it is to fully understand them intellectually: in so doing, he demands that the audience confront the shadows triggered in its own inherited, primeval memory and acknowledge their existence (and connotations) at a conscious level.

Having examined the way in which Shaffer integrates mythological elements into his play at the dramatic and theatrical level, we can now move on to an investigation of the connections between these myths and the central moral debate presented here. This debate claimed the vast majority of newspaper column inches when the play was first performed in London in December 1992 since it plugged into an emotively topical issue. The majority of critics, however, offering only a partial and emotive reading of the play, made a serious error in minimizing the role of myth in the ethical exploration presented here and were thus guilty of misinterpreting its dialectic.

Peter Hall notes: 'Shaffer has always divided the critics. His blend of genuine popular drama with subjects that question the conventional morality of the age has constantly aroused extravagant fury as well as extravagant praise'.[18] In this case, Shaffer's examination of 'conventional morality' involved asking questions such as 'what do we *feel* about terrorists? How can we deal with them – and with our feelings of rage and revenge?'.[19] It should be stressed that the issue of terrorism is by no means the sole focus of such questions in this play, but since both Hall and the critical establishment emphasize its centrality, this discussion will follow suit.

Though terrorism, through the 'Irish question', hovers on the peripheral vision of modern English consciousness, there are times when the issue achieves an insistent voice, usually following some event or 'outrage' which catapults it into urgency. Two such recent incidents include the Enniskillen Remembrance Day bombing in November 1987 (referred to within the play as the motivation for Edward's writing of *I.R.E.*) and the Warrington bomb which exploded days before the first night of *The Gift of the Gorgon*, killing a young boy. Given the proximity of this terrorist attack to the play, Shaffer's drama achieved a contemporaneity which intensified an already guaranteed focus upon it. Shaffer, with some bitterness, notes that not one critic mentioned the innovative staging or the reinvention of theatrical grammar involved in his drama, so focused were they on the play's underlying, richly topical debate.[20]

This debate revolves around two conflicting moral positions. Bitterly opposed attitudes towards the morality of revenge are voiced through the two central protagonists, Helen and Edward, whose positions are informed by their interpretation of mythic structures and ancient attitudes. The central question of the play can be paraphrased as, 'should acts of outrage be revenged through blood, or does revenge inevitably lead to a cycle of destruction which maims more than it cures'? Related to this is the matter of whether there is such a thing as an 'unforgivable act' (p.62), an act which projects the transgressor beyond the pale of pardon. These questions are initially posited in relation to mythic or historic tales of violence and horror (the Empress Irene, Cromwell), but focus increasingly on contemporary acts of terrorism as the play develops: an ongoing history of human violence and retribution is therefore presented.

Edward's belief that revenge purifies not only man but society as a whole is inherited from the forms and attitudes of Greek theatre. In the ancient world, he perceives, the theatre was an arena where a communal purgation of violent instincts could be effected (the connection with Artaudian doctrine, as outlined in Chapter 2, should be clear); it was a powerful quasi-religious forum where the audience gathered 'in communion' to witness the 'sacred and indispensable' (p.22).[21] As the Dionysian representative in the play, 'Extreme Edward' (p.17) places his faith in the dramatic ethos that this necessarily involves, insisting that his plays should re-enact and revalidate the cleansing violence of ancient forms. Though, as Helen points out, this drama 'never showed violence onstage', the Greeks realizing that 'Measure is everything' (p.47), it nevertheless presented a mental world of retribution and extreme response wherein terror was central to a clear moral scheme. Responding to this view, Edward declares that it is 'the playwright's duty to appal' by forcing an audience 'out of moral catalepsy' (p.57) and, to these ends, he aims to create a modern theatre that reclaims the moral power intrinsic to the logic of ancient drama by staging plays that confront man's terrors, explore the dark regions of man's psyche, and that allow man's instincts to walk murderously over the stage. Theatre that refuses this task, he asserts, is symptomatic of a contemporary society dying of 'avoidance' (p.57): 'avoidance', in short, of its unconscious urges.

In Edward's view, theatre should therefore express and validate the revenge ethic which, in modern, 'civilized' man, lies dormant but silenced. A society that ignores the archaic voice which stipulates that only through revenge can the 'slate' be 'cleaned' will be destroyed by a corrosive cancer of repressed hate. Edward's is, essentially, an Old Testament philosophy ('an eye for an eye') that sees 'rightness' in Clytemnestra's planned, ritual revenge which offered 'sacrifice for sacrifice' (p.15); similarly, such a philosophy sees 'justice' in the Empress Irene's blinding of her son since, 'What fitter punishment could there be for a man who made war on pictures – to have all pictures taken away from him for ever?' (p.47). For Edward, then, revenge purifies and cleanses man and society; it responds to rather than represses instinct: above all, in Edward's terms, 'pure revenge […] means pure justice' (p.16).

For Helen, however, revenge is 'not justice' and can never be (p.16). Helen is, perhaps, the clearest and most persuasive carrier of Apollonian impulses that we have ever seen in Shaffer's work, a character who personifies the archetypal values of moderation and restraint.[22] Reared by a father who rejects the ethos of war and violence in favour of peace and reconciliation, Helen has inherited the belief that violence simply breeds more violence and that in revenge lies only the perpetuation of an inadequate, destructive cycle. Her reading of the Agamemnon myth, for example, would point out that Clytemnestra's revenge leads to Orestes' revenge which leads in turn to the Furies' attempted revenge; only when the voice of peace is heard in Apollo and Athena's pleas is the flow of blood stemmed. In addition, she would argue that there can be no moral difference between the revenger who murders (Clytemnestra) and he who murders the revenger (Orestes). After all, as Helen states in reference to the Perseus myth, the man who kills the Gorgon, *'becomes* the Gorgon!' (p.84).

Throughout the play, she combats Edward's position with force and conviction, arguing that a society which accepts the precepts of violence, blood and revenge cannot be said to operate on any grounds of moral, psychological or emotional health. Edward, of course, argues exactly the opposite. His reading of the Agamemnon myth centralizes the 'hallowed, health-giving peace of Clytemnestra' (p.60), and that society has been similarly 'cleansed', he would argue, is implied by the fact that it is subsequently launched into a period of peace. Similarly, for Edward, Perseus is a hero who rightly kills a dreaded killer and is venerated for so doing. The opposition between them, then, is profound: Edward's position constitutes a Dionysian demand for extreme reaction to extreme horrors, a reaction which is capable of purging man and society; Helen proposes an Apollonian plea for moderation and understanding in the face of obscenity, a call for restraint which guards man and society from the archaic taint of blood-soaked instinct.

The connection between myth and morality within this ethical opposition is clear in relation to the Agamemnon and Perseus myths, but it is also manifested in the terms in which Edward argues his position. The ambiguity associated with the Goddess Athena, and the projection of this ambiguity onto Helen, has been outlined above, and it is significant that Edward configures his arguments against Helen's ethos upon the double-aspect that he perceives in both. Edward equates Helen's rationalist philosophy with personal and societal castration, constantly returning to the idea of emasculation. When he refers to a 'deballed' society (p.16), metaphorically castrated through its refusal of the revenge ethic, he initiates a later connection he will make between Helen (upholder of the 'castrating' values) and his own situation in which he also feels himself to be castrated, paralysed and disempowered: when Helen interprets Edward's inability to finish a play as evidence that he is simply keen to delay judgement, Edward's extreme response (which suggests the justness of her comment) is delivered in a classic 'masculine' offensive: 'Just cut them off, why don't you? [*Grabbing his testicles.*] It's what you want to do, isn't it?...I presume that's what you finally want to do!' (p.36).

Though a rare comic moment in the play, this episode also alerts us to Edward's sense that he is being emasculated at the hands of the rational, austere Helen/Athena who seems to him to represent the twin roles of saviour and judge.[23] He is torn between worship and loathing as a result. For Edward, Helen/Athena has come to personify those values which seem to immobilize him at a personal and creative level, and which he perceives are condemning society to a state of timid passivity – hence his question: 'Can't you see it has become a vice, your fairness? How it's castrating us?' (p.59). For Edward, then, the restraint and moderation inscribed within Athena in one of her manifestations connotes all the 'deballed' hesitations of a society characterized by 'liquefied defeat' (p.34) while Helen, in his terms, carries this castrating potential into the heart of the personal and creative sphere.

The connections between mythic allusion and the moral debate presented here thus multiply at every level. We have seen such an ethical conflict before in Shaffer's work; in *Shrivings*, the moral battlelines are clearly drawn between Mark Askelon's belief that man is essentially 'unimprovable' and will always revert to his base instinct, and between Gideon's belief that man can, through an act of will, defeat the archaic call to bloodshed. In the earlier play, of course, Gideon's creed was revealed to be a self-deluding fraud, and the philosopher emerged from the drama fatally discredited. In *The Gift of the Gorgon* too, the ethos proposed by Jarvis is undermined by the fact that he fails to convert his beliefs into actions, refusing to forgive Edward for stealing his daughter from him. However, in Helen, the humanist claim is challenged, wavers, but finally emerges intact: brought face-to-face with an 'unforgivable act', Helen can finally forgive. The effort this costs her is enormous and she is torn in two by it, but her final rejection of the revenge ethic suggests that the essentially Apollonian plea for reason, order and restraint (emanating from the conscious realm of man's psyche) at last stands triumphant on Shaffer's stage.

This constitutes an entirely new development in Shaffer's drama. In earlier plays, the Dionysian voice of passion, excess and unconscious instinct has been defeated but fundamentally celebrated, while the Apollonian representative of moderation and emotional numbness is shown to be spiritually, morally and emotionally shattered by his hollow 'victory'. Here, however, the position is reversed as not only the Dionysian, but also the ethos he expounds, is categorically rejected. But the matter of where the audience stands in relation to this movement is an interesting question.

In Shaffer's earlier dramas, we saw how the conflicts centralized in the plays resolve themselves into 'two kinds of Right', this forcing the audience to mediate in a complex debate where neither 'side' can be unequivocally dismissed. In *The Gift of the Gorgon*, however, the matter becomes more complex still: the contemporary audience has been reared with an intellectual acceptance of Helen's position and understands at a conscious level that 'blood' does not solve the problem of violence. In this sense, it accepts that Helen is intellectually 'right' where Edward is almost certainly 'wrong'. In emotional and psychological terms, however, the waters become rather more muddied. Faced with 'outrages' such as the Enniskillen and Warrington bombings, the archaic voice demanding retribution is naturally called forth from the unconscious, and the audience cannot help but respond to it.

Peter Shaffer describes how, when Edward and Helen each argue their cases following the Enniskillen incident, the tension in the auditorium is tangible as the audience tears itself between conscious intellect and unconscious instinct in its response.[24] But one of the several achievements of the play is that it succeeds in doing what Edward's theatre had signally failed to do: it brings an audience face-to-face with its darker, violent instincts, forces it to consider them seriously, and purges the audience of them. The play does not deny the validity of these instincts, but it shows clearly where they inevitably lead. Edward's form of 'right' cannot, we know, be morally sanctioned and can be validated only in emotional terms: the majority of us, though, would be less than truthful if we denied that Edward's position has never been entertained by us in the face of some atrocity. However, when this position is both verbalized and enacted before us in Edward's play *I.R.E.* (which illustrates his philosophy in brutal terms) and in the 'Sacred Gift of Vengeance' that Edward bestows, as he insists, on Helen's behalf (p.88), when we witness his ethos in concrete rather than in abstract terms, Helen's philosophy becomes the only feasible alternative.

This becomes emphatically the case when both the protagonist's ritual murder in *I.R.E.* and Edward's own revenge upon Helen chill the audience with their planned cruelty: a momentary loss of control leading to horrific violence it can perhaps understand and even accept, but calculated cruelty (whether 'cleansing' or not) is another matter.[25] The phrase 'in cold blood' begins to carry connotations that are far from 'sanative' (p.59). In this light, it becomes clear that there is no moral, emotional or intellectual difference between the terrorist act Edward's play condemns and the revenge taken for it by his protagonist. Similarly, there is no moral, emotional or intellectual difference between Edward's planned revenge upon Helen's behalf (and upon Helen *herself*) and Helen's calculated attempt to orchestrate her own revenge through Philip. This, Helen and Shaffer's audience must ultimately accept. Representing the unconscious impulse towards blood in Edward, Shaffer leads the audience through an investigation of it, teaches the audience to listen to and respect it, and finally persuades the audience to reject it. As in Helen's assessment of *Hamlet*, Shaffer's play thus reaches 'beyond the *need* for revenge' and takes a 'naturally blood-thirsty audience to that same point' (p.16).

However, Shaffer warns that this rejection of 'blood' is neither simple nor unequivocal. As indicated above, throughout the course of the play, while Helen has been stating her non-violent philosophy to both Philip and Edward, she has, it transpires, been attempting to persuade Philip of the 'rightness' of revenging his father. Edward has finally taught her that the 'unforgivable act' may exist after all, and he has shown her that such an 'act' calls for slate-cleaning revenge. Her desire to 'erase' his work, his memory and his still dominant voice which urges her from beyond the grave, originates in her bitter recognition that Edward has defeated her cool, rational logic and has awakened her to the insistent demands of her own un-conscious urges. However, when Philip (a non-revenging Orestes) refuses to be the instrument of her retribution, Helen is forced to pause and to engage in a fight between intellect and instinct. Finally, her screamed 'I FORGIVE!' (p.94) indicates that, even in the face of personal atrocity, her ethos cannot be defeated. Her agony at this point suggests not that her belief is ultimately in doubt, but that the 'battle for deliverance' between her conscious mind and her uncon-scious instincts involved in accepting this conclusion is overwhelm-ing.[26] The extremity of her state validates her earlier assertion that 'to kill our own passion when it's wrong' is a passion in itself (p.60). It is not an easy option, a surrender to inactivity or to passivity: Helen's scream is *aggressive* in its connotations.

In a Brechtian manoeuvre, the audience is forced to think about what it has seen and heard on stage far beyond the limits of the action, and to investigate the nature of its responses and of the judgements it has made. The archaic voice of revenge is not, after all, easily silenced, but nor is the voice of conscious reason. For the first time in Shaffer's work, one 'kind of Right' has clearly tri-umphed and, again for the first time, this 'Right' has not been focused in emotional and psychological territories of instinct. Helen, the arch-Apollonian, emerges from the play as the final carrier of moral meaning; she is, by now, a battered, screaming wreck, but her ethos, insisting upon the moral validity of conscious response, though shaken, nevertheless survives. We could finally conclude that her form of intellectual 'Right' has ultimately become a form of 'emotional' 'Right' where Edward's gory revenge, planned and enacted on her behalf, has become a form of fundamental emotional 'wrong'.

The moral scheme in this play is thus highly complex: here we find Shaffer's familiar technique of planting two opposing beliefs in two opposing protagonists, but where, in earlier plays, difference melted into likeness in an imitation of a dialectic which presented 'two kinds of Right' and which mimicked the dualism inherent in the human psyche, here, opposition remains necessarily diametric. Launched between the conflicting positions, the audience must respond either to intellect or to instinct but it is refused the option of evasion. The 'unforgivable act', when finally presented to the audience in the form of Edward's cruel revenge enacted on Helen's behalf, brings the debate to its crisis. But the audience must ultimately concede, like Helen, that when man accepts that the 'unforgivable' can exist, he simultaneously 'creates Hell'.[27]

Shaffer's achievement in this play is to give voice to an urgent, silent contemporary dilemma; in so doing, he offers modern theatre as a medium in which such issues can be debated as they were in ancient drama. The mythological infrastructure of the play is essential to this project since it not only forges direct physical connections between modern man and the ancient world (in terms of staging devices, etc.), but also extends these connections into mental territories. Ancient instinct does not change over the course of millenia, argues Edward: man's urges remain essentially stable. The myths of Agamemnon, Athena and Perseus are appropriated in the interests of corroborating this statement and are used to forge absolute links between ancient and contemporary man, society and situation. These myths, positioned one on top of the other, are woven into the play so that parallels become concrete through a network of allusion. The path through history is forged through the centralization of Empress Irene and Cromwell, and is then brought up to date through the debate focusing on terrorism, a syndrome for contemporary issues. *The Gift of the Gorgon*, then, extends Shaffer's reach towards myth (initiated in earlier plays such as *Equus*) into new and innovative territories, the underlying project being to trace a clear path between the mental worlds that inform man's essential condition.

At the centre of the play stands a group of massive moral questions which ask the audience to examine the nature of its psyche and society. As Sheridan Morley notes, 'Shaffer has always been able, even in the heart of the commercial theatre jungle, to engage an audience in adult and literate debate about the way we live now', and the relentless scrutiny noted here reaches a new intensity in this play.[28] The questions the playwright asks here are deeply uncomfortable since they involve confronting terrifying regions of unconscious instinct that we would rather ignore; further, these instincts are not simply dismissed out of hand but are respected, verbalized and examined: as such, an urgent, yet repressed, contemporary debate dominates the stage and insists on being heard.

The critical battering that this play received at the hands of some critics derived at least in part from a reluctance to confront, or even to refuse to acknowledge, the archaic voice that screams from Shaffer's play. This resulted in misreadings of the ethical debate centralized here since most responses ignored the profound connection in the drama between myth and morality. Both elements had appeared on Shaffer's stage before, myth being centralized in *Equus* and an ethical opposition being centralized in *Shrivings*, but never had the two been conjoined in such absolute terms. If we mistake the mythological allusions, we mistake also the moral debate, and this is the trap into which many critics fell. The purpose of this chapter has been to ensure that readers do not make a similar error.

The Gift of the Gorgon will certainly increase in reputation and approval as the years go by.[29] While it would be misjudged to label the play Shaffer's 'masterpiece', its innovative revision of theatrical grammar and its bold dialectic demand sustained and serious attention. As the 1990s unfold, the playwright's insistence that the stage is a forum for the exploration of fundamental ethical, psychological and metaphysical questions shows no signs of becoming any less urgent.

9

Conclusion

This discussion has analysed the plays of Peter Shaffer from several points of view and has presented a variety of ways in which they can be interpreted. The concern throughout, however, has been to emphasize the point that Shaffer is a writer both for and of the theatre, producing ideas and words which rely on the theatrical environment for the achievement of their full emotional, psychological and intellectual effect. Here, this point will be enforced for a final time through a brief analysis of the adaptation of Shaffer's stage work to the cinema. In this discussion it will be argued that the transfer of this drama into another medium fails aesthetically purely because it belongs quite specifically to the theatrical arena and to nowhere else.

Shaffer's astonishing ability to draw audiences (evident even from his earliest plays) has proved attractive to film executives who see certain profit in the adaptation of his material to the cinema. In all, six cinematic 'treatments' of his dramas have been released, the very term suggesting a perceived corrective to the 'theatricality' (a purely pejorative word in film circles) of the original stage material. Each 'treatment' has, however, proved that 'theatricality' is entirely the point of Shaffer's dramatic success. All have attempted to 'naturalize' the highly metaphorical environments and ideas of the stage originals and all have proved disastrous either commercially or aesthetically (and often both) in adaptation. As Shaffer himself comments: 'Really, I think my films are best left alone. They are all terrible...They bore and depress me, even in retrospect'.[1]

Two central problems lie at the heart of the resistance of Shaffer's work to the cinematic environment: firstly, film is, above all, a literal medium; it does not accept easily either metaphor or ambiguity, elements upon which Shaffer's theatre relies. Secondly, a glass barrier separates the drama from the reception of it so that direct communication (physical and psychological) can never be achieved in this arena; Shaffer's drama, as has been argued in this book, centralizes the communal responses of an audience who engage emotionally and imaginatively with the images created in the 'magic' space of live theatre – when engagement can only be achieved at 'second hand', this communal 'magic' cannot materialize. So, despite the undisputed appeal of Shaffer's drama in the theatre, the very characteristics that create this appeal cannot possibly be transferred to the cinematic medium. The adaptation is bound, in short, to fail simply as a result of relative environmental restrictions.

This point has obviously never occurred to the film producers and directors who have each believed that they hold the key to unlocking the secret of adapting Shaffer's plays to film; despite repeated failures over the years, a further attempt is sure to be made. The first of these attempts was made in 1962 when a dully uninspired adaptation of *Five Finger Exercise* appeared in the cinemas; of all the plays that were later to seek transfer to the cinema, this should potentially have been the most successful aesthetically since the overwhelming naturalism of its form did not militate against filmic representational convention to the extent that some of the later dramas were bound to do. Its 'success', however, was hardly dazzling in whatever terms we could define that word and the adaptation received only a mixed and unexcited response from critics and audiences alike.

Remarkable then, that it should have been followed in 1968 by the attempt to adapt *The Royal Hunt of the Sun*, a play which relied heavily on non-realistic elements such as mime and narration. Its means of communication were thoroughly metaphorical and herein lay its power; as Alan Brien noted, the mimed climb of the mountain of ice, enacted 'in blinding light against a wooden wall', was as 'exhausting and exhilarating as any Hollywood sequence filmed by cameras hanging over the edge of a real precipice'.[2] The film, however, had no choice but to literalize the ascent as the theatrical power of the metaphor that Brien responded to had been made redundant when the 'real precipice' could, of course, be filmed. Combined with the loss of metaphor, a 'mishmash of acting and directorial styles' produced a truly 'dreadful' film that is best forgotten.[3]

But this fiasco did not deter the makers of the next adaptation which appeared in 1972; this was an attempt to transfer Shaffer's delicate one-act play *The Private Ear* to the big screen under the dubious title, *The Pad (and How to Use It)*. This was again a disaster for altogether different reasons than the previous failures: it could be argued that Shaffer's intimate grouping of characters, confined within a grubby living area and involving only three players, was simpy too 'small' for the screen, while the communal identification which arose with Bob in the theatrical auditorium could not materialize in the impersonal atmosphere of the cinema. Further, Shaffer's crafted dialogue had been mangled out of all recognition in the 'treatment' process, Penelope Gilliat deciding that the 'excruciating film' that resulted had been 'drawn and quartered' by a 'script-conference of boneheads' who had wrecked the delicate metaphors of the stage original.[4]

Nor did the next adaptation, *The Public Eye*, also appearing in 1972, fare any better, being described by a critic known only as 'J.C.' as a 'sad travesty'.[5] Five years later, however, hopes were riding high for Sydney Lumet's adaptation of the worldwide hit *Equus*, especially as its cast included such 'heavyweight' actors as Richard Burton, Joan Plowright and Peter Firth (Burton and Firth having played the roles of Dysart and Strang to great acclaim on stage). In addition, its screenplay was written by Shaffer himself who had learned to his cost the perils of entrusting scriptwriters with his intricate material. The film, however, when it finally emerged, was disappointing. C.J. Gianakaris correctly notes that the main problem with the adaptation was its 'extreme literalness'[6] where the 'stable of Superhorses to stalk through the mind', far from suggesting archetypal figures of the communal unconscious, became instead a group of ordinary horses led by a chestnut mare.[7] In the theatre, Equus could be represented as a metaphorical and stylized nightmare paradigm, but in the cinema, a horse is a horse is a horse.

Shaffer was himself bitterly disappointed with the failure to capture on film the levels of imaginative and psychological experience that had made *Equus* so remarkable a play in the theatrical arena. In particular he expressed dissatisfaction with the 'visual side' of the film, complaining that he had done 'much more imaginative work' on the script 'than was shot'.[8] Little surprise, then, that it was seven years before he ventured into the realms of adaptation again, this time working with Milos Forman on the adaptation of *Amadeus*, a play that, as Peter Hall reports, captivated Forman the first time he saw it on stage at the National Theatre in London.[9] This time, Shaffer insisted on a close collaboration with his director whose adaptational technique involved 'tearing the play apart and putting it together in a new form'.[10]

The result of this strategy was that *Amadeus* on screen bore little resemblance to *Amadeus* on stage. Shaffer himself prefers to regard the adaptation as a 'parallel work'[11] to the stage play, one which contains, as he states elsewhere, 'coarsenesses [...] which I deplore'.[12] Such 'coarsenesses' undoubtedly include the expansion in the role of Mozart and his family (to the cost of the focus on Salieri) and the simplification of the conflict at stake in the stage play. Where in the theatre Salieri's battle had been with a mocking, unjust God, and where the aptly named Amadeus had been the battleground, in the cinema the battle became an unsophisticated tale of professional rivalry. In addition, the audience's relationship with the sly mediocrity Salieri, so close on stage, became an impossibility in the cinema not only as a result of the loss of the live medium, but also as a result of the decision to replace the audience as Salieri's 'confessor' with a third-party priest who fulfilled this role. Meaning and emotional identification were forfeit. With the narrator as ringmaster and stage-manager displaced, the direct channel of communication between Salieri and the audience was resolutely closed while the disturbing intensity of man's war against God, so powerful in the theatre, was made redundant. As a result, those who have seen the adaptation of *Amadeus* have little or no idea of what the original stage version was about, and have still less idea of the emotional and imaginative power Shaffer's work ignites in its natural home – the theatre.

To date, there have been no more adaptations of Shaffer's work to the cinema though plans are afoot for a film version of *Lettice & Lovage*. Given the bitter experiences of the previous efforts, however, it is a matter of debate whether this can be a good idea. Shaffer's plays constitute, to paraphrase Peter Hall, an invitation to imagine; they resist the literal and thrive on metaphor, transporting audiences to levels of experience that transcend the concrete and the rational.[13] To persuade them to do otherwise is to destroy the tangible psychological forcefield they create in the theatre and is to attempt to mould them into a form they will always reject.

If the theatre is, in the words of Edward Damson (here clearly articulating a sentiment close to the playwright's heart), a place of 'faith and True Astonishment', then the plays of Peter Shaffer similarly belong in the territories of intense, irrational experience.[14] For this reason, all attempts to interpret this work solely in intellectual terms will lead to partial analysis since the whole point of Shaffer's theatre is to access unconscious areas of response. We can, in other words, explain by way of semiotics, performance analysis, or psychoanalytic theory why certain images or passages of dialogue transmit such power on stage, but this is always to avoid discussion of reactions which perhaps can never be articulated in words. In addition, analysing these reactions (even in non-academic terms) only drives them further away.

Finally, we have to admit that analysis can take us only so far along the road to a full understanding of this playwright's work: at a certain and obvious point, it is necessary to surrender to experience. Peter Shaffer's drama allows entry into an imaginative realm in which dramatic craft and theatrical skill conspire to elevate an audience from the daily and into the transcendent; as such, a theatre is created in which we find, in Lotte's words, 'Enlargement for shrunken souls. Enlivenment for dying spirits. Enlightenment for dim, prosaic eyes'.[15] In a plastic postmodern world of stock, numbed response, this is surely Shaffer's supreme gift to his audience.

Notes

CHAPTER 1

1. Simon Trussler, 'General Editor's Introduction', in Virginia Cooke and Malcolm Page (eds), *File on Shaffer* (London: Methuen, 1987), p.6.
2. Peter Shaffer, quoted in Oleg Kerensky, *The New British Drama: Fourteen Playwrights Since Osborne and Pinter* (London: Hamish Hamilton, 1977), p.58.
3. Peter Shaffer, 'A Personal Essay', *The Royal Hunt of the Sun*, ed. Peter Cairns (London: Longman, 1983), p.vii.
4. Walter Kerr, quoted in Virginia Cooke and Malcolm Page, 1987, p.16.
5. Peter Shaffer, interview with the author, 22 November 1996, Chichester Festival Theatre.
6. John Russell Taylor, *Peter Shaffer* (London: Longman, 1974), p.32.
7. John Dexter himself was fully aware that the success of Shaffer's plays had often been attributed to his directorial skills. He was obviously responding to this claim when, as Peter Hall reports, he demanded a share of Shaffer's receipts for *Amadeus* if he agreed to direct it. Since this was unprecedented and unreasonable, Shaffer refused and Hall directed the play at the National Theatre in his place. Dexter had, in short, believed the critics who argued that, without him, Shaffer's dramas would undoubtedly fail. The success of *Amadeus* in front of worldwide audiences (achieved without Dexter's input) suggests the spuriousness of this claim. See John Goodwin (ed.), *Peter Hall's Diaries: The Story of a Dramatic Battle* (London: Hamish Hamilton, 1983), p.445.
8. The whole debate revolving around Shaffer's supposed habit of taking liberties with historical fact is largely an irrelevant smokescreen. Critics who quibble with Shaffer's historical accuracy (see James Fenton's attacks on *Amadeus*, for example) are actually objecting not to inaccuracy in itself, but to the uncomfortable sensation of having preconceptions questioned.

   In relation to this issue, Shaffer himself comments that the playwright has to be 'faithful to a vision of some kind which does consort with historical fact'; he adds that he had 'read almost everything that was published about Mozart before I started *Amadeus*', and that 'every scene in the play has its basis in truth *except* for the final confrontation between them' (which arose from the need to provide a dramatic conclusion). He finally interprets much of the hostility that greeted this de-mythologized creature as emanating from a communal desire for 'sentimental mythology in our creators', a desire which resisted the essential truth of Shaffer's representation of the musical genius. Peter Shaffer, interview with the author, 22 November 1996.
9. It is worth pointing out that Tom Stoppard (like Shaffer, a skilled and popular wordsmith and dramatic craftsman) is similarly prone to this split between audience approval and critical hostility.

10. Peter Shaffer, interview with the author, 22 November 1996.
11. Peter Shaffer, interview with the author, 22 November 1996.
12. Peter Shaffer quoted in Virginia Cooke and Malcolm Page (eds), 1987, p.42.
13. Peter Shaffer, quoted in Virginia Cooke and Malcolm Page (eds), 1987, pp.41–2.
14. Peter Shaffer, interview with the author, 22 November 1996.
15. Peter Shaffer, interviewed by Brian Connell, 'The Two Sides of Theatre's Agonized Perfectionist', *The Times*, 28 April 1980, p.7.
16. Peter Shaffer, quoted by Gene A. Plunka, *Peter Shaffer: Roles, Rites and Rituals in the Theater* (London: Associated University Press, 1988), p.209.
17. Peter Shaffer, quoted by Oleg Kerensky, 1977, p.57.
18. Peter Shaffer, interviewed by Brian Connell, 1980, p.7.
19. Peter Shaffer, interviewed by Brian Connell, 1980, p.7.
20. Martin Esslin, 'Drama and the Media in Britain', *Modern Drama*, 28 (1985), 99–109, p.109.
21. Oleg Kerensky, 1977, p.32.
22. Peter Shaffer quoted in Oleg Kerensky, 1977, p.58.
23. Peter Shaffer, 'Labels Aren't for Playwrights', *Theatre Arts*, February 1960, 20–1, p.20.
24. Shaffer is himself an extremely gifted pianist and music plays a significant part in his dramas in both theatrical and dramatic terms. This point will be returned to in later discussions.
25. Alan Brien, review of *The Royal Hunt of the Sun*, quoted in Gareth Lloyd-Evans and Barbara Lloyd-Evans (eds), *Plays in Review 1956–1980: British Drama and the Critics* (London: Batsford Academic and Educational, 1985), p.127.
26. Bernard Levin, 'Yes, It's the Greatest Play in My Lifetime', *Daily Mail*, 10 December 1964, p.18.
27. Shaffer adds that similar 'blocks' have occurred throughout his career, and readily admits that a recent problem has been 'finding a subject that really engaged my attention to the degree of devoting two or three creative years' work to it'. Peter Shaffer, interview with the author, 22 November 1996.
28. Christopher Ford, 'The *Equus* Stampede', *The Guardian*, 20 April 1976, p.8.
29. Shaffer was also awarded the CBE in 1987, together with the Hamburg Shakespeare Prize.
30. To complete this overview of Shaffer's writing career, it should be noted that, in 1994, he succeeded the producer Michael Codron as Cameron Mackintosh Professor of Contemporary Theatre at St Catherine's College, Oxford. Professors, who are leading members of the professional theatre, are appointed for one year. In early 1995, a heavily revised version of *Yonadab* was presented by Oxford University Dramatic Society in a highly successful run at the Oxford Playhouse with students taught by Shaffer during his tenure at the University.
31. Since 1965, Shaffer has divided his time equally between New York and London, spending half the year living in each city.

32. John Russell Taylor, *Anger and After: A Guide to the New British Drama* (London: Methuen, 1962), p.178. Taylor also raises the interesting point that Shaffer, being born in 1926, is 'three or four years older than John Osborne, Harold Pinter and John Arden, two or three years younger than Robert Bolt, Brendan Behan and John Mortimer'. As a result, Taylor argues, Shaffer belongs fully to neither 'camp'. John Russell Taylor, *Peter Shaffer* (London: Longman, 1974), p.3.
33. John Russell Taylor, 1974, p.3.
34. C.J. Gianakaris, *Peter Shaffer* (London: Macmillan, 1992), p.106.
35. Gareth Lloyd-Evans and Barbara Lloyd-Evans (eds), 1985, p.188.
36. Peter Hall, in John Goodwin (ed.), 1983, p.473.
37. Simon Callow, *Being an Actor* (London: Penguin, 1984), pp.118–19.
38. Peter Hall, in John Goodwin (ed.), 1983, p.448. In response to Hall's description of *Amadeus* as a 'sincere right-wing play' in its celebration of the individuality of talent, Shaffer comments: 'Don't left-wing people celebrate the individuality of talent? Is it necessarily 'right-wing' to do so? Maybe what Hall means is that left-wing minds might raise the proposition that we're all equal in all fields of endeavour, and that's palpably untrue. We're all equal in *no* fields of endeavour, actually, except perhaps in our disappointment, rights, and somewhat in our needs'. In relation to the whole issue of his political affiliation and to the glib labelling of him as an 'Establishment playwright', Shaffer continues: 'I hardly think that *The Gift of the Gorgon* is a play written by an Establishment figure, nor for that matter *Equus*, or *The Royal Hunt of the Sun*. But critics have fixed mind-sets about issues like this and they have gone on for such a long time that they have actually set very hard in this case'. Peter Shaffer, interview with the author, 22 November 1996.
39. Peter Shaffer, *The Public Eye*, in Peter Shaffer, *Four Plays: The Private Ear, The Public Eye, White Liars, Black Comedy* (London: Penguin, 1981), p.86.

CHAPTER 2

1. Peter Shaffer, quoted in C.J. Gianakaris, *Peter Shaffer* (London: Macmillan, 1992), p.77
2. Peter Shaffer, quoted in Virginia Cooke and Malcolm Page (eds), *File on Shaffer* (London: Methuen, 1987), p.24.
3. John Russell Taylor, *Peter Shaffer* (London: Longman, 1974), p.32. Taylor's comment is also used as the title for this chapter.
4. Jack Kroll, 'Mozart and his Nemesis', *Newsweek*, 29 December 1980, p.58.
5. Peter Shaffer, *The Gift of the Gorgon* (London: Viking, 1993), p.51.
6. Peter Shaffer quoted in Gene A. Plunka, *Peter Shaffer: Roles, Rites and Rituals in the Theater* (London: Associated University Press, 1988), p.38.
7. Peter Shaffer, in Philip Oakes, 'Shaffer Gallops to Glory and Explains what Makes Him Run'. *Sunday Times*, 29 July 1973, p.33.

8. Peter Shaffer, quoted in Gene A. Plunka, 1988, p.40.
9. Peter Shaffer, *Black Comedy*, in Peter Shaffer, *Four Plays: The Private Ear, The Public Eye, White Liars, Black Comedy* (London: Penguin, 1981), p.196.
10. Peter Shaffer, *The Gift of the Gorgon*, 1993, p.22.
11. Peter Shaffer, in Peter Adam, 'Peter Shaffer on Faith, Farce and Masks', *The Listener*, 14 October 1976, pp.476–7. Commenting on this phenomenon 20 years later, Shaffer recalls that the audiences had asked: '"How do you get them to move, to change expression?" It sounded so pretentious to say "well, whose expression do you think it is?" It's projection: the audiences were hoping so much that Atahuallpa would rise that they were imbuing their own hope into whatever material those masks were made of. And this was done so *passionately*'. A form of transubstantiation, of a quasi-religious nature, resulted. Peter Shaffer, interview with the author, 22 November 1996, Chichester Festival Theatre.
12. Peter Shaffer, quoted in Gene A. Plunka, 1988, p.41.
13. These ideas are presented in Peter Shaffer's essay, 'The Cannibal Theatre', *Atlantic Monthly*, CCVI (October 1960), pp.48–50.
14. Peter Shaffer, quoted in C.J. Gianakaris, 1992, p.29.
15. Simon Callow, *Being an Actor*, (London: Penguin, 1984), p.106.
16. John Russell Taylor, *Anger and After: A Guide to the New British Drama* (London: Methuen, 1962), p.227.
17. Michael Wall, in Virginia Cooke and Malcolm Page (eds), 1987, p.15.
18. Walter Kerr, in Virginia Cooke and Malcolm Page (eds), 1987, p.16.
19. John Simon, in Virginia Cooke and Malcolm Page (eds), 1987, p.19.
20. Antonin Artaud, *The Theatre and Its Double: Essays by Antonin Artaud* [first published 1938], trans. by Victor Corti (London: John Calder, 1981), p.22.
21. Antonin Artaud, 1981, p.27.
22. Antonin Artaud, 1981, p.40, p.42. Gene A. Plunka decides that Artaud's theatrical agenda was motivated by 'a selfish reason'. Plunka notes: 'Throughout his life, Artaud claimed he was possessed by demons (he even worshipped Satan at one point) [...] For Artaud, theater was thera-peutic – a means of purging his soul of vices...'. It is in this context that the comment quoted here should perhaps be interpreted. Gene A. Plunka, 1988, p.207.
23. For a detailed description of the various staging strategies employed in this play, see C.J. Gianakaris, 1992, pp.86–8.
24. Antonin Artaud, 1981, p.62.
25. Antonin Artaud, 1981, p.81.
26. Antonin Artaud, 1981, pp.85–6.
27. Antonin Artaud, 1981, p.85.
28. Peter Shaffer, *The Royal Hunt of the Sun* (London: Penguin, 1981), p.90.
29. In a discussion of 'Theatre of Cruelty', Shaffer categorically insisted: 'When [Artaud] says the psychological drama is dead, this seems to me to be absolute rubbish – it has hardly begun'. Peter Shaffer, partici-pant in discussion, transcribed in 'Artaud for Artaud's Sake', *Encore*, no.49 (May–June 1964), pp.20–31, p.24. In addition, a weak link in Artaud's argument that Western psychological drama is redundant in

contemporary theatre is that the effect of his concept of 'theatrical language', which triggers the senses and leads to psychic elevation, cannot be described in terms *other than* the 'psychological'.

30. Peter Shaffer, 'A Note on the Text' [*Equus*], in Peter Shaffer, *Three Plays: Equus, Shrivings, Five Finger Exercise* (London: Penguin, 1976), p.199.

31. That Shaffer's attitude towards Artaudian theory is ambivalent is made clear in his play *The Gift of the Gorgon* where Edward Damson's notions of theatre are clearly modelled on 'Theatre of Cruelty' (together with Classical precepts). This is evident in his statement : 'It is the playwright's duty to appal. Tear an audience out of moral catalepsy' (Peter Shaffer, *The Gift of the Gorgon*, 1993, p.57). However, Damson's work demonstrates the potential pitfalls of Artaudian doctrine when its precepts are taken to their natural conclusions; a critic of Damson's play *I.R.E.* comments: 'At the end we get to see clearly just how nasty and exploitative his ideal of ultimate theatre really is. It is actually an attempt to seduce it into abetting mental and physical torture' (Peter Shaffer, *The Gift of the Gorgon*, 1993, p.69). The phrase 'ultimate theatre', of course, deliberately recalls Artaud's phrase 'total theatre' which is central to 'Theatre of Cruelty'.

32. In *The Theatre and Its Double*, Artaud suggests that the actor is akin to the athlete in terms of the 'support points' each must develop and in terms of breathing control (Antonin Artaud, 1981, pp.88–9). The athleticism of the central performances in *The Royal Hunt of the Sun* points to a link between its director, John Dexter, and the theoretician, as also does Simon Callow's description of Dexter during rehearsal: 'he generally wears a tracksuit and plimsolls, circling the acting area, shouting out comments, criticism or advice. His conception of acting is at heart athletic: it's a skill, requiring physical address and mental stamina'. Simon Callow, 1984, p.109.

33. Judith Thompson makes a similar point in her essay '"The World Made Flesh": Women and Theatre', in Adrian Page (ed.), *The Death of the Playwright?: Modern British Drama and Literary Theory* (London: Macmillan, 1992), p.38.

34. This is not, of course, to argue that Shaffer's plays are 'non-political': the matter of Shaffer's political position has been addressed in the previous chapter. The point here, though, is that Shaffer is not emerging from the Marxist tradition as is Brecht. It is also worth noting that Artaud's ideological agenda is also at odds with Shaffer's vision, Artaud stating: 'to my mind the present state of society is iniquitous and ought to be destroyed. If it is theatre's role to be concerned with it, it is even more a matter for machine guns'. Antonin Artaud, 1981, p.31. Brecht and Artaud's political and ideological positions condition their theatrical project to varying degrees, but for Shaffer, this emphasis is not part of his aesthetic agenda.

35. Gene A. Plunka, 1988, p.167.

36. Peter Shaffer, 'Labels Aren't for Playwrights', *Theatre Arts*, XLIV (February 1960), pp.20–1.

37. Peter Shaffer, *Equus*, 1976, p.250. Subsequent references to this play are placed after quotations in the main text.

38. The detective format is again evident in *Amadeus* where Salieri opens the drama by titling his 'last composition', *'The Death of Mozart, or Did I Do It?'*. Peter Shaffer, *Amadeus*, 1981, p.21.
39. Peter Shaffer, *Amadeus* (London: Penguin, 1981), p.78.
40. Colin Blakely, in Christopher Ford, 'The *Equus* Stampede' *The Guardian*, 20 April 1976, p.8.
41. For an example of the split stage technique, see Act 2 of *Amadeus* where Mozart's rooms are represented on stage along with those of Salieri, this allowing for a period of simultaneous action.
42. The intensity of audience response is remarked upon by several actors who have appeared in Shaffer's plays. Simon Callow, for example, states of *Amadeus*: 'Everyone who appears in the play feels the same thing: there's a magnetic pull coming from the auditorium [...] not one performance of the two hundred or so that we did failed to ignite an electric charge in the audience'. Simon Callow, 1984, p.119. Similarly, Colin Blakely, discussing his role as Dysart in *Equus*, notes that 'when you're playing it you can feel this atmosphere all around you...in the dark'. Colin Blakely, quoted in Christopher Ford, 'The *Equus* Stampede', *The Guardian*, 20 April 1976, p.8. The actors' awareness of this response seems to be unique to Shaffer's theatre.
43. Antonin Artaud, 1981, p.101.

CHAPTER 3

1. The essential instability of language is an issue noted by Carl Jung whose work has had a profound influence on Shaffer (as Chapters 5 and 6 detail). Jung decided that one of the reasons why language is not 'fixed' is that 'each word means something slightly different to each person, even among those who share the same cultural background. The reason for this variation is that a general notion is received into an individual context and is therefore understood and applied in a slightly individual way'. Jung's analysis at least partially accounts for the problematic relationship between words, communication and meaning that is so often centralized in Shaffer's drama. Carl G. Jung, 'Approaching the Unconscious', in Carl G. Jung (ed.), *Man and his Symbols* (London: Picador, 1978), p.28.
2. It is worth noting that a short sketch written by Shaffer for BBC TV's *That Was The Week That Was* relied for its joke on a simple inversion of the meaning of words. 'But My Dear' (1963) involves a junior Civil Service clerk being roundly berated by his superior for producing a letter of apparently unmitigated obscenity. Phrases such as 'Pursuant to your letter' and 'Thanking you in anticipation' are interpreted by him as being of an explicitly sexual nature while the letter's final 'Your obedient servant' he finds 'just plain perverted'. Here, interpretation has little to do with meaning and words cause the gap between the two. Peter Shaffer, 'But My Dear', in David Frost and Ned Sherrin (eds), *That Was the Week That Was* (London: W.H. Allen, 1963), p.50.

3. Peter Shaffer, *Equus*, in Peter Shaffer, *Three Plays: Equus, Shrivings, Five Finger Exercise* (London: Penguin, 1976), p.210.

4. For an interesting discussion of this idea, see Werner Huber and Walter Zapf, 'On the Structure of Peter Shaffer's *Amadeus*', *Modern Drama* 27 (1984), pp.299–313.

5. Peter Shaffer, *Amadeus* (London: Penguin, 1981), p.21.

6. Peter Shaffer, *Amadeus*, 1981, p.20.

7. Peter Roberts, review of *Five Finger Exercise*, in Gareth Lloyd-Evans and Barbara Lloyd-Evans (eds), *Plays in Review 1956–1980: British Drama and the Critics* (London: Batsford Academic and Educational, 1985), p.68.

8. Peter Griffith, 'Bakhtin, Foucault, Beckett, Pinter', in Adrian Page (ed.), *The Death of the Playwright? Modern British Drama and Literary Theory* (London: Macmillan, 1992), p.99.

9. Peter Shaffer, *Five Finger Exercise*, in Peter Shaffer, *Three Plays: Equus, Shrivings, Five Finger Exercise* (London: Penguin, 1976), p.13. Subsequent references to this play are placed in the main text following quotations.

10. Related to the idea of 'non-sense' or 'nonsense' language raised here and above in relation to *Amadeus*, it is worth pointing out that Pamela and Clive have devised a range of games that convert language into a joke they share between themselves. Puns recur (as in Clive's remark that his mother suffers from 'a plaster-gilt complex', p.45), slang punctures Pamela's speech, nicknames are bestowed and parodic language patterns are adopted in a constant game of 'pretend'. It is possible that the tensions associated with language with which Clive and Pamela have been brought up have been unconsciously converted by them into this harmless, though significant, 'play'.

11. The choice of this phrase should recall Frank Strang's favourite cliché in *Equus*: 'If you receive my meaning' is used so frequently by him that Alan parodies him in conversation with Dysart. As implied in *Equus* and in relation to *Five Finger Exercise*, however, the phrase carries deeper connotations that it at first appears. Peter Shaffer, *Equus*, 1976, p.245.

12. John Russell Taylor also suggests that Stanley refuses to understand what Clive is saying to him because 'he fears the challenge it may pose to everything he has built his life on'. John Russell Taylor, *Peter Shaffer* (London: Longman, 1974), p.11.

13. John Carey is one critic who comments usefully on the Oedipal and homosexual inferences of this play, and his analysis which connects the two emphases is worth quoting here. Carey writes: 'Oedipus remains discreetly unmentioned, but vulgar Mrs Harrington half-recalls seeing a play where the hero put out his own eyes just before she withdraws with her son to the sofa for mutual caresses. Like Phaedra, both she and Clive carry lying tales to Mr Harrington in a bid to pay out Walter, the young German tutor, for resisting their advances'. John Carey (on the BBC TV production of *Five Finger Exercise*), 'Oh Come All Ye Separate', *The Listener*, 31 December 1970, p.928.

14. Peter Shaffer, *The Private Ear*, in Peter Shaffer, *Four Plays: The Private Ear, The Public Eye, White Liars, Black Comedy* (London: Penguin, 1981), p.37. Subsequent references to this play are placed after quotations in the main text.

15. This phrase draws attention to Ted's easy relationship with the 'world' which is placed in contrast to Bob's alienation from it.

16. The inability of the alienated protagonist to make himself 'understood' within the realm of words is an emphasis central to Thomas Mann's short story *Tonio Kröger*, a work which Shaffer deeply admires. In Mann's tale, the agonized artist stands watching the two loves of his youth dancing together and longs to make contact with them. However, he realizes that the wall of non-comprehension that had separated him from them years before necessarily remains: 'He thought out what he might say; but he had not the courage to say it. Yes, this too was just as it had been: they would not understand him, they would listen like strangers to anything he was able to say. For their speech was not his speech'. Thomas Mann, *Tonio Kröger*, in Thomas Mann, *Death in Venice, Tristan, Tonio Kröger*, trans. by H.T. Lowe-Porter (London: Penguin, 1994), p.186. A corresponding emphasis is at work in Bob and Clive's doomed attempts to speak and to be understood.

17. This exchange is directly reminiscent of 'Pinteresque' dialogue in plays such as *The Caretaker* where communication is so fraught with dangers and private terrors that interaction becomes impossible. The technique of two separate conversations running concurrently is surely borrowed from this playwright.

18. Peter Shaffer, interview with the author, 22 November 1996, Chichester Festival Theatre. Shaffer adds that only the 'insensitive' can avoid being 'orchestrated' by these 'unverbalized' 'messages' which are both detected and responded to at the level of non-articulated (and inarticulable) intuition.

19. Peter Shaffer, *The Public Eye*, in Peter Shaffer, *Four Plays: The Private Ear, The Public Eye, White Liars, Black Comedy* (London: Penguin, 1981), pp.88–9. Subsequent references to this play are placed after quotations in the main text.

20. Julian's speculations on his strange name suggest the issue of identity that will be explored in the next chapter. They also draw our attention to the connotations of 'Christoforou' through the emphasis that Julian places on the *'for'* syllable. His initials 'J.C.' possibly suggest a link with Jesus Christ while the surname perhaps implies 'Christ for you': in his role as the 'redeemer' of Charles and Belinda, Julian certainly enjoys a peculiar Christ-like quality.

21. Never satisfied with this play, Shaffer has rewritten it extensively and has produced several versions of it. The version referred to here is the (to date) unperformed text titled *White Liars* published in Peter Shaffer, *Four Plays: The Private Ear, The Public Eye, White Liars, Black Comedy* (London: Penguin, 1981). References to this version are placed after quotations in the main text.

CHAPTER 4

1. Rodney Simard, *Postmodern Drama: Contemporary Playwrights in America and Britain* (Boston: University Press of America, 1984), p.104.
2. Shaffer's frequent use of a narrator who fulfils the function of commentator, stage manager, director of experience, etc., recalls the techniques of Classical Greek theatre, as also does his use of ceremonial masks and choruses.
3. Una Chaudhuri, 'The Spectator in Drama/Drama in the Spectator', *Modern Drama*, 27 (1984), pp.281–323, p.289.
4. Peter Shaffer, *Equus*, in *Peter Shaffer: Three Plays – Equus, Shrivings, Five Finger Exercise* (London: Penguin, 1976), p.210. Subsequent references to this text are placed in the main text following quotations.
5. Peter Shaffer, *Black Comedy*, in *Peter Shaffer: Four Plays – The Private Ear, The Public Eye, White Liars, Black Comedy* (London: Penguin, 1981), p.198.
6. Peter Shaffer, *Yonadab*, in *Peter Shaffer: Lettice and Lovage and Yonadab* (London: Penguin, 1989), p.161. Subsequent references to this text are placed in the main text following quotations.
7. Cited in Virginia Cooke and Malcolm Page (eds), *File on Shaffer* (London: Methuen, 1987), p.70.
8. Peter Shaffer, *Shrivings*. in *Peter Shaffer: Three Plays – Equus, Shrivings, Five Finger Exercise* (London: Penguin, 1976), p.162. Subsequent references to this text are placed in the main text following quotations.
9. Some critics have attempted (with mixed success) to explore Shaffer's preoccupation with issues of identity in relation to his status as a twin. The playwright himself has doubts about this potentially invasive and misleading form of criticism, and it is also true that many of these explorations have been conducted by psychoanalysts with little or no grasp of basic dramatic and theatrical techniques. Michael Hinden's essay, '"Where All the Ladders Start": The Autobiographical Impulse in Shaffer's Recent Work', in C.J. Gianakaris (ed.), *Peter Shaffer: A Casebook* (London and New York, 1991) is the illuminating exception to this usually reductive and tenuous strand of analysis, while Dr Jules Glenn has perhaps been the worst offender in this field suggesting, as Gene A. Plunka reports, that 'Shaffer may have unconsciously misspelled Atahuallpa using two *l*'s to indicate twinship'. Gene A. Plunka, *Peter Shaffer: Roles, Rites and Rituals in the Theater* (London: Associated University Press, 1988), p.108. This is by no means Dr Glenn's wildest speculation. Shaffer's twinship may partially account for his consistent emphasis on crises of identity, but the evidence is flimsy and, as detailed in the following note, the playwright's upbringing and personality account for this preoccupation more fully. This argument will not be expanded upon here as a result.
10. There is an interesting connection here between the notions of invisibility and chameleonism and Shaffer's statements about his own history and character. As Gene A. Plunka reports, 'when Shaffer wrote the preface to his collected plays, he commented that *Five Finger Exercise* "expressed a great deal of my own family tensions and

also a desperate need to stop feeling invisible"'. Gene A. Plunka, 1988, p.73. Based on an interview with the playwright, Plunka also records that Shaffer 'compares himself to a chameleon because his sense of identity is amorphous and constantly in flux' (p.30). However, Shaffer by no means feels himself to be unique in this, commenting that 'the world sharply divides between those people who are different with each person, and between people (who are usually, I suspect, rather less what the world calls "sensitive"), who are always the same'. (Peter Shaffer, interview with the author, 22 November 1996, Chichester Festival Theatre.) This is worth noting but, as before, interpreting the writer's work in sole relation to his life has frequently led to poor analysis.

11. Dennis A. Klein, 'Game-Playing in Four Plays by Peter Shaffer: *Shrivings, Equus, Lettice and Lovage,* and *Yonadab'*, in C.J. Gianakaris (ed.), *Peter Shaffer: A Casebook* (London and New York: Garland, 1991), p.144.

12. Peter Shaffer, 'A Note on the Text', *Equus*, 1976, p.200.

13. Peter Hall in John Goodwin (ed.), *Peter Hall's Diaries: The Story of a Dramatic Battle* (London: Hamish Hamilton, 1983), p.465.

14. Charles A. Pennell cited in Gene A. Plunka, '"Know Thyself": Integrity and Self-Awareness in the early Plays of Peter Shaffer', in C.J. Gianakaris (ed.), 1991, p.68.

15. Shaffer comments that the 'incapacity for Immediate Life' is a 'lack' of which he is conscious in himself, stating: 'one of the greatest things I envy in people is the capacity to exult, exult in life, and exult in moments when they arise. I sometimes deplore in myself the fact that I live half the time in some remembered, and no doubt altered, past, and/or am apprehensive about a future that, of course, never comes because it's the present. And I think that is not a way to live'. This observation forms a direct link between the playwright (who adds that, in his youth, he 'suffered very strongly from a sense of feeling "outside"') and his alienated protagonists who are unable to experience 'the moment' in direct and 'exultant' terms. As before, however, biographical criticism should be treated with some caution. Peter Shaffer, interview with the author, 22 November 1996.

16. The emphasis on eyes in *Equus* relates conspicuously to the fact that, as Barbara Lounsberry points out in her fascinating essay, eyes are 'a traditional symbol of divinity'. In *Yonadab*, we find a similar implication. Barbara Lounsberry, 'The Cosmic Embrace: Peter Shaffer's Metaphysics', in C.J. Gianakaris (ed.), 1991, p.86.

17. Gene A. Plunka, 1988, p.32.

18. In addition, the suggestion of homosexual attraction between these two men is weakened by Peter Shaffer's statement that 'the theme which lies behind their relationship is the search for god'. Shaffer quoted in Christopher Innes, *Modern British Drama 1890–1990* (Cambridge: Cambridge University Press, 1992), p.408.

19. Charles R. Lyons, 'Peter Shaffer's *Five Finger Exercise* and the Conventions of Realism', in C.J. Gianakaris (ed.), 1991, p.53.

20. Peter Shaffer, *The Gift of the Gorgon* (London: Viking, 1993), pp.43–4.

21. Peter Shaffer, 'Preface' to *Yonadab*, 1989, p.vii.
22. As in the case of paralysis, the concept of voyeurism is incorporated
     into the staging of this play. Christopher Innes notes that 'the elabo-
     rate staging becomes a form of sensationalistic voyeurism', this re-
     minding the theatre audience that in the very act of spectatorship,
     they too are fellow voyeurs. Innes' use of the word 'sensationalistic' is
     also interesting here since it corroborates the argument presented
     throughout this chapter that Shaffer's alienated voyeurs are at-
     tempting to connect self with sensation through the witnessing and
     appropriation of experience. Christopher Innes, 1992, p.406.
23. Shaffer quoted in Michael Hinden, '"Where All the Ladders
     Start": The Autobiographical Impulse in Shaffer's Recent Work', in
     C.J. Gianakaris, 1991, p.156.
24. The motif of barriers, curtains and obstacles recurs in several of
     Shaffer's plays. This visual metaphor connects with a passage from
     Thomas Mann's short story *Tonio Kröger*, a passage that, as Shaffer
     recalls, affected him profoundly when he first came upon it. In the
     story, Tonio Kröger stands outside a room where a dance is in
     progress and, in an act (and statement) of alienated voyeurism,
     watches the dancers within and from behind a glass window: 'his skin
     prickled with the thievish pleasure of standing unseen in the dark and
     spying on the dancers there in the brightly lighted room'. In Shaffer's
     words, he subsequently 'becomes aware of the distancing of himself
     by the glass', which comes to represent 'a description of his whole
     mental state'. (Peter Shaffer, interview with the author, 22 November
     1996). *Yonadab* is a play littered with such moments of 'distancing' via
     barriers, while the episode related by Edward Damson in *The Gift of
     the Gorgon*, where the playwright stands outside a window watching
     his son lecture on his work and shouts unheard abuse at him, pro-
     vides a further example of the same motif of alienation. Yonadab,
     Edward, Dysart, Salieri and indeed all Shaffer's alienated protago-
     nists, could each, like Thomas Mann's Tonio Kröger, describe them-
     selves as standing 'between two worlds. I am at home in neither, and I
     suffer in consequence'. Thomas Mann, *Tonio Kröger*, in Thomas Mann,
     Death in Venice, Tristan, Tonio Kröger, trans. by H.T. Lowe-Porter
     (London: Penguin, 1994), p.183, p.190.

CHAPTER 5

1. Peter Shaffer quoted in Christopher Innes, *Modern British Drama
    1890–1990* (Cambridge: Cambridge University Press, 1992), p.406.
2. Peter Shaffer, quoted in Virginia Cooke and Malcolm Page (eds), *File
    on Shaffer* (London: Methuen, 1987), p.61.
3. Peter Shaffer, *Amadeus* (London: Penguin, 1981), p.58. It should be
    noted that quotations are taken from the revised edition of this play
    staged at the Broadhurst Theater, New York City in 1980. Subsequent
    references to this play are placed after quotations in the main text.

4. Joan Fitzpatrick Dean quoted in Rodney Simard, *Postmodern Drama: Contemporary Playwrights in America and Britain* (Boston: University Press of America, 1984), p.104.

5. Peter Shaffer, *Equus*, in Peter Shaffer, *Three Plays: Five Finger Exercise, Shrivings, Equus* (London: Penguin, 1976), p.300. Subsequent references to this play are placed after quotations in the main text.

6. Peter Shaffer quoted in Barbara Lounsberry, 'The Cosmic Embrace: Peter Shaffer's Metaphysics', in C.J. Gianakaris (ed.), *Peter Shaffer: A Casebook* (London and New York: Garland, 1991), p.76.

7. This phrase derives from Barbara Lounsberry, in C.J. Gianakaris (ed.), 1991, p.128.

8. Peter Shaffer quoted in Barbara Gelb, '...And Its Author', *New York Times*, 14 November 1965, sec.2, p.4.

9. Peter Shaffer, 'To See the Soul of a Man...', *New York Times*, 24 October 1965, sec.2, p.3.

10. Alexander S. Murray, *Who's Who in Mythology: Classic Guide to the Ancient World: Revised Edition* (London: Bracken Books, 1995), p.7

11. Antonin Artaud, *The Theatre and Its Double: Essays by Antonin Artaud*, trans. by Victor Corti (London: John Calder, 1981), p.21.

12. It could be argued that these gods' ability to transcend time and space is mimicked in the staging of Shaffer's plays where tenses collide and where multi-environment arenas represent several locations simultaneously. In *Equus*, for example, there is a constant interchange between the past and the present while the boxing-ring stage set becomes the stables, the Strang's home and the doctor's consulting room according to the needs of the action. The staging therefore potentially echoes the properties of divinity which loom over the play.

13. Joseph L. Henderson, 'Ancient Myths and Modern Man', in Carl G. Jung (ed.), *Man and His Symbols* (London: Picador, 1978), p.98.

14. Peter Shaffer, *The Royal Hunt of the Sun* (London: Penguin, 1981), p.43. Subsequent references to this play are placed after quotations in the main text.

15. Not only does Atahuallpa suggest a Christ-figure (the son of 'god' dying at the same age as Jesus), but, according to several critics, Pizarro also has Christ-like characteristics. Barbara Lounsberry argues that the wound Pizarro has suffered in his side forms a parallel with Jesus and that Pizarro also spends roughly 40 days in the wilderness before entering Cajamarca just as Jesus did before entering Jerusalem. She continues: 'Pizarro tells his men to move over the land as if they were "figures from a Lent Procession" and indeed the road is lined with eucalyptus trees'. Barbara Lounsberry, '"God-Hunting": The Chaos of Worship in Peter Shaffer's *Equus* and *Royal Hunt of the Sun*, *Modern Drama* 21 (1978), 13–28, p.23. p.27.

16. Peter Shaffer, interviewed by John Russell Taylor, 'Shaffer and the Incas', *Plays and Players*, April 1964, p.12.

17. Peter Shaffer, interviewed by John Russell Taylor, 'Shaffer and the Incas', April 1964, p.13.

18. Alexander S. Murray, 1995, p.15.

19. Carl G. Jung, 'Approaching the Unconscious', in Carl G. Jung (ed.), 1978, p.71.

20. Carl G. Jung cited in Una Chaudhuri, 'The Spectator in Drama/ Drama in the Spectator', *Modern Drama* 27 (1984), 281–323, p.292.

21. Gene A. Plunka mentions several references in this argument, among them the fact that Dysart 'has not kissed his wife in six years', that Alan blinds six horses in the stables, and that he had had his first encounter with horses aged six on the beach: 'Six years later, aged twelve', the picture of Jesus is replaced with the picture of the horse's head, and six years later again, the mutilations occur. Plunka concludes: 'the three episodes, each taking place in six-year intervals, suggest the mark of the devil: 666'. Gene A. Plunka, *Peter Shaffer: Roles, Rites and Rituals in the Theater* (London: Associated University Press, 1988), p.234.

22. Bettina L. Knapp quoted in Una Chaudhuri, 1984, p.293.

23. Alexander S. Murray, 1995, p.11.

24. It is worth mentioning here that Laing is, in effect, arguing that societal definitions of 'normality' constitute a dominant ideological myth (shared by the majority of people) and that any challenge to it is regarded as a dangerous counter-myth (proposed by an individual, a minority or a sub-culture). Here, the word 'myth' shifts into ideological territory as it will later do in *Amadeus* where Shaffer challenges our assumption that genius is necessarily equated with moral goodness: as several critical responses to this play revealed when the play was first performed, 'counter-myth' is most often interpreted as a destabilizing threat to comfortable belief and is rejected on the grounds of its subversive potential. See note 29 below where this point is developed.

25. John Russell Taylor, *Peter Shaffer* (London: Longman, 1974), p.31.

26. John Russell Taylor, 1974, p.29.

27. Alexander S. Murray notes that ancient myth enjoyed 'an intense hold [...] upon the great mass of the people' and exercised an 'important influence' on the civilization. Alexander S. Murray, 1995, p.2.

28. In his dream, Dysart is flanked by two priests: we have already been told that he shares his rooms with two 'highly competent psychiatrists' whose professional certainty may be aligned with the priests' zeal and with the threat they potentially pose to him.

29. This connection between moral virtue and genius is central to Western concepts of art: it is, in effect, an ideological myth that is deeply ingrained in our cultural consciousness. When it is challenged, as mentioned above, it shakes normative assumptions relating to the 'value' of art and to its social function. That this involves an uncomfortable reassessment (which is often blankly refused) is suggested in Peter Hall's anecdote where he relates Margaret Thatcher's reaction to the London production of *Amadeus*: 'She told me it was disgraceful for the National Theatre to be doing a play in which Mozart used four-letter words. I said they were splattered throughout his letters, but she said "Nonsense, impossible"'. Peter Hall, quoted in Kate Saunders, 'The Peter Principals', *The Sunday Times*, 29 November 1992, sec.10, p.8.

30. Peter Shaffer, quoted in Virginia Cooke and Malcolm Page (eds), 1987, p.60.

CHAPTER 6

1. Peter Shaffer, 'A Personal Essay', in Peter Shaffer, *Equus*, ed. T.S. Pearse (London: Longman, 1983), p.ix. Shaffer is here following Aristotle in his argument that tragedy does not necessarily involve a wicked antagonist nor a virtuous protagonist but characters who, often with the finest motives, simply fall into error (*hamartia*). All believe they are behaving impeccably (socially, personally or politically) but enter into conflict with others who believe the same. Tragedy, as in Shakespeare's *King Lear*, results.
2. Rodney Simard, *Postmodern Drama: Contemporary Playwrights in America and Great Britain* (Boston: University Press of America, 1984), p.105.
3. Doyle W. Walls, '*Equus*: Shaffer, Nietzsche, and the Neursoses of Health', *Modern Drama*, 27 (1984), pp.314–23, p.315. Walls uses the spelling 'Apollinian' throughout his article as this is faithful to the original translation; my spelling of the word in this chapter is the more widely used 'Apollonian'.
4. Peter Shaffer, quoted by Brian Connell in 'Peter Shaffer: The Two Sides of Theatre's Agonised Perfectionist', *The Times*, 28 April 1980, p.7. Shaffer uses the spelling 'Dionysiac' but, again, I am using the more usual 'Dionysian' throughout this chapter.
5. The labels 'Apollonian' and 'Dionysian' derive from Greek mythology. Apollo was the God of the sun whose light is an emblem of 'mental illumination, knowledge [and] truth'. In this respect, the connotations of Apollo's symbolization are positive. Also positive is his reputation for purifying individuals polluted with disease and crime which gives rise to his title, 'the God of medicine' (in this, his connection with Dysart is clear). However, since the sun's heat produces plague in the summer, Apollo is also titled 'the God of death', the sun's rays viewed as 'unerring arrows' which 'carry destruction with them'. The duality implied in the notion of godhead (discussed in the previous chapter) is thus inscribed within Apollonian signification.
   Dionysus similarly implies a double aspect. Also named Bacchus, Dionysus was the God of the vine and of the theatre. Usually represented as a jovial benefactor of mankind, he is also represented as a fierce and stubborn retributive force following 'copious indulgence in wine': in one tale, Dionysus punishes Lykurgos, the king of Thrace who had opposed him, by driving him mad and causing him to kill his son and thereafter himself. Again, the duality of godhead (whether ancient or modern) is implied. See Alexander S. Murray, *Who's Who in Mythology: Classic Guide to the Ancient World: Revised Edition* (London: Bracken Books, 1995), pp.96, 104, 98, 119.
6. C.J. Gianakaris, *Peter Shaffer* (London: Macmillan, 1992), p.18.

7. As will be argued later in the discussion, we should be careful not to regard Dysart's status as the 'Apollonian representative' as unambiguous and absolute in this play. Though his profession and intellect tempt us to regard him as the repository of Apollonian forces in *Equus*, his situation is rather more complex than this assumes. The debate will return to this issue in due course.

8. Christopher Innes, *Modern British Drama 1890–1990* (Cambridge: Cambridge University Press, 1992), p.407. It is significant that the Dionysian representatives in Shaffer's plays feel no tension between conflicting forces within themselves: only the Apollonians are subject to such torments. Lacking intellectual development, the Dionysians have no capacity for such analysis but, more than this, they feel no need for it since they are perfectly accommodated within their own visions and belief-systems. In addition, the playwright, a Western intellectual, is clearly more interested in exploring the limitations of Apollonianism than he is in investigating the limitations of an impulse he clearly values. This situation holds true until we reach Shaffer's most recent play, *The Gift of the Gorgon* (see Chapter 8).

9. Peter Shaffer, *Equus*, in Peter Shaffer, *Three Plays: Equus, Shrivings, Five Finger Exercise* (London: Penguin, 1976), p.210. Subsequent references to this play are placed in the main text following quotations.

10. John Freeman, 'Introduction', in Carl G. Jung (ed.), *Man and His Symbols* (London: Picador, 1978), p.xi.

11. Joseph L. Henderson, 'Ancient Myths and Modern Man', in Carl G. Jung (ed.), 1978, p.110.

12. Carl G. Jung, 'Approaching the Unconscious', in Carl G. Jung (ed.), 1978, p.75.

13. Carl G. Jung, quoted by Joseph L. Henderson, 'Ancient Myths and Modern Man', in Carl G. Jung (ed.), 1978, p.110.

14. Peter Shaffer, *The Royal Hunt of the Sun* (London: Penguin, 1981), p.14. Subsequent references to this play are placed in the main text following quotations.

15. Christopher Innes, 1992, p.407.

16. Christopher Innes, 1992, p.407.

17. Peter Shaffer, quoted in Virginia Cooke and Malcolm Page (eds), *File on Shaffer* (London: Methuen, 1987), p.24.

18. Peter Shaffer aligns Dionysian impulses with the capacity for worship when he discusses the 'tension' he feels within himself between Apollonian and Dionysian forces (quoted above). Having associated the former with 'order and restraint', and the latter with 'violence of instinct', he then proceeds to connect his Apollonian impulse with 'the secular side of me' and his Dionysian impulse with 'the inescapable fact that to me life without a sense of the divine is perfectly meaningless'. Peter Shaffer quoted by Brian Connell is 'Peter Shaffer: The Two Sides of Theatre's Agonised Perfectionist', *The Times*, 28 April 1980, p.7.

19. Christopher Innes, 1992, p.408.

20. Carl G. Jung, 'Approaching the Unconscious', in Carl G. Jung (ed.), 1978, p.16.

21. Christopher Innes, 1992, p.407.

22. C.J. Gianakaris, 1992, p.103.
23. A number of critics have seized on this notion of 'oneness' between two separate entities as further evidence of Shaffer's unconscious obsession with his own twinship. Since there is little value in this dubious approach, this idea will not be expanded upon here but it is, at least, worth noting in relation to this issue.
24. Doyle W. Walls, 1984, p.318.
25. This label is incorrectly applied to Dysart in Gene A. Plunka, *Roles, Rites and Rituals in the Theater* (London: Associated University Press, 1988), p.161.
26. Carl G. Jung, 'Approaching the Unconscious', in Carl G. Jung (ed.), 1978, p.6.
27. Wendy J. Wheeler and Trevor R. Griffiths, 'Staging "The Other Scene": A Psychoanalytic Approach to Contemporary British Political Drama', in Adrian Page (ed.), *The Death of the Playwright? Modern British Drama and Literary Theory* (London: Macmillan, 1992), p.203.
28. Werner Huber and Walter Zapf, 'On the Structure of Peter Shaffer's *Amadeus*', *Modern Drama*, 27 (1984), 299–313, p.300.
29. Christopher Innes, 1992, p.411.
30. Mozart's music, rejecting the legends and forms beloved by the Emperor's feudal Court, reflects his anti-establishment position. As Walter Huber and Hubert Zapf note: 'Mozart, the innovator, disregards the norms. His art becomes republican and democratic'. Walter Huber and Hubert Zapf, 1984, p.304. Similarly, Mozart chooses to base *The Marriage of Figaro* on a story by Beaumarchais, an agitator and political nuisance in pre-Revolutionary France: in this, his anti-establishment impulses are again suggested.
31. C.J. Gianakaris, 1992, pp.119–20.
32. That Salieri's mission to destroy Mozart originates less from artistic rivalry than from a desire to eliminate an 'aberration' is enforced by the fact that Mozart's music would have failed in the Viennese context whether Salieri plotted against him or not. Salieri immediately perceives the presence of divine beauty in Mozart's music but it is clear from the beginning of the play that the citizens of Vienna, steeped in shallowness and mediocrity, do not. All Salieri has to do is wait for Mozart to be rejected further and watch the 'giggling child' slide into poverty and self-destruction (p.59). But Salieri chooses not to wait for the inevitable because Mozart constitutes a living insult, a manifestation of divine mockery, and a projection of unconscious drives within himself which he cannot (or will not) acknowledge: he must, therefore, be eliminated.
33. Peter Shaffer, interview with the author, 22 November 1996, Chichester Festival Theatre.
34. Walter Huber and Hubert Zapf, 1984, p.303.
35. Walter Huber and Hubert Zapf, 1984, pp.304–5.
36. It is worth briefly considering why the audience responds more to the tragedies of the 'victimizers' (Pizarro, Dysart and Salieri) than to the tragedies of their 'victims' (Atahuallpa, Alan and Mozart). To begin with, Shaffer is more interested in the conflicts raging within the

former and his plays, despite their titles, focus upon them as a result. Related to this point is the fact that the audience enters the plays through the minds of the 'Apollonians' and its identification with their struggles and torments is therefore more acute and sustained than is its identification with the victims who it never knows as well. In addition, of course, the struggles of average man (as opposed to those of 'gods' and geniuses) align the audience with tormented 'everyman'. This is not to argue that the victims' destruction does not move us profoundly, but it is to suggest that any audience feels for the destroyer in Shaffer's plays more than it feels for the destroyed.

37. Simon Callow, *Being an Actor*, (London: Penguin, 1984), p.115. The 'little beast' that Callow describes here was his original attempt at the role, a characterization which he later tempered with 'real grace and lightness' (p.119). These negative characteristics, however, further align Shaffer's Mozart with the Dionysian archetype: where on the one hand, he represents celebration and human happiness (in his music), he also represents childlike malice. An echo of Dionysian dualism is provided. In addition, where Dionysus was said to have driven the King of Thrace, Lykurgos, insane (causing him to commit suicide), Mozart has a similar effect upon Salieri. The connection between Mozart and Dionysianism is everywhere apparent.

It should be stressed, particularly in relation to critical objections that Shaffer exaggerated Mozart's negative traits to an offensive degree, that the 'creature' he presents in this play is not necessarily *the* Mozart but is '*Salieri's* Mozart; Salieri brought up in a prim Lombard family and seeing this little man giggling, running about and showing off – *showing off*, that would be the thing'. Though Shaffer adds that he 'regrets the giggle' he gave his Mozart, he insists that his representation of the composer was faithful to contemporary records of the man, and implies that much of the critical hostility towards his creation was based on illogical sentimentality. After all, as he states, 'there's nothing remarkable about Mozart except that he was Mozart: I'm drawing a portrait of a perfectly ordinary person endowed with one sovereign and extraordinary quality'. Peter Shaffer, interview with the author, 22 November 1996.

38. Peter Shaffer, interview with the author, 22 November 1996.

CHAPTER 7

1. Throughout this discussion, the word 'femaleness' will be used in preference to the word 'femininity'. Where the former is a neutral term connoting qualities and values associated with the female gender, the latter is a loaded term, carrying with it a weight of cultural baggage. 'Femininity' is often used to convey a value judgement and, while both words easily rely on preconception and stereotype for their definitions, 'femaleness' is more easily removed from the sphere of gender-driven cliché.

2. John Russell Taylor, *Anger and After: A Guide to the New British Drama* (London: Methuen, 1962), p.274.

3. This tendency towards cliché is, in addition, evident in the male protagonists in these plays; Charles Sidley, Colonel Melkett, Harold Gorringe and Ted are all recognizable as 'types' and are thus, inevitably, underexplored as dramatic characters. This is, of course, an effect of the form of these dramas: the one-act play does not allow for in-depth investigation of character and motivation. The question here, however, is whether Shaffer's female stereotypes can be connected with wider impulses evident in this drama in relation to Shaffer's presentation and use of the female voice in his work.

4. Gene A. Plunka, *Peter Shaffer: Roles, Rites and Rituals in the Theater* (London: Associated University Press, 1988), p.119.

5. Shaffer adds that the characters who surround Clea correspond to the figures on 'an old-fashioned pack of cards: the Colonel, the Queen and the spinster. The only thing that's missing is the vicar, with or without trousers. That was the kind of game I was trying to play'. Clea alone refuses such farce stereotype. Peter Shaffer, interview with the author, 22 November 1996, Chichester Festival Theatre.

6. The term 'think-piece' derives from John Russell Taylor, *Peter Shaffer* (London: Longman, 1974), p.16.

7. It is interesting to note that perceptions of gender difference in Shaffer's plays do not always emanate from directions within the dramas themselves: critics may often bring their own preconceptions to bear on their analyses of individual characters and situations, and these are frequently based on perceptions of gender function. One example of this occurs in the case of Lois when her situation is compared with that of Walter Langer in *Five Finger Exercise*. Both characters have abandoned their families, faiths and homelands in search of fulfilment; Lois is sexually unresponsive while Walter is celibate and may or may not have homosexual tendencies. However, where Gene A. Plunka describes Walter as 'primitive' and 'independent', as a person like Alan Strang and Mozart who have 'fashioned their lives for themselves, not for others' (p.81), he has no hesitation in describing Lois as 'an insecure rebel, a transient who has lost her family and her sense of religion' (p.137). Further, he refers to her as 'basically a weak person' (p.137) whose 'aversions to sexual activities are abnormal in a woman of her age' (p.138). This difference in interpretation may disguise the fact that Walter and Lois are highly similar characters in highly similar situations: the most crucial difference between them in these terms is their gender. This, however, is more than enough to radically condition critical response to them. The 'problem with women' here lies less in the way that they are written than in the way that they are interpreted. Gene A. Plunka, 1988, pp.81, 137, 138.

8. Barbara Lounsberry, 'The Cosmic Embrace: Peter Shaffer's Metaphysics', in C.J. Gianakaris (ed), *Peter Shaffer: A Casebook* (London and New York: Garland, 1991), p.83.

9. It is worth noting here that scenes in the original London version of *Amadeus* which portrayed Constanze as a caring, protective wife, were

cut in revision. As a result, Constanze becomes a more selfish, greedy and sexually untrustworthy character in the version of the play referred to throughout this book. This has the result of focusing dramatic sympathy on Mozart (particularly in the second Act), and rendering female presence in this play more problematic still.

10. The drama is shared equally between the two female protagonists, providing two rare and powerful central roles for its actresses. Maggie Smith and Margaret Tyzack both won Tonys in 1990 for recreating their original roles in this play on Broadway.

11. Peter Shaffer, 'Preface', in Peter Shaffer, *Lettice and Lovage and Yonadab* (London: Penguin, 1989), p.ix.

12. Peter Shaffer, *Lettice and Lovage and Yonadab* (London: Penguin, 1989), p.9. Subsequent references to this play are placed in the main text following quotations. It should be noted that the version of the play referred to here is the revised edition with the altered conclusion where Lettice and Lotte, rather than planning to blow up ugly buildings, decide to use the weapon of words and conduct satiric tours around them. This revision was marked in a change to the title; the original 'and' disappears to be replaced with the ampersand with all its connotations of business partnership. Unfortunately, this change was not registered in the published version of the play referred to here: the 'and', incorrectly, remains. This important mistake should be noted by readers.

13. It is worth remembering, in relation to this point, that Dionysus was the God of the theatre.

14. Lettice's potent concoction, Lovage, also connects her with Dionysus, otherwise known as Bacchus, since both are strongly associated with the transforming, 'enlarging' effects of alcohol.

15. Michael Hinden argues that the attachment between Lettice and Lotte at the end of the play suggests a deviation from 'the heterosexual norm', and cites the fact that the toast to the audience connotes the marriage ceremony with which Shakespearean comedy habitually concludes. In addition, he interprets the use of words such as '*swells*', 'cascade' and '*brimming*' as 'positively orgiastic', and concludes that 'Lettice and Lotte constitute a comic version of the divine incestuous couple of which Yonadab dreamed'. The play is certainly about love, but Hinden's case here, though well argued, is tenuous to say the least. It is tempting to read Hinden's analysis as evidence of a male inability to penetrate female/female relationships without recourse to sexual interpretation. Michael Hinden, '"Where all the Ladders Start": The Autobiographical Impulse in Shaffer's Recent Work', in C.J. Gianakaris (ed), 1991, p.165.

16. Peter Shaffer, in C.J. Gianakaris, 'A Conversation with Peter Shaffer', in C.J. Gianakaris (ed.), 1991, p.34.

17. One reason why Lettice may be more closely associated with the quality of perception than Lotte in this play is perhaps because she is characterized as the more 'feminine' of the two women. We step into hazardous territory here because the definition of the word 'feminine' relies heavily upon traditional stereotypes and on cultural

conditioning. It is, however, true to state that, in performance, Lettice emerges as the 'feminine' focus while Lotte carries strong 'masculine' traits. Where Lettice is emotional and artistic, Lotte is contained and logical; where the former is dressed whimsically, the latter is costumed in austere business clothes; where Lettice is associated with the theatre and with her idiosyncratic lair, Lotte is connected with her office and with the 'non-doer's desk' (p.48). These associations, of course, constitute arbitrary definitions of 'masculinity' and 'femininity', but, on stage, any audience will be tempted to categorize the characters along these lines. Further, if we apply the commutation test as outlined above, we find that Lotte's words do not sound inappropriate in a male voice where Lettice's words most certainly do. As a result, 'female' qualities such as imagination and perception are more obviously attached to Lettice than to the more 'male' Lotte.

18. Peter Shaffer, *Whom Do I Have the Honour of Addressing?* (London: André Deutsch, 1990), p.15, p.11. Subsequent references to this play are placed in the main text following quotations.

19. The idea for this play came from a story told to Peter Shaffer by a stranger; within the space of five minutes, Shaffer learned of a young film fan, who had for years worshipped a famous film star. By chance, he had met the 'object of his obsession' in London, a correspondence between them had ensued, and the fan was finally invited to visit California. The trip went disastrously wrong, 'and was followed by a traumatized return to England, and an even grimmer sequel'. Shaffer continues: 'I can still see the distraught face of my narrator, his eyes filled with bewildered tears. A few months afterwards, I became possessed with the need to write a play for radio, with his agonised recital as my jumping-off point'. Writing the drama some months later, Shaffer found that, since the details of the story had vanished from his mind, he was forced to create new characters, change their genders and devise an original plot. However, as he states, 'paradoxically I truly believe that the emotional essence of the story to which I had so briefly listened, and by which I had been so highly disturbed, remains intact'. The play was written for Maggie Smith who, as it transpired, could not perform the role due to ill-health, and the part of Angela was subsequently played by Judi Dench for BBC Radio on 20 November 1989. Peter Shaffer, 'The Play: A History', in Chichester Festival Theatre Programme for *Whom Do I Have the Honour of Addressing?*, November 1996.

20. Peter Shaffer, 'Introduction', *Whom Do I Have the Honour of Addressing?* (London: André Deutsch, 1990), p.ii.

21. That cinema is a medium in which separation (and thus alienation) is embedded in the fact of production is a point noted by Christian Metz who comments that, during a film, the audience is present while the actors are absent, whereas, during shooting, this situation is reversed. Christian Metz, 'History/Discourse: A Note on Two Voyeurisms', in John Caughie (ed.), *Theories of Authorship: A Reader* (London: Routledge/British Film Institute, 1990), pp.228–9.

22. Peter Shaffer, interview with the author, 22 November 1996.
23. It is significant that Tom has codified Angela in gendered terms, casting her in the role of 'Super-mom' (p.26). Angela resents this positioning because it ignores who she really is ('it was actually absurd as I was quite obviously nobody's Mom and wasn't ever going to be', p.27), and also because it ignores what she wants to be: as she notes, 'Whatever else I felt for him, it wasn't what Super-mom should feel!' (p.28). As an orphan, Tom (or 'Tommy', as Angela later calls him in a child-like endearment) has projected his longing for a mother onto Angela who does not want this role; simultaneously, he confuses her further by apparently deliberately arousing her sexually, hugging and massaging her. Oedipal impulses may be at work in this, but Angela's resistance to inaccurate, gendered codification is the point here. This is, of course, what motivates her furious statement to Tom: 'I'll be what I please [...] What I damn please!' (p.38).
24. Peter Shaffer, interview with the author, 22 November 1996.

CHAPTER 8

1. Press release, *The Gift of the Gorgon*, quoted by Kate Saunders, 'The Peter Principals', *The Sunday Times*, 29 November 1992, p.8.
2. Peter Shaffer, in C.J. Gianakaris, 'A Conversation with Peter Shaffer (1990)', in C.J. Gianakaris (ed.), *Peter Shaffer: A Casebook* (London and New York: Garland, 1991), p.37.
3. Peter Shaffer, in C.J. Gianakaris, 'A Conversation with Peter Shaffer (1990)', in C.J. Gianakaris (ed.), 1991, p.37.
4. Peter Shaffer, interview with the author, 22 November 1996, Chichester Festival Theatre.
5. Peter Hall, 'Introduction', in Peter Shaffer, *The Gift of the Gorgon* (London: Viking, 1993), p.x.
6. Carl G. Jung, 'Approaching the Unconscious', in Carl G. Jung (ed.), *Man and His Symbols* (London: Picador, 1978), p.57.
7. Peter Shaffer, *The Gift of the Gorgon* (London: Viking, 1993), pp.15, 29. Subsequent references to this play are placed after quotations in the main text. It should be noted that the version of the play referred to here was not the version performed on stage: Shaffer advised the publisher to delay printing the text until after the play had been staged since he correctly anticipated that certain elements would be revised during the rehearsal process: the publisher, however, was impatient. Since most readers will have access to this published version (and since the revised text has not been published) it is to this that the discussion will refer.
8. Edward's communication difficulties are many and various: upon his exile to Greece, he retreats into futile secrecies, begins to ventriloquize the hated opinions of his father, and finally constructs a silent statement to Helen in his 'revenge'. In addition, when he tells Helen that he had stood outside a lecture hall where his son was speaking about

his work, he resembles a retributive spirit, separated by a glass screen, shouting bitter words that no-one can hear. For a playwright (a communicator by profession) and for a man who appears to have little trouble in expressing himself, Edward is, in fact, ill-accommodated within the realm of words.

9. In Jungian terms, Edward's choice of Perseus is significant since, as Joseph L. Henderson notes, Perseus (like Theseus, who killed the Minotaur) could be said to slay the Gorgon in order to overcome his 'fear of unconscious demonic maternal powers'. This should be considered in relation to the later discussion focusing on the problematic relationship between Edward and Helen. Joseph L. Henderson, 'Ancient Myth and Modern Man', in Carl G. Jung (ed.), 1978, p.117.

10. Alexander S. Murray, *Who's Who in Mythology: Classic Guide to the Ancient World: Revised Edition* (London: Bracken Books, 1995), p.218.

11. Though Edward forces Helen into making a choice between staying with him and having children (she selects the former option) and is thus childless, she returns insistently to the idea that she has 'delivered' her husband into the world of creativity, his plays becoming her surrogate children: she refers to *Icons*, for example, as 'my child by him. My firstborn' (p.49). Helen is thus both the 'mother' of Edward in a metaphorical sense, nurturing him physically, emotionally and creatively, and the 'mother' of his work. Ultimately, however, she realizes that he has rendered her 'barren' (p.85) in terms wider than her reproductive capacity. The word links with her perception that, like the Gorgon, he has 'laid waste' to all that surrounds him (p.84).

12. Alexander S. Murray, 1995, p.89.

13. Edward and Mark Askelon from *Shrivings* have more than this wandering, homeless state in common: both have also rejected their sons, exiling them abroad; both are men of letters, a playwright and a poet; both inflict small revenges on their wives through blatant infidelities; both finally 'paralyse' their wives emotionally or physically. Further similarities are equally obvious. In addition, Edward's alienation recalls not only Mark but also the eponymous Yonadab: all are characters defined by disconnection and psychic disintegration.

14. Peter Shaffer, interview with the author, 22 November 1996.

15. Alexander S. Murray, 1995, p.345.

16. Edward's desk dominates the room in which the play is set. Described as 'remarkable' and 'impressive' in the author's stage notes (Peter Shaffer, 'The Set', *The Gift of the Gorgon*, 1993, p.xv), it is also referred to as Edward's 'altar' to be used solely by 'Russian madmen' (p.9). Reputed to be Rasputin's table, it is also the sacred 'relic' upon which Philip must swear to Helen that he will write the version of Edward's life that she is about to reveal to him. Edward's plays, written at this desk, also become enacted upon them when the metaphorical 'stage' literally becomes a performative platform.

17. These episodes constitute 'plays-within-the-play' conducted in the midst of two realities and two tenses. The complexity of Shaffer's drama becomes apparent.

18. Peter Hall, 'Introduction', *The Gift of the Gorgon*, 1993, p.ix.
19. Peter Hall, 'Introduction', *The Gift of the Gorgon*, 1993, p.ix.
20. Shaffer adds that it is the 'job' of the critic to comment on issues such as staging rather than to offer personal opinions about the moral positions advanced in a play to the exclusion of all else. Peter Shaffer, interview with the author, 22 November 1996.
21. That Edward 'worships' at the altar of theatre is indicated throughout, and drama becomes a form of religion as a result. Edward, for example, describes himself in his role as a dramatist as 'the quaint priest of a spent religion' (p.81), while Philip, drawing a connection between himself and his father, declares: 'His worship. *That's* my disease, if you like: worship of theatre' (p.6). That Philip selects the word 'disease' here is interesting since the 'dis-ease' worship gives rise to in both father and son in this play connects with Shaffer's equivocal attitude towards religious impulse in earlier dramas such as *The Royal Hunt of the Sun, Equus, Amadeus* and *Yonadab*.

   The word 'disease', in addition, recurs throughout the play, being used by Edward to describe the festering infection of hate that results when revenge is not taken in *'proper, proper rage'*, and being used by Helen to argue that 'all revenge is diseased' (p.56). Further, Helen refers to the 'darkness' in Edward that consumed him 'like some un-stoppable cancer' following his self-imposed exile to Greece (p.70). Similar references to disease and infection abound, all being in some way connected with the central moral questions posited here in relation to the revenge ethic.
22. The breach between the Dionysianism of Edward and the Apollonianism of Helen is fully communicated in Edward's choice of red ink and Helen's choice of blue: when Helen pens her last 'scene' to Edward in blue ink on one side of a piece of paper and Edward responds in red ink on the other, the archetypal clash they embody is communicated in one economical, symbolic gesture.
23. In relation to this issue of emasculation, it is significant that Edward's small revenges upon his wife involve blatant infidelities which seem designed to assert his sexuality. In Edward's terms, he is insisting upon his continued masculinity which survives despite the efforts of his 'castrating' wife/saviour/judge. This 'castration' is felt at the creative level when Helen demands that Edward's drama be tempered; it is no coincidence that Edward's resentment against her when she is proved correct in the wake of his first huge success is manifested in these sexual terms. It is also no coincidence that the most vicious re-vengers in his plays are women, the Empress Irene, who blinds her son, being particularly revealing since blinding is a traditional metaphor of castration.
24. Peter Shaffer, interview with the author, 22 November 1996.
25. It should be stressed that while Edward's revenge supposedly taken upon Helen's behalf involves casting her as his unwitting murderer (which, in his moral scheme, she has every right to be and is a role that she should celebrate), the revenge he takes upon *her* in this action is infinitely more destructive. As Helen tells Philip, the emotional and

psychological pain of lying awake at night, unable to sleep for feeling Edward's blood between her fingers, suggests that the 'revenge' taken has not been Helen's, but Edward's.

26. Carl G. Jung quoted by Joseph L. Henderson, 'Ancient Myths and Modern Man', in Carl G. Jung (ed.), 1978, p.110.
27. Shaffer adds: 'Hell is a place where you mentally or physically put people who are literally unforgivable, to whom you do not extend the possibility of absolution'. Peter Shaffer, interview with the author, 22 November 1996.
28. Sheridan Morley, 'Cheers for Maggie Smith', *Playbill: The National Theatre Magazine*, 30 June 1990, p.12.
29. Premiering at the Barbican's Pit Theatre in December 1992, the play survived the initial critical furore that greeted it and transferred to Wyndham's Theatre in March 1993; it ran, to great acclaim, until early July. At the time of writing productions of the play are scheduled in several capital cities worldwide.

CONCLUSION

1. Peter Shaffer quoted in C.J. Gianakaris, 'Drama into Film: The Shaffer Situation', *Modern Drama*, 27 (1984), 81–109, p.85.
2. Alan Brien, review of *The Royal Hunt of the Sun*, quoted in Gareth Lloyd-Evans and Barbara Lloyd-Evans, *Plays in Review 1956–1980: British Drama and the Critics* (London: Batsford Academic and Educational, 1985), p.127.
3. C.J. Gianakaris, 'Drama into Film: the Shaffer Situation', 1985, p.84.
4. Penelope Gilliat, quoted in Virginia Cooke and Malcolm Page (eds), *File on Shaffer* (London: Methuen, 1987), p.16.
5. 'J.C.', quoted in Virginia Cooke and Malcolm Page (eds), 1987, p.20.
6. C.J. Gianakaris, 'Drama into Film: the Shaffer Situation', 1985, p.87.
7. Peter Shaffer, 'A Note on the Text', in Peter Shaffer, *Three Plays: Five Finger Exercise, Shrivings, Equus* (London: Penguin, 1976), p.200.
8. Peter Shaffer, quoted in C.J. Gianakaris, 'Drama into Film: the Shaffer Situation', 1985, p.87.
9. Peter Hall reports that Forman was 'extremely excited' after seeing *Amadeus* on stage, stating that it was 'a great play, the first he had ever seen, about the problems of the creative artist in all ages'. John Goodwin (ed.), *Peter Hall's Diaries: The Story of a Dramatic Battle* (London: Hamish Hamilton, 1983), p.470.
10. Forman quoted in Henry Kamm, 'Milos Forman Takes his Cameras and "Amadeus" to Prague', *New York Times*, 29 May 1983, sec.2, 1, 15, p.15.
11. Peter Shaffer, quoted in C.J. Gianakaris, 'Drama into Film: the Shaffer Situation', 1985, p.92.
12. Peter Shaffer, quoted in Gene A. Plunka, *Peter Shaffer: Roles, Rites and Rituals in the Theater* (London: Associated University Press, 1988), p.228.

13. Peter Hall comments that 'an old strength of the theatre' is 'its ability to invite an audience to imagine'. He adds that 'this is something the cinema can never do'. Peter Hall, 'Introduction', in Peter Shaffer, *The Gift of the Gorgon* (London: Viking, 1993), p.x.
14. Peter Shaffer, *The Gift of the Gorgon*, 1993, p.22.
15. Peter Shaffer, *Lettice and Lovage*, in Peter Shaffer, *Lettice and Lovage and Yonadab* (London: Penguin, 1989), p.78.

Bibliography

The following bibliography provides a comprehensive reference guide to published material on the work of Peter Shaffer. All the texts used in this book are itemized here and additional references are also included for further reading.

PRIMARY SOURCES

Play Texts Referred to in this Book

Shaffer, P. *The Royal Hunt of the Sun*. London: Penguin, 1981.
Shaffer, P. *Four Plays: The Private Ear, The Public Eye, White Liars, Black Comedy*. London: Penguin, 1981.
Shaffer, P. *Three Plays: Equus, Shrivings, Five Finger Exercise*. London: Penguin, 1976.
Shaffer, P. *Amadeus*. London: Penguin, 1981.
Shaffer, P. *Lettice and Lovage and Yonadab*. London: Penguin, 1989.
Shaffer, P. *Whom Do I Have the Honour of Addressing?* London: André Deutsch, 1990.
Shaffer, P. *The Gift of the Gorgon*. London: Penguin, 1993.

Articles and Essays by Peter Shaffer

'Labels Aren't for Playwrights', *Theatre Arts*, XLIV (Feb. 1960) 20–1.
'The Cannibal Theatre', *Atlantic Monthly*, CCVI (Oct. 1960) 48–50.
'Artaud for Artaud's Sake', *Encore*, No.49 (May–June 1964) 20–31 [participant in discussion on Artaudian Theatre of Cruelty].
'In Search of a God', *Plays and Players*, Oct. 1964, p.22.
'Peter Shaffer's Personal "Dialogue"', *New York Times*, 24 Oct. 1965, Sec.II, p.1, p.3 [self-interview].
'To See the Soul of a Man', *New York Times*, 24 Oct. 1965, Sec.II, p.3.
'End of Empire', *The Listener*, 13 Aug. 1970, 220–1.
'What We Owe to Britten', *Sunday Times*, 18 Nov. 1973, p.35.
'*Equus*: Playwright Peter Shaffer Interprets its Ritual', *Vogue*, CLXV (Feb. 1975), p.136, p.192.
'Figure of Death', *The Observer*, 4 Nov. 1979, p.37.
'Mozartian Magic Behind the Masks', *The Times*, 16 Jan. 1985, p.9.
'The Play: A History', Chichester Festival Theatre Programme, *Whom Do I Have the Honour of Addressing?*, November 1996.

Interviews with Peter Shaffer

Adam, Peter. 'Peter Shaffer on Faith, Farce, and Masks', *The Listener*, 14 Oct. 1976, 476–7.

Buckley, Tom. 'Why Are There Two Us in "Equus"?', *New York Times*, Magazine, 13 April 1975, 20–1, 25–6, 28, 30, 32, 34, 37–8, 40.

Chambers, Colin. 'Psychic Energy', *Plays and Players*, Feb. 1980, 11–13.

Colvin, Clare, 'Quest for Perfection', *Drama*, 1986 (1), 11–12.

Connell, Brian. 'The Two Sides of Theatre's Agonized Perfectionist', *The Times*, 28 April 1980, p.7.

Ford, Christopher. 'High Horse', *The Guardian*, 6 Aug. 1973, p.8.

Gelatt, Roland. 'Mostly *Amadeus*', *Horizon*, Sept. 1984, 49–52.

Gelb, Barbara. 'And Its Author', *New York Times*, 14 Nov. 1965, Sec.II, pp.1, 2, 4.

Gilliard, David, 'Deadly Rivals', *Radio Times*, 22–28 Jan. 1983, p.4.

Gussow, Mel. 'Shaffer Details a Mind's Journey in *Equus*', *New York Times*, 24 Oct. 1974, p.50.

Higgins, John. 'The Challenge of Jumping Into the Unknown', *The Times*, 28 Nov. 1985, p.15.

Hobson, Harold, 'Shaffer Gallops to Glory and Explains What Makes Him Run', *The Sunday Times*, 29 July 1973, p.33.

Saunders, Kate, 'The Peter Principals', *Sunday Times*, 29 Nov. 1992, p.8.

Taylor, John Russell. 'Shaffer and the Incas', *Plays and Players*, April 1964, pp.12–13.

Webb, W.L. 'Committed to Nothing but the Theatre', *Manchester Guardian*, 27 Aug. 1959, p.4.

Full-length Studies

Cooke, V. and Malcolm Page (eds). *File On Shaffer*. London: Methuen, 1987.

Gianakaris, C.J. (ed.), *Peter Shaffer: A Casebook*. London and New York: Garland, 1991.

Gianakaris, C.J. *Peter Shaffer*. London: Macmillan, 1992. [Macmillan Modern Dramatists Series].

Klein, Dennis A. *Peter Shaffer*. Boston: Hall/Twayne, 1979.

Plunka, Gene A. *Peter Shaffer: Roles, Rites and Rituals in the Theater*. London: Associated University Press, 1988.

Taylor, John Russell. *Peter Shaffer*. London: Longman, 1974. [Writers and Their Work Series].

Chapters on Shaffer in Books

Carlson, Ralph S. 'Peter Shaffer', in *Critical Survey of Drama*, IV, ed. Frank N. Magill. Englewood Cliffs, N.J.: Salem Press, 1985. 1676–88.

Cohn, Ruby. *Retreats from Realism in Recent English Drama*. Cambridge: Cambridge University Press, 1991, 183–5.

Elsom, John. 'Peter Shaffer', in *Contemporary Dramatists*, ed. James Vinson. 3rd edn. London: Macmillan, 1982, 708–11.

Hayman, Ronald. *British Theatre Since 1955: A Reassessment*. Oxford: Oxford University Press, 1979, 52–5.

Innes, Christopher. 'Peter Shaffer (1926–): Symbols of the Divine', in Christopher Innes, *Modern British Drama 1890–1990*. Cambridge: Cambridge University Press, 1992, 403–16.

Kerensky, Oleg. 'Peter Shaffer', in Oleg Kerensky, *The New British Drama: Fourteen Playwrights Since Osborne and Pinter*. London: Hamish Hamilton, 1977, 31–58.

Simard, Rodney. 'Peter Shaffer: Epic Psychoquester', in Rodney Simard, *Postmodern Drama: Contemporary Playwrights in America and Britain*. Boston: University Press of America, 1984, 99–115.

Taylor, John Russell, 'Art and Commerce', in *Contemporary English Drama*, ed. C.W.E. Bigsby. London: Edward Arnold, 1981, 178–81 [Stratford-Upon-Avon Studies, No.19].

Taylor, John Russell. 'Peter Shaffer', in John Russell Taylor, *Anger and After: A Guide to the New British Drama*. London: Methuen, 1962, 272–8.

BACKGROUND INFORMATION/SECONDARY READING (BOOKS)

Anderson, M. *Anger and Detachment*. London: Pitman, 1976.

Ansorge, Peter. *Disrupting the Spectacle*. London: Pitman, 1975.

Artaud, Antonin. *The Theatre and Its Double*, trans. Victor Corti. London: John Calder, 1981.

Barnes, Philip. *A Companion to Postwar British Theatre*. Buckingham: Croom Helm, 1986.

Brown, John Russell, and Bernard Harris (eds). *Modern British Dramatists*. Englewood Cliffs, N.J.: Prentice-Hall, 1984.

Bull, John. *Stage Right: Crisis and Recovery in British Contemporary Mainstream Theatre*. London: Macmillan, 1994.

Bull, John. *New British Political Dramatists*. London: Macmillan, 1983.

Callow, Simon. *Being An Actor*. London: Penguin, 1984.

Caughie, John. *Theories of Authorship: A Reader*. London: Routledge/British Film Institute, 1990.

Cohn, Ruby. *Currents in Contemporary Drama*. Bloomington: Indiana University Press, 1969.

Cook, Judith. *Director's Theatre*. London: Harrap, 1974.

Costick, J.F. *Antonin Artaud*. Boston: G.K. Hall, 1978.

Eagelton, T. *Criticism and Ideology*. London: Verso, 1976.

Edwards, Sydney. *Celebration: 25 Years of British Theatre*. London: W.H. Allen, 1980.

Elsom, John. *Postwar British Theatre Criticism*. London: Routledge and Kegan Paul, 1981.

Elsom, John. *Postwar British Theatre*. London: Routledge and Kegan Paul, 1976.

Esslin, Martin. *The Field of Drama: How the Signs of Drama Create Meaning on Stage and Screen*. London: Methuen, 1987.
Esslin, Martin. *Antonin Artaud*. London: John Calder, 1976.
Frost, David, and Ned Sherrin (eds). *That Was The Week That Was*. London: W.H. Allen, 1963.
Goodwin, John (ed.). *Peter Hall's Diaries: The Story of a Dramatic Battle*. London: Hamish Hamilton, 1983.
Graves, Robert. *The Greek Myths: 1*. London: Penguin, 1988.
Graves, Robert. *The Greek Myths: 2*. London: Penguin, 1960.
Hayman, Ronald. *Theatre and Anti-Theatre*. London: Secker & Warburg, 1979.
Hayman, Ronald. *Playback*. New York: Horizon, 1974.
Hayman, Ronald. *Playback 2*. London: Davis-Poynter, 1973.
Hildesheimer, Wolfgang. *Mozart*, trans. Marion Faber. New York: Vintage Books, 1983.
Hilton, Julian. *Performance*. London: Macmillan, 1988.
Hinchliffe, Arnold. *British Theatre 1950–70*. Oxford: Oxford University Press, 1974.
Itzin, Catherine. *Stages in the Revolution*. London: Methuen, 1980.
Jacobson, Dan. *The Rape of Tamar*. New York: Macmillan, 1970.
Jung, Carl Gustav (ed.). *Man and his Symbols*. London: Picador, 1978.
Jung, Carl Gustav. *Psychology and Religion: West and East*, trans. R.F.C. Hull. Princeton: Princeton University Press, 1955.
Kennedy, Andrew. *Dramatic Dialogue*. Cambridge: Cambridge University Press, 1983.
Lloyd-Evans, G. and B. Lloyd-Evans (eds). *Plays in Review 1956–80: British Drama and the Critics*. London: Batsford Academic and Educational, 1985.
Lloyd-Evans, G. and B. Lloyd-Evans. *The Language of Modern Drama*. London: J.M. Dent, 1977.
Lumley, Frederick. *New Trends in Twentieth-Century Drama*. Oxford: Oxford University Press, 1967.
Mann, Thomas. *Death in Venice, Tristan, Tonio Kröger*, trans. H.T. Lowe-Porter. London: Penguin, 1994.
Marowitz, Charles, Tom Milne and Hale Owen (eds). *New Theatre Voices of the Fifties and Sixties: Selections from 'Encore' Magazine 1956–1963*. London: Methuen, 1965.
McGrath, John. *A Good Night Out — Popular Theatre: Audience, Class and Form*. London: Eyre Methuen, 1981.
Murray, Alexander. S. *Who's Who in Mythology: Classic Guide to the Ancient World: Revised Edition*. London: Bracken Books, 1995.
Nightingale, B. *An Introduction to Fifty Modern British Plays*. London: Pan Books, 1982.
Page, Adrian (ed.). *The Death of the Playwright? Modern British Drama and Literary Theory*. London: Macmillan, 1992.
Pick, John. *The Arts In A State*. Bristol: Bristol Classical Press, 1988.
Prescott, William. H. *The Conquest of Peru*. 2 vols. London: J.M. Dent & Sons, 1933.
Roberts, Peter. *Theatre in Britian*. London: Pitman, 1973.

Shaffer, P. and Anthony Shaffer. *Withered Murder*. New York: Macmillan, 1956.

Shaffer, P. *The Woman in the Wardrobe*. London: Evans Brothers, 1951.

Smith, Leslie. *Modern British Farce*. London: Macmillan, 1989.

Styan, J.L. *Drama, Stage and Audience*. Cambridge: Cambridge University Press, 1975.

Taylor, John Russell. *The Second Wave: British Drama for the Seventies*. London: Methuen, 1971.

Wandor, Michelene. *Look Back in Gender: Sexuality and the Family in Post-War British Drama*. London: Methuen, 1987.

Wandor, Michelene. *Carry On Understudies: Theatre and Sexual Politics*. London: Methuen, 1986.

Willett, John (ed.). *Brecht on Theatre*. London: Methuen, 1974.

Worth, Katherine. *Revolutions in Modern English Drama*. London: G. Bell, 1973.

Wright, Elizabeth. *Postmodern Brecht: A Re-Presentation*. London: Routledge, 1989.

ARTICLES IN JOURNALS

Baldwin, Hélène L., 'Equus: Theater of Cruelty or Theater of Sensationalism?', *Philological Papers* [West Virginia University], 25 (1978), 118–27.

Berman, Jeffrey, 'Equus: After Such Little Forgiveness, What Knowledge?', *The Psychoanalytic Review*, 66, No.3 (1979), 406–22.

Chaudhuri, Una, 'The Spectator In Drama/Drama in the Spectator', *Modern Drama*, 27 (1984), 281–323.

Dallas, Ian, 'The Naturalists', *Encore*, 10 (Sept. 1958), 24–8.

Dean, Joan Fitzpatrick, 'Peter Shaffer's Recurrent Character Type', *Modern Drama*, 21, No.3 (1978), 297–305.

Esslin, Martin, 'Drama and the Media in Britain', *Modern Drama*, 28 (1985), 99–109.

Gianakaris, C.J., 'Placing Shaffer's *Lettice and Lovage* in Perspective', *Comparative Drama*, 22, No.2 (Summer 1988), 145–61.

Gianakaris, C.J., 'Drama into Film: The Shaffer Situation', *Modern Drama*, 28 (1985), 83–98.

Gianakaris, C.J., 'Shaffer's Revisions in *Amadeus*', *Theatre Journal*, 35, No.1 (1983), 88–101.

Gianakaris, C.J., 'A Playwright Looks at Mozart: Peter Shaffer's *Amadeus*', *Comparative Drama*, 15 (Spring 1981), 37–53.

Gianakaris, C.J., 'Theatre of the Mind in Miller, Osborne, and Shaffer', *Renascence*, XXX (1977), 33–42.

Glenn, Jules, 'Alan Strang as an Adolescent: A Discussion of Peter Shaffer's *Equus*', *International Journal of Psychoanalytic Psychotherapy*, 5 (1976), 473–87.

Glenn, Jules, 'Anthony and Peter Shaffer's Plays: The Influence of Twinship on Creativity', *American Imago*, 31 (Autumn 1974), 270–92.

Glenn, Jules, 'Twins in Disguise: A Psychoanalytic Essay on *Sleuth* and *The Royal Hunt of the Sun*', *Psychoanalytic Quarterly*, 43, No.2 (1974), 288–302.

Hinden, Michael, 'When Playwrights Talk to God: Peter Shaffer and the Legacy of O'Neill', *Comparative Drama*, XVI, No.1 (Spring 1982), 49–63.

Hinden, Michael, 'Trying to Like Shaffer', *Comparative Drama*, 19, No.1 (1985), 14–29.

Huber, Walter and Hubert Zapf, 'On the Structure of Peter Shaffer's *Amadeus*', *Modern Drama*, 27 (1984), 299–313.

Jacobson, Harlan, 'As Many Notes as Required', *Film Comment* (Sept/Oct 1984), 50, 53–5.

Klein, Dennis A., '*Amadeus*: The Third Part of Peter Shaffer's Dramatic Trilogy', *Modern Language Studies*, 13, No.1 (1983), 31–8.

Loney, Glenn, 'Recreating *Amadeus*: An American Team Recreates John Bury's Design', *Theater Crafts*, (March 1981), 10–15.

Lounsberry, Barbara, 'Peter Shaffer's *Amadeus* and *Shrivings*: God-Hunting Continued', *Theatre Annual*, 39 (1984), 15–33.

Lounsberry, Barbara, '"God-Hunting": The Chaos of Worship in Peter Shaffer's *Equus* and *Royal Hunt of the Sun*', *Modern Drama*, 21, No.2 (1978), 13–28.

MacCabe, Colin, 'The Revenge of the Author', *Critical Quarterly*, Vol.31, No.2 (1989), 3–13.

Pennell, Charles A., 'The Plays of Peter Shaffer: Experiments in Convention', *Kansas Quarterly*, lll, No.2 (1979), 100–9.

Plunka, Gene A., 'The Existential Ritual: Peter Shaffer's *Equus*', *Kansas Quarterly*, No.4 (1980), 87–97.

Rosenwald, Peter J., '*Amadeus*: Who Murdered Mozart?', *Horizon*, 23, No.2 (1980), p.33.

Vandenbroucke, Russell, '*Equus*: Modern Myth in the Making', *Drama and Theater*, 12, No.2 (1975), 129–33.

Walls, Doyle W. '*Equus*: Shaffer, Nietzsche, and the Neurosis of Health', *Modern Drama*, 27 (1984), 314–23.

Witham, Barry, 'The Anger in *Equus*', *Modern Drama*, 22, No.1 (1979), 61–6.

ARTICLES/REVIEWS IN NEWSPAPERS

Barber, John, 'Mozart Depicted as a Popinjay', *Daily Telegraph*, 5 November 1979, p.15.

Barber, John, 'Fascinating Play on an Obsession', *Daily Telegraph*, 27 July 1973, p.13.

Billington, Michael, 'A Voyeur of Divinity', *Manchester Guardian Weekly*, 22 December 1985, p.5.

Billington, Michael, 'Divining for a Theme', *The Guardian*, 5 November 1979, p.11.

Brien, Alan, 'Middle-Aged Absurdity', *The Sunday Telegraph*, 25 February 1968, p.14.

Brien, Alan, 'Silent Epic – With Words', *The Sunday Telegraph*, 13 December 1964, p.12.

Brien, Alan, 'Eating People is Wrong', *The Spectator*, 25 July 1958, pp.133–4.

Brustein, Robert, 'The Triumph of Mediocrity', *The New Republic*, 17 January 1981, pp.23–4.

Bryden, 'Echoes of Russell', *The Observer*, 8 February 1970, p.31.

Bryden, Ronald, 'Ruin and Gold', *New Statesman*, 17 July 1964, pp.95–6.

Buckley, Tom, '"Write Me" Said the Play to Peter Shaffer', *The New York Times Magazine*, 13 April 1975, pp.20–1, 25–6, 28, 30, 32, 34, 37–8, 40.

Carey, John, 'Oh Come All Ye Separate', *The Listener*, 31 December 1970, p.928.

Christie, Ian, 'Not a Lot of Horse Sense', *Daily Express*, 27 July 1973, p.10.

Cushman, Robert, 'Horsemanship at the National', *The Observer*, 29 July 1973, p.30.

Darlington, W.A., 'Conquistador in Search of a Faith', *Daily Telegraph*, 9 December 1964, p.18.

Davies, Russell, 'Horses for Courses', *New Statesman*, 3 August 1973, pp.165–6.

Edwards, Sydney, 'What the Riots Did to Peter Shaffer', *Evening Standard*, 9 January 1970, pp.20–1.

Fenton, James, 'Can we Worship this Mozart?', *The Sunday Times*, 23 December 1979, p.43.

Flood, Gerry, 'God's Flute', *Opera News*, 31 January 1981, p.18.

Ford, Christopher, 'The *Equus* Stampede', *The Guardian*, 20 April 1976, p.8.

Gascoigne, Bamber, 'All the Riches of the Incas', *The Observer*, 12 July 1964, p.24.

Gascoigne, Bamber, 'Touched by Pleasure', *The Spectator*, 18 May 1962, p.653.

Gelatt, Roland, 'Peter Shaffer's *Amadeus*: A Controversial Hit', *Saturday Review*, November 1980, pp.11–14.

Gifford, Sanford, 'Psychoanalyst Says Nay to *Equus*', *New York Times*, 15 December 1976, Sec.2, p.1, p.5.

Gill, Brendan, 'Bargaining with God', *The New Yorker*, 29 December 1980, p.54.

Gill, Brendan, 'Unhorsed', *The New Yorker*, 4 November 1974, pp.123–4.

Gilliatt, 'A Huge Stride Backwards – With the Inca', *The Observer*, 13 December 1964, p.24.

Grant, Steve, 'Much Ado About Mozart', *The Observer*, 11 November 1979, p.16.

Hayman, Ronald, 'John Dexter: Walking the Tightrope of Theatrical Statement', *The Times*, 28 July 1973, p.9.

Henehan, Donal, 'Never Mind Salieri: Süssmayr Did It', *New York Times*, 23 September 1984, Sec.2, p.1, p.21.

Hobson, Harold, 'Gielgud, Shaffer, and Hall — Had a Great Fall', *The Christian Science Monitor*, 13 February 1970, p.6.

Hobson, Harold, 'All too Black and White', *The Sunday Times*, 8 February 1970, p.53.

Hope-Wallace, Philip, 'Joan Littlewood's Panto at Wyndham's', *The Guardian*, 20 December 1963, p.7.

Kakutani, Michiko, 'How *Amadeus* Was Translated From Play to Film', *The New York Times*, 16 September 1984, Sec.2, p.1, p.20.

Kalem, T.E., 'Blood Feud', *Time*, 29 December 1980, p.57.

Kalem, T.E., 'Freudian Exorcism', *Time*, 4 November 1974, pp.119–20.

Kamm, Henry, 'Milos Forman Takes his Cameras and "Amadeus" to Prague', *New York Times*, 29 May 1983, sec.2,1,15, p.15.

Karsten Larson, Janet, '*Amadeus*: Shaffer's Hollow Men', *Christian Century*, 98 (May 1981), pp.578–83.

Kauffmann, Stanley, 'Shaffer's Flat Notes', *Saturday Review*, February 1981, p.78–9.

Kretzmer, Herbert, 'More Sparkle from Off-Beat Mr Shaffer', *Daily Express*, 12 May 1962, p.7.

Kroll, Jack, 'Four from the London Stage', *Newsweek*, 13 January 1986, pp.64–5.

Kroll, Jack, 'Mozart and his Nemesis', *Newsweek*, 29 December 1980, p.58.

Kroll, Jack, 'Horse Power', *Newsweek*, 4 November 1974, p.60.

Levin, Bernard, 'Out of the Darkness, a Blind Farce', *Daily Mail*, 29 July 1965, p.12.

Levin Bernard, 'Yes, It's the Greatest Play in My Lifetime', *Daily Mail*, 10 December 1964, p.18.

Nightingale, Benedict, 'Some Immortal Business', *New Statesman*, 13 February 1970, p.227.

Pennell, Charles A., 'Peter Shaffer Restores the Spectacle', *Evening Standard*, 8 July 1964, p.6.

Schikel, Richard, 'Showman Shaffer', *Time*, 11 November 1974, p.117, p.119.

Shorter, Eric, 'Gielgud and Magee as Mouthpieces of Ideas', *Daily Telegraph*, 6 February 1970, p.16.

Shorter, Eric, 'Exotic Epic Play by Peter Shaffer', *Daily Telegraph*, 8 July 1964, p.16.

Shulman, Milton, 'Arguments without Soul', *Evening Standard*, 6 February 1970, p.24.

Shulman, Milton, 'A Search for Faith in a Feast of Spectacle', *Evening Standard*, 9 December 1964, p.14.

Shulman, Milton, 'Mr Shaffer – First Sex-War Reporter', *Evening Standard*, 11 May 1962, p.21.

Wardle, Irving, 'Shaffer's Variation on a Theme', *The Times*, 27 July 1973, p.15.

Wardle, Irving, 'Philosopher of Peace', *The Times*, 6 February 1970, p.13.

Worsley, T.C., '*Merry Rooster's Panto*', *Financial Times*, 6 February 1970, p.3.

Worsley, T.C., '*The Private Ear: The Public Eye*', *Financial Times*, 11 May 1962, p.26.

Worsley, T.C., 'Give me a Good Play', *New Statesman*, 26 July 1958, pp.112–13.

Young, B.A., '*Amadeus*', *Financial Times*, 5 November 1979, p.15.

Young, B.A., '*The Battle of Shrivings*', *Financial Times*, 6 February 1970, p.3.

Young, B.A., '*The Royal Hunt of the Sun*', *Financial Times*, 8 July 1964, p.24.

Index